Theatre for Living

the art and science of community-based dialogue

David Diamond

Foreword by Fritjof Capra

Note for Librarians: A cataloguing record for this book is available from Library and Archives Canada at www.collectionscanada.ca/amicus/index-e.html
Theatre for Living – the art and science of community-based dialogue / by David Diamond
ISBN # 978-1-4251-2458-8
Version 1.1

Editors: Graham Hayman, Jackie Crossland, Vicki McCullough
Book and cover design / layout: Dafne Blanco

Theatre for Living is printed on 100 percent chlorine bleach-free recycled paper.
Printed in Victoria, BC Canada.
Trafford's print shop runs on "green energy" from solar, wind and other environmentally-friendly power sources.

Order online at:
Trafford.com/06-3181

www.trafford.com

North America & international
toll-free: 1 888 232 4444 (USA & Canada)
phone: 250 383 6864 ♦ fax: 250 383 6804
email: info@trafford.com

The United Kingdom & Europe
phone: +44 (0)1865 487 395 ♦ local rate: 0845 230 9601
facsimile: +44 (0)1865 481 507 ♦ email: info.uk@trafford.com

10 9 8 7 6 5 4

"At all levels of life, beginning with the simplest cell, mind and matter, process and structure, are inseparably connected."

Fritjof Capra
The Hidden Connections, p. 38

"Whatever is not expressly forbidden, is allowed."

Augusto Boal
in person, many times

CONTENTS

READER TIPS AND ACKNOWLEDGEMENTS

Reader tips

The English language has limitations, in particular when dealing with gender. In an attempt to make the writing gender neutral and avoid the cumbersome him/her, s/he conundrum, I have used 'she' and 'he' interchangeably throughout the book, except when speaking about obviously male or female people or characters.

I have explained some games and exercises in detail as part of the narrative structure when it supports the understanding of concepts under discussion. All other games and exercises that I currently draw on are detailed in the section *Games and Exercises* at the end of the book.

Acknowledgements

Thank you, of course, to Brazilian theatre director and originator of the *Theatre of the Oppressed*, Augusto Boal.[1] He has been an inspiration, a

---

[1] http://www.theatreoftheoppressed.org

mentor and a friend. His courage and joyful creativity continue to be a beacon in my world. Thanks to him for first suggesting that it was time for me to write a book and also for feedback on drafts in 2003 and 2005.

Dr. Fritjof Capra, physicist, systems theorist and a founder of the Centre for Ecoliteracy[2] has been an inspiration since 1986 when I first encountered his book *The Turning Point*.[3] His work has helped me bridge a lifelong interest in science with my passion for the theatre. Thanks also to him for feedback on science sections of the book in 2005 and for his foreword. It is an honour for me to include it here.

It is only in the writing of this book that I have gained a perspective on how so many of my own insights have happened in the midst of collaborations with various First Nations communities. We have gone to places of risk and innovation together. For that I am very grateful and want to mention, in particular, the following Nations: the Sto:Lo; the Gitxsan, in particular the Blackwater family (Bill Sr., Gloria and Hal) in Kispiox, BC, and Don Ryan; the Wet'suwet'en, in particular Alfred Joseph; the Nuu-Chah-Nulth, in particular Lisa Charleson and Mary Martin; and the Passamaquoddy, in particular Gail Marie Dana and Vera Francis. Also Ron George and the 1991 Board of Directors of United Native Nations.

There are so many people who were participants in workshops – people whose generosity has been an integral part of my learning – it is an impossible task to name them. I have tried to be diligent in naming cast members and production team members for mainstage projects.

Finding the time to write would not have been possible without taking a sabbatical from my work at Headlines Theatre. Thanks for this to the Canada Council for the Arts and in particular: André Courchesne (who suggested the sabbatical), and theatre officers Sheila James and Bob Allen; also thanks to Jane Heyman and Jan Selman for the supporting recommendations to Canada Council.

My own journey as a theatre artist has been supported and made possible by many people who have given time and energy to Headlines:

[2] http://www.ecoliteracy.org
[3] First published by Simon & Schuster, New York 1982.

The Co-Founders: Anne Hungerford, Beth Kaplan, Suzie Payne, Jay Samwald, Nettie Wild (and me).

The 2003/04 Board of Directors: Barbara A. Buckman, Marjorie MacLean, Darlene Marzari, Kevin Millsip, Bill Roxborough, Kamal Sharma, Kirk Tougas, Nettie Wild and Tad Young, who were so supportive of my sabbatical writing period.

Core Headlines' Staff from 1981 to 2007: Marjorie MacLean, Gwen Kallio, Doug Cleverley, Honey Maser, Jackie Crossland, Saeideh Nessar Ali, Denise Golemblaski, Lola Sim, Siobhan Barker, Mirjana Galovich, Sheelagh Davis, Harry Hertscheg, Jen Cressey, Jennifer Girard, Dylan Mazur, Dafne Blanco, Mumbi Tindyebwa.

People who worked with me as Jokers: Sherri-Lee Guilbert, Patti Fraser, Saeideh Nessar Ali, Victor Porter, Jacquie Brown.

And very special thanks to Headlines' 2003/04 staff, whose hard work made it possible for me to take the time away to do the primary writing: Dafne Blanco, Jackie Crossland, Jen Cressey, Jennifer Girard, Harry Hertscheg, Dylan Mazur.

Thanks also to:
Hal B. Blackwater for feedback on the *Dancers of the Mist* chapter;
Jackie Crossland for feedback on early drafts in 2003 and 2005;
Jagdeep Singh Mangat for feedback on the *Here and Now (ਏਥੇ ਤੇ ਹੁਣ)* chapter;
James Nicholas for the eagle feather;
Lisa Charleson for feedback on the *Reclaiming Our Spirits* chapter;
Dr. Michelle La Flamme for cultural feedback and guidance on various First Nations sections;
Mike Keeping for feedback on the *Television and the World Wide Web* chapter;
Dr. Mukti Khanna for her section on morphogenetic fields;
Ronald Matthijssen for feedback on the first draft in 2003;
Ronnie Tang for her nurturing support;
Victor Porter for feedback on the *Oppressed Leader of the Death Squad* section.

FOREWORD

by Fritjof Capra

During the past 25 years, a new conception of life has emerged at the forefront of science that is radically different from the mechanistic world view of Descartes and Newton, which has dominated our culture for over 300 years. The new world view, or paradigm, is holistic and ecological. Instead of seeing the universe as a machine composed of elementary building blocks, scientists have discovered that the material world, ultimately, is a network of inseparable patterns of relationships; that the planet as a whole is a living, self-regulating system. The view of the human body as a machine and of the mind as a separate entity is being replaced by one that sees not only the brain, but also the immune system, the bodily tissues and even each cell as a living, cognitive system. Evolution is no longer seen as a competitive struggle for existence, but rather a co-operative dance in which creativity and the constant emergence of novelty are the driving forces.

With this change of world view, there has been a fundamental change of the metaphors we use to express our understanding of the world. For Descartes and Newton, the universe worked like a clock, and the clock became the central metaphor of the mechanistic paradigm. In the new ecological view, by contrast, the central metaphor is the network.

In science, the network perspective began in the 1920s in the field of ecology, when ecological communities were seen to consist of organisms linked together in food webs, i.e., in networks of feeding relations. Subsequently, scientists began to use network models at all levels of living systems, viewing organisms as networks of cells and cells as networks of molecules, just as ecosystems are understood as networks of individual organisms. Gradually it became evident that the network is a pattern that is common to all life.

Life in the social realm can also be understood in terms of networks, but here we are not dealing with chemical and biological processes. Living networks in human society are networks of communications. They involve language, culture and the experience of community.

In my own work, I have used the concepts and ideas developed recently in complexity theory and the theory of living systems to create a synthesis of the new scientific conception of life. I have also applied this "systems view of life" to various practical fields, including education and the management of human organizations. When I met David Diamond, I was amazed to discover that our approaches to living systems, networks and communities have much in common, even though our methods, language and practice are quite different.

David Diamond has spent more than 30 years in the theatre, first as a professional actor and then as the artistic director of his own company, Headlines Theatre. With this company he has created a special form of political theatre called *Theatre for Living*, which is strongly influenced by the revolutionary works of two Brazilians – Paulo Freire's *Pedagogy of the Oppressed* and Augusto Boal's *Theatre of the Oppressed*.

The unique feature of Diamond's company is that, instead of producing theatre *for* communities, it makes theatre *with* communities. In hundreds of projects and workshops, the company has used theatre as a means to create political change by empowering communities to use the language of the theatre – words, movement, gestures, dance – to tell their stories, open up new channels of communication, and face difficult problems such as racism, gender stereotypes, addiction and violence.

In the present book, Diamond gives us an extensive and eloquent account of the theory and praxis of his *Theatre for Living*. As the author "weaves the science into the theatre," he brings to light many fascinating connections with the new systemic conception of life.

According to this new understanding of life, the key characteristic of a living network is that it is self-generating. In a social network, each communication creates thoughts and meaning, which give rise to further communications, and thus the entire network generates and regenerates itself. As the communications continue, they form multiple feedback loops that eventually produce a shared system of beliefs, explanations and values – a common context of meaning known as culture, which is continually sustained by further communications.

Organizational theorists and consultants who work with these systemic concepts have come to realize that the aliveness of a human organization or community – its flexibility, creative potential and learning capability – resides in its informal, fluid and ever-changing networks of communications. This realization also lies at the core of David Diamond's *Theatre for Living*. In this book he shows us, with examples of numerous games and practices from his workshops, how communities can better experience their interconnections, create intentional feedback loops, and use symbolic language to express themselves in new ways. These practices, he explains, result in a deeper understanding of the dynamics in the community and lead to changes in relationships and behaviour. Ultimately, they empower communities to bring about political change. The author emphasizes that a *Theatre for Living* workshop is a theatre workshop, not a group therapy session. However, "like any good theatre, it can and often does have therapeutic value."

In these workshop practices, special attention is paid to nonverbal communications – gestures, synchronization (or "entrainment") of rhythmic movements, and "blind games" in which interconnections and closeness among the members of the group are sensed by touch and by subtle signals. All these interactions are highly nonlinear; hence, the results are impossible to predict. The role of the director, accordingly, is not to give strategic instructions, but to create an environment in which meaningful change is likely to occur.

David Diamond is well aware of the unconventional role of the artistic director in his community-based theatre. In fact, he does not even refer to himself as director, but instead, following Augusto Boal, uses the term "Joker" to denote his position. I find this term very evocative and inspiring. It is reminiscent of the medieval court jester, who had a license to mock the ruling establishment and to address inconvenient truths in playful and entertaining ways. The joker, fool or jester embodied creative power and was often pictured as a juggler, skillfully manipulating multiple elements.

Many of these qualities are displayed by the Joker in the *Theatre for Living*. As Diamond explains, a *Theatre for Living* project happens because a community wants to deal with certain issues and has invited the Joker into the community. His role there is often to create disturbances by giving a voice to people who would normally not be heard, or by enabling individuals to manifest conflicting voices. These disturbances then set in motion the group dynamics that lead to change. The role of the Joker, as conceived by Boal and Diamond, reflects the recent discovery in science that living systems respond to disturbances in their own self-organizing ways. One can never direct a living system; one can only disturb it.

Another important advance in the scientific understanding of life has been the realization that creativity is inherent in all living systems. Although they generally remain in a stable state, every now and then such systems will encounter a point of instability where there is either a breakdown or, more frequently, a spontaneous emergence of new forms of order. This spontaneous emergence of order at critical points of instability, which is often referred to simply as "emergence", is one of the hallmarks of life. It has been recognized as the dynamic origin of development, learning and evolution. In other words, creativity – the generation of new forms – is a key property of all living systems.

The detailed theory of emergence shows that the instabilities and subsequent jumps to new forms of organization are the result of fluctuations amplified by feedback loops. The system encounters a small disturbance, which then circulates around multiple feedback loops and is amplified until the system as a whole becomes unstable. At this point, it will either break down or break through to a new form of order.

In a human community, the event triggering the process of emergence may be an offhand comment that does not seem important to the person who made it, but is meaningful to some members of the community. Because it is meaningful to them, they choose to be disturbed and to amplify the information. As it circulates through various feedback loops in the community's network, the information may get amplified and expanded to such an extent that the community can no longer absorb it in its present state. When that happens, a point of instability has been reached. The result is a state of chaos, confusion, uncertainty and doubt; and out of that chaotic state a new form of order, organized around new meaning, emerges. The new order was not designed by any individual, but emerged as a result of the community's collective creativity.

In Diamond's *Theatre for Living*, the principal task of the Joker seems to be to bring forth this collective creativity by putting in place conditions in which the emergence of novelty is likely to occur. This means, first of all, building up and nurturing active networks of communications. As Diamond puts it: "Praxis, the creation of intentional feedback loops, is an essential part of group process."

The process of emergence also requires that the community be open to outside influences that provide the disturbances. Facilitating emergence, therefore, includes creating that openness. "We are making theatre that is an expression of the larger community," the author explains. "In order to do this, we must trust the knowledge in the room, and the fact that it is connected to the larger community outside the physical boundaries of our workspace."

And finally, a crucial role of the Joker is to create a climate of trust and mutual support to help the community go through the feelings of uncertainty, fear, confusion or self-doubt that always precede the emergence of novelty. The issues addressed in the *Theatre for Living* workshops are emotionally highly charged, and the vivid stories in this book make it clear that the author is fully aware of the critical importance of the emotional dimension of his work.

Throughout the book, David Diamond emphasizes that his *Theatre for Living* is about empowerment, about using the language of theatre to help communities become more connected within themselves and thus more alive, creative and capable of bringing about meaningful change. Today, this is highly relevant for all human communities and organizations. As our global economic system increases social inequality, accelerates environmental destruction, and threatens local communities around the world, bringing life into human organizations to enhance their integrity, creativity and potential for change has become a critical task. This book, therefore, can be inspiring to anyone concerned about the future of humanity, both inside and outside the theatre.

PROLOGUE

We know now that, if we don't express ourselves as individuals, if we keep our stories bottled up inside us, eventually we will get sick. The stress will manifest as disease. The human body is, after all, an integrated system.

I suggest that, in the same way our bodies are made up of cells that constitute the living organism, a community is made up of individual people that comprise the organism I call the living community. Communities are alive and need to express themselves just like people; if they don't, they get sick, just like people. The proof of this is all around us. As cultural life has become more and more consumer oriented, living communities have manifested more and more disease.

This is because communities have become fragmented into individualized consumers and have lost their ability to collectively tell their stories.

Theatre, like all other forms of cultural expression, used to be ordinary people singing, dancing, telling stories. This was the way a living community recorded and celebrated its victories, defeats, joys, fears. As the Cartesian or mechanistic model took root, and later as colonialism spread across the planet, coinciding with the mechanization of capitalism, this primal activity of storytelling also evolved in a mechanistic way. Like many other things we can think of, cultural activity became commodified. It transformed from something that people did naturally "in community", into a manufactured consumer product. Today a vast majority of people buy theatre, buy dance, buy paintings, buy books, buy movies; the list goes on and on. We now pay strangers to tell us stories about strangers. But when do we use the symbolic language of theatre, dance, etc., to tell our own stories about our collective selves?

What is the result of the living community's inability to use primal language to tell its own stories? Alienation, violence, self-destructive behaviour on a global level. Living communities have fallen into a stupor, hypnotized by a steady diet of manufactured culture.

Between 1987 and 1990 I spent a lot of time in Kispiox, a Gitxsan community in the Northwest part of British Columbia, working on a project called *NO' XYA' (Our Footprints)*.[4] One of the things I came to understand there is that culture is attached to geography. The Gitxsan have lived on that spot, in the Kispiox Valley by the Kispiox River, for approximately 10,000 years. They have songs, dances and community rituals that are rooted in the geography of the place. All of my grandparents came to Canada from Russia as young adults. When they left, they brought the theatricality of their songs, dances and rituals with them. The act of relocating halfway across the planet severed their physical connection with their geographic home. They all matured in Winnipeg, married and had children who grew up, married and had children. I am the result of that story. I now live approximately 1,600 miles from where I was born, having made Vancouver my home.

My 31-year history living near the Straight of Georgia has relevance when held up against my Gitxsan friends' 10,000-year ancestry in the Kispiox Valley. I am, and it is very likely you are (especially if you live

---

4 Written by: David Diamond with Hal B. Blackwater, Marie Wilson and Lois Shannon. Cast: Sylvia-Anne George, Hal B. Blackwater, Sherri-Lee Guilbert and Ed Astley. Director: David Diamond. Co-producer: Maasgaak (Don Ryan). Administrators: Doug Cleverley, Honey Maser. Technical Directors/Stage Managers: Paul Williams, Marian Brandt. Consultants: Gitxsan Chief Baasxya laxha (Bill Blackwater Sr.) and Wet'suwet'en Chief Gisdaywa (Alfred Joseph). Designers: (poster graphic) Maas Likinisxw (Ken N. Mowatt); (sound) Skanu'u (Ardythe Wilson), Ray Cournoyer; (set) Vernon Stephens; (regalia and masks) Gitxsan Chief Wii Muk'wilsxw (Art Wilson), Gitxsan Chief Wii' Elaast (Jim Angus), Gitxsan Chief Sekwan (Silena Jack), Gitxsan Chief Iswoox (Lorraine Morgan), 'Alluksa'xw (Cheryl Stevens), Gitxsan Chief Niiyees Haluubist (Rita Williams); (cartoons) Don Monet. For a fuller description of the project, see *Dancers of the Mist* in the *Case Studies*.

in North America), part of a new culture the likes of which the Earth has never seen before. A very mobile, essentially rootless culture.

I am not suggesting that local storytelling never happens. It is impossible to stop this entirely. It happens in small gatherings of family around dinner tables in homes around the world; it happens in Gitxsan Territory in the Feast Hall and in many, but no longer all, surviving Aboriginal communities. I witnessed it years ago in a bar in Saint John's, Newfoundland, when most of the patrons of the bar burst into a song about Newfoundland. I was very struck in that moment at how this would never happen in a public gathering in my own community in Vancouver, BC.

Physicist Fritjof Capra starts his book *The Hidden Connections*[5] with a quote from Czech president Václav Havel, who was speaking to the Forum 2000 conference[6] in Prague, on October 15, 2000:

> *"Education is the ability to perceive the hidden connections between phenomena."*

I have tried, in this book, to bring together what appear to be disconnected worlds, and to make the connections tangible through specific examples in theatre projects. I am a theatre artist, but want to begin with René Descartes.

In the 1600s Descartes, who was to become known as the father of modern philosophy, began a systematic exploration of nature. Not wanting to follow in his predecessor Galileo's footsteps and be threatened with execution for heresy, Descartes agreed to base his views of nature on the fundamental division between two realms – mind and matter. In the early 1700s, Sir Isaac Newton, and then others, deepened Descartes' work. As a result, a mechanistic model, a pervasive image of the universe as a machine, slowly developed in European thought. The human body was imagined to be a machine. The ecosystems of the earth were imagined to be like machines. Nature itself was

---

[5] Published by Doubleday, New York 2002.
[6] The first Forum 2000 conference was held at Prague Castle in September 1997 on the initiative of president Václav Havel and Nobel peace laureate Elie Wiesel. Prominent representatives of the world's religions and internationally recognized politicians, scholars, writers and artists (including Fritjof Capra) came together in 1997 and years following to discuss global issues.
For more information see http://www.forum2000.cz/

perceived to be a machine. The solar system worked like a timepiece, as did the essence of matter (molecules, atoms, electrons). Although seeded in Europe, over time colonialism spread this mechanistic image across the globe; the image extended to the (nuclear) family, to corporations and, in the privatizing world of today, to governments. Did culture escape this image of mechanization? Of course it didn't.

The mechanistic model, an artificial separation of mind (consciousness) and matter (the physical body), has had many negative impacts on the planet. What has made it possible to imagine clear-cutting mountains? The idea that the earth is a machine and the trees were not connected to the river, or the fish in the river. What has made it possible to turn our collective backs on, or to criminalize, people who are living in poverty? The idea that society is a machine made up of disconnected individuals and that the person dying of hunger in a seemingly remote part of the world, or begging for small change on the street corner, was disconnected from you and me.

It also became possible, in this mechanistic model, to create an artificial construct: the separation of oppressor and oppressed.

We live, however, in a remarkable and challenging time. In the 21st century, science is coming around full circle and once again meeting what got labelled mysticism. Many disciplines, e.g., physics, mathematics, biology, sociology, philosophy, psychology, ecology, cognitive science, economics and even business administration, are incorporating systems theory into an analysis of how all aspects of life and the world around us are interconnected. Systems theory abandons the Cartesian view of mind being separated from matter and, instead, recognizes mind and matter as complementary aspects of the phenomenon of life. Will culture escape this reintegration? It will not.

I don't pretend that this book is an academically coherent understanding or clear set of concepts about systems theory. Systems theory does, however, help me explain in what I think is a clear and cogent way, what I have been seeing happen organically over many years in theatre processes with living communities.

This book is about making connections – the connections between theatre and systems theory. My intention is to make apparent the ancient connections between two seemingly separate worlds, by weaving the science into the theatre, along with practical case study examples. In doing so, perhaps I can understand my own evolving work better and in the process stimulate discussion about the central role that storytelling and art play in creating and living in healthy communities.

This book is also about my own evolution from an actor working in the mainstream theatre, to a politicized artist encountering Brazilian pedagogue Paulo Freire, then becoming an avid practitioner of Brazilian director Augusto Boal's *Theatre of the Oppressed*, and the further evolution of that work into what I now call *Theatre for Living*. It is about how communities function as living, conscious organisms and about how we can use theatre, a symbolic and primal language, as a vehicle for living communities to tell their stories.

The best way to illustrate how the concepts in this book actually work in a community setting is to share some in-depth case studies from actual projects. Every time I work in community, I write daily after each workshop or rehearsal session. The writing helps me get some perspective on what has happened during the day, which helps me plan the next day. If I am going to make a document about a *Theatre for Living* workshop public, I will always run the report past the organizers and/or participants first. If the project is not a mainstage project that may have gone to television or the web, I will also make the document anonymous, changing names of participants. There are sections of case studies throughout the book and full case studies near the end.

The final pages of the book are detailed explanations of the games and exercises I use the most when working with living communities. I have felt it necessary to include this section, even though many of the games or exercises can be found in other theatre books, because they have evolved in my work in a very particular direction. Each one has been revised to provide an opportunity for integrated learning inside a larger process of *epoché*, of awakening of a group consciousness.

Some people may see the development of *Theatre for Living*, and the notion that the separation between oppressor and oppressed is an artificial construction, as being in opposition to the work of Boal and the *Theatre of the Oppressed*. Nothing could be further from the truth. My work has been influenced by Boal more than any other person mentioned in this book. *Theatre for Living* is an outgrowth of *Theatre of the Oppressed* in the same way that Boal's work has grown from the work of socially conscious artists before him.

The name *Theatre for Living* describes all of my community-based theatre work, including the six-day *Power Play* workshop that leads to performance, which will be explained later. The name came to me one day in the middle of a Tai Chi routine. It bubbled up out of that mysterious, subconscious place where knowledge resides. After encountering Freire and Boal and doing what I saw as Boal's work for about 10 years, I suddenly realized that I lived in Canada, not Brazil, and that naturally, with the passage of time, my work was evolving. It wasn't focused on oppressor/oppressed relationships any more (why and how will be explained), but was investigating ways to help us live together in healthier ways. Theatre, for living in healthy communities ... *Theatre for Living.*

In 2003 when I started the writing process for this book, and now in 2007 upon publication, there is a rising hunger for stories that are a true voice. The emergence of community cultural development and artist-in-community practices are a sign of this. Sometimes the steps towards this are small, but they are significant. At least 90 percent of my work involves invitations to enter communities in order to create issue-based theatre with community members about subjects that the living community is struggling to understand or resolve.

Since 1992 that invitation has involved, more and more, finding ways to create theatre that does not polarize the living community into 'good guys' and 'bad guys', but rather recognizes that the community is an integrated, and perhaps dysfunctional organism that is struggling to resolve difficult issues.

Today, my hope is that this book operates at the level of image; that each idea, each story, sits amidst other ideas and stories and together they create a picture for the reader.

It has been asked of me that I articulate what I would like the reader to take away from reading this book. Not only am I incapable of doing this, I believe attempting to do so would be presumptuous. Anything I could articulate would be relevant to only a small percentage of readers and irrelevant to the rest. The irrelevance of my presumption would in itself be a negation of ideas, questions and insights that I cannot imagine. Such is the power of the image.

point and turn[7]

> "There is no such thing as a neutral educational process. Education either functions as an instrument which is used to facilitate the integration of the younger generation into the logic of the present system and bring about conformity to it, or it becomes 'the practice of freedom,' the means by which men and women deal critically and creatively with reality and discover how to participate in the transformation of their world. In other words, education either helps reinforce the status quo, or it helps break the rules."[8]

I believe that the words "theatrical" and "theatre" can be substituted for "educational" and "education" in this quote, and not just for younger generations. Regardless of the form it takes, theatre educates both its practitioners and its audience in some way.

We all live our lives by many rules. Some of them are good rules. When a child learns not to put her hand on a hot stove because she will get burned, she is learning a good rule. The rules that limit us, that keep us trapped in old patterns when shifts in thinking or new ways of seeing are appropriate, are not good rules. One of the important roles of artists is to challenge the status quo. In order to create vibrant art that has transformational value we must break the rules.

---

7 This game exists in the *Several senses* category. See the *Games and Exercises* section for an explanation of these game categories.
8 Richard Shaull, in the final paragraph of the introduction to Paulo Freire's *Pedagogy of the Oppressed*, first published in Great Britain by Sheed & Ward, 1972, and subsequently by Penguin, UK 1972, and Continuum, New York 1997.

Point and turn is a game I use to introduce the idea that the work we are about to do together involves breaking rules:[9]

> Everyone find a place to stand in the room where you can swing your arms and not hit anyone. Now with your eyes open, stand in neutral (arms by your sides) and lift your right arm, point in front of you and then twist around as far as you can without straining. Remember where you got to and return to neutral. Now close your eyes. Just in your mind – do not use your body – see yourself raise your arm, point, and then twist around, going further than you did before. Return to neutral. Again, just in your mind, see yourself raise your arm, point, twist even further than before, return to neutral. One last time, just in your mind, raise your arm, point, and then twist 180 degrees around – go nuts, do the impossible. See it! And return to neutral. Now open your eyes. Using your body, raise your arm, point, and then twist. What happens?

I facilitate this game a lot and can say with 90+ percent assurance that, once you read the instructions, if you actually do it, you will go further than you did the first time. Why? Did you warm up physically? No. "I imagined it – I saw it – I visualized it," people in workshops say. Yes, I agree. I think you also did something else: you broke a rule.

---

[9] Unless otherwise indicated, all games and exercises detailed in this book were originally published in my *Joker's Guide to Theatre for Living* in 1991 and distributed to participants in training workshops. Whenever appropriate and possible, cross-reference has been made to Boal's *Games for Actors and Non-Actors*.

A SHORT PERSONAL HISTORY

Everything imagined, uttered and done has a context. Here is some of mine.

I was born in Winnipeg, Manitoba, in 1953 and grew up in a home touched by alcohol, drugs and violence. My childhood experiences are not as extreme as the experiences of many people I have met later in life. The experiences are, nevertheless, mine, and have shaped me and the way I view the world.

By the time I was 15, I knew I wanted to be a writer and for the better part of a year tried to organize a creative writing course in my high school. I was not successful. There was, however, a theatre course in the school course catalogue and so I lobbied vigorously for theatre. In 1970 the school administration did start that program and so I dove into theatre.

In 1971 I auditioned for and entered the University of Alberta's Drama Department for an intensive four-year professional acting program, and emerged from there with a Bachelor of Fine Arts in acting and a solid classical theatre training. This led to acting work in television and on live stage in Edmonton, which precipitated a move to Vancouver in 1976.

By 1980 I was working in theatre, television, radio and film throughout Western Canada, almost making a living, and supplementing my income with driving taxi and going door to door fundraising for the environmental group Greenpeace (founded in Vancouver). Such is the working actor's lot – certainly one who has politics brewing in his heart.

As fate would have it, this was also a moment when the Canadian government made quite massive cuts in funding to culture. A meeting was called by Canadian actor Janet Wright to discuss what to do. At this meeting, I met Nettie Wild,[10] who was to become a renowned documentary filmmaker and dear friend. Nettie, a small core of others and I founded the Vancouver Artists' Alliance (VAA), the purpose of which was to represent artists' interests to all three levels of government (federal, provincial and municipal). Membership grew very quickly to almost 800 and the VAA became a full-time (unpaid) job for Nettie and me.

Some of the group – Nettie, John Lazarus, Beth Kaplan, Suzie Payne, Anne Hungerford and Norbert Rubesaat – started to meet in my living room once a month to complain about the state of theatre in Vancouver. Where was the activist theatre? This complaining went on for some time, until we got so frustrated we imagined doing something ourselves.

Some of us decided to do a socially relevant play. We all had housing problems of one sort or another, and so, in 1981, we did research on people who were feeling the housing crunch, the activists who were organizing on their behalf, and the developers who were making a lot of money from an exploding market. Then we wrote and performed the resulting play (with music) on organizing for affordable housing called *Buy, Buy, Vancouver*.[11] We thought we were doing a single project. This play, though, struck a nerve in the city, and Headlines Theatre was born.

---

[10] See www.canadawildproductions.com
[11] Writers: Beth Kaplan, Anne Hungerford, Suzie Payne, Jay Samwald, Nettie Wild, David Diamond. Cast: Heidi Archibald, Colin Thomas, Jay Samwald, Nettie Wild, David Diamond. Directed by: Suzie Payne. Design: Barbara Clayden and Phillip Tidd.

By 1984 Headlines had also produced a video documentary, *Right to Fight*,[12] and a play on militarism called *Under the Gun*,[13] which toured nationally. At the beginning, Nettie and I had done the producing together (fundraising, venue booking, organization of sponsoring groups, etc.), but her journey into film had escalated and so *Under the Gun* had been produced almost entirely by me. The company structure had evolved into a pseudo-collective, in which I was making many decisions every day and reporting to the collective once a month. The collective, through no ill intent, would very often say, "yes, but..." I felt hamstrung.

After the national tour was finished, I asked the collective to either come back together to share in the administrative work, or to give me the ability to make decisions. I had expected the former. They chose the latter. I inherited Headlines, never having directed anything in my life.

What to do now? I approached the Canada Council for the Arts for a travel grant that would pay for an airline ticket to Europe, and I set up visits with various political theatre companies. Invitations came from 7:84 Theatre in Scotland, which was under the guidance of John McGrath and Liz MacLennan, and Theatre Centre in London, under the directorship of Dave Johnstone. Canada Council said yes, and, after growing a beard in order to look more like my vision of a theatre director, I was set to go.

Days before leaving I was in a bookstore looking for something to read along the way and happened upon *Pedagogy of the Oppressed* by Brazilian educator Paulo Freire. I had never heard of Freire, but liked the title.

Headlines' work had been very successful. I felt, though, that something was missing. We had been very good at making theatre *for* and *about* people living the issues under scrutiny, but how did one make

---

[12] Co-producer/Director: Nettie Wild. Co-producer/Associate Director/Sound: David Diamond. Editor: Bill Roxborough. Cinematographer: Kirk Tougas.
[13] Writers: Nettie Wild, David Diamond, Karen Draisey, Colin Thomas, Bob Bossin and Suzie Payne. Original cast: Reid Campbell, Craig Davidson, Patrick Keating, Nettie Wild, David Diamond and Karen Draisey. Directed by: Suzie Payne. National tour cast: Reid Campbell, Wayne York, Patrick Keating, Nettie Wild, David Diamond and Karen Draisey. Directed by: Suzie Payne. Design: Barbara Clayden and Phillip Tidd.

theatre *with* people living the issues? Freire's monumental book helped me start to imagine how to do that.

Then, in Manchester, England, while attending a Theatre in Education conference, I witnessed a demonstration given by Chris Vine[14] of something called *Forum Theatre*. I couldn't believe what I was seeing! This theatre was *exactly* what Freire was writing about! The originator of the work, Augusto Boal, also a Brazilian, was in Paris, and would be giving a 10-day training workshop in three weeks! After a series of telephone calls, a group of us from the conference went off to Paris.

The Paris workshop and this first encounter with Boal and the *Theatre of the Oppressed* changed the direction of my work and life. Perhaps it was always headed in this kind of direction and was crystallized by Freire and Boal's work.

The workshop space was filled with participants from around the world – South Africa, Brazil, Finland, Britain, France, Canada and the US spring to mind immediately, but I am fairly certain there were others as well. There was a sense of deep experimentation, of rehearsing for life, of using the theatre for a purpose much more profound than entertainment or storytelling. Boal was very open about some of the techniques he was using not being fully developed and many being experiments that he was doing with us. They were, for the most part, very simple ideas – simplicity being achieved by a lot of weeding work to get to the essentials. The simplicity of an image – a human tableaux – and of the power of the artistry of that image and the richness of our various, global perspectives on the image. The creativity in the room was infectious. I took a lot of notes.

One of the things that struck me during this 10 days was how much fun we were all having investigating very serious issues like poverty, family relations and the miner's strike in the UK at the time. Our fun was a direct result of the fun Boal was having; here was a person who was on fire, who saw the world through very confident and yet critical eyes, who had a strong political message to his work, and who had not forgotten that the making of theatre had to be filled with joy. His joy filled us with enthusiasm and our enthusiasm fed his joy. The techniques were

---

[14] In 2006 Chris Vine was the artistic and education director of the Creative Arts Team (CAT) of City University of New York. See http://portal.cuny.edu/

important, but just as important to me (and many others there, I believe) was the modelling of the theatre-maker.

Upon returning home I wrote my first play, *The Enemy Within*,[15] named after the label then British prime minister Margaret Thatcher had given the striking miners in 1984. (I had gotten involved in the strike and, while living with a mining family in Clipstone, had done soup kitchen and picket duty.) The play was about then premier of British Columbia Bill Bennett and his plan to break the BC unions in order to pave the way for Expo '86, a world's fair, in Vancouver, and the resulting growth of international trade.

What to do with the *Theatre of the Oppressed*? I asked a group of friends if they would help me out and booked a hall. We spent two days together, me looking at my notes, trying to understand basic games, exercises and philosophical concepts. Often, what I was trying to do with them would fall apart. The two days was not for them; it was for me. Their generosity helped me gain a tentative understanding of Boal's work, which in turn let me venture into the public with the techniques.

The beginning of Power Plays

In 1986, two years after returning from the *Theatre of the Oppressed* workshop with Boal in Paris, I started to wonder if it was possible to create a structure in which people who did not know each other well, or maybe even at all, could create theatre about issues in their own community in one week. Creating a definable package seemed like a good way to accomplish this. *Power Plays* was the result.

I had already been experimenting with the vocabulary of *Theatre of the Oppressed* in one and two-day workshops and felt confident about facilitating a more complex process. I imagined a series of activities that made up a five-day workshop. Each day was self-contained but also built on the next; each day had a beginning, a middle and an end.

---

[15] Playwright: David Diamond. Directed by: Sue Astley. Cast (Vancouver run): Colin Thomas and Suzie Payne. Cast (BC tour): Craig Davidson and Meredith Woodward. Design: Barbara Clayden. Stage Manager: Patrick Keating.

During the process a group of people who had never met before would, in theory, be able to focus together on issues that they shared, discover what their connecting points were, and create a work of art that asked the most difficult questions possible about the struggles contained in those issues.

This was an attempt to design a process that could contain whatever content came from the community. The process would adapt for each situation, depending on the needs of particular workshop participants, while still retaining a sense of the steps necessary to get to public theatrical performance at the end of the week.

The first day was almost entirely spent doing games from what Boal calls "the arsenal",[16] carefully chosen and ordered to provide the potential for building trust and the development of theatre language in a group of strangers. As the days progressed, we would shift to fewer games and more exercises that could be used to explore various perspectives on an issue in the community. By the end of the fourth day, the process would move to play creation and, finally, on the fifth day, interactive Forum Theatre with an audience from the community.

It looked good on paper, but there was only one way to see if it would work. Headlines had done two extensive tours of the province of BC by this time[17] and so the company had working networks in place made up of people who were interested in social justice issues. I got on the phone and in a very short period of time booked a workshop tour: seven week-long workshops, one after the other, in seven communities across the province.[18] Some of the sponsors were First Nations, some were local arts councils and some were local unions. I was very open with the organizers that this was a big experiment, a learning experience for all of us. I really didn't know if it would work.

We were going to need promotional material (posters, flyers, press releases) and that necessitated a name for the tour. I came up with the name *Power Plays*. This fit very nicely with the idea I had of the work at the time, that it was an opportunity for a community to make an

---

[16] See *Games for Actors and Non-Actors* by Augusto Boal, published by Routledge, Oxford 1992.
[17] *Under the Gun* in 1983/84 and *The Enemy Within* in 1985/86.
[18] Port Alberni, Chilliwack, Telkwa, Hazelton (Gitanmaax), Kitimat, Old Massett, Prince Rupert.

exerted effort to overcome oppression in the same way a hockey team, having a one-player advantage during an opposing team's penalty, uses a power play to score a goal and win the game.

Karen Draisey, who had been in the Paris workshop in 1984 and then on an extended visit to Canada from the UK, had been an integral part of Headlines' previous production on militarism, *Under the Gun*. She had been developing the workshop work with me in Vancouver, but was offered other theatre opportunities, so opted out of the tour. Karen eventually returned to the UK. I didn't want to do this two-month-long tour alone. Kevin Finnan, a dance/theatre artist, also from the UK, who I had met at the Paris workshop, agreed to come on the road with me, but could not make it until the second workshop and had to leave after the sixth. This meant doing the first one alone. Margo Kane, a friend and well-known First Nations theatre artist based out of Vancouver, agreed to join me for the final workshop.

The first workshop, sponsored by a non-government organization called Canadian University Students Overseas (CUSO), was in Port Alberni, BC, in late May 1986. Because of scheduling difficulties with many of the people who wanted to take the workshop, it was three days long, not five. This wasn't a bad thing. It afforded me the opportunity to focus on *Image Theatre*[19] without the pressure of making plays for public performance – something I would not attempt in three days. The participants were mostly young women who were interested in development issues in underdeveloped countries. My challenge in this workshop turned out to be to try to help them understand that the work we could do needed to be about them, not about people they wanted to help in another part of the world. If they were pretending to be people they were not, how could the work we were doing be an authentic voice?

This was a big red flag. Had we not explained what the work was well enough in the telephone conversations and promotional material? Or was it something particular to this group of people who, with the best of intentions and from a place of living in relative privilege, wanted to focus outside their own community to do good work? Gwen Kallio was

---

[19] *Image Theatre* is the exploration of issues through frozen tableaux, or pictures, that are created by the workshop participants, using their own bodies to make the images. *Image Theatre* is discussed in the chapter *In the Workshop Room*. There is a section on *Image Theatre* in Boal's *Games for Actors and Non-Actors*, p. 164.

doing administrative work for Headlines at the time. Phone calls were made to all sponsors and material was rewritten to make it clear that the focus of the work would be the people who were in the room.

It was in the next workshop in early June 1986, with the Sto:Lo Nation,[20] that Kevin and I got to really test the *Power Play* model for the first time. The workshop was organized by Marcia Krawll, who was working for the Chilliwack Area Indian Council. The Council, after consulting with people in the community, decided that they wanted the workshop to be focused into issues of violence in the community. The 15 community participants who entered the room that first day came to investigate these issues and create interactive theatre so that the community could rehearse solutions to these problems. We asked for, and received, a support person from the community who was present at all times, in case anyone needed one-on-one support.

The participants loved being able to play; there was a tremendous freedom for them in the games. They also appreciated being able to make theatrical images by placing themselves and other participants in shapes to tell a silent, frozen story of a moment of the violence in their lives, and how this made it possible to analyze, from a more objective perspective, what was going on in the frozen images. The moments of recognition, of seeing that their neighbours had the same experiences as they did behind closed doors, were very powerful. The connections this built in the room were palpable and may have been enough to satisfy the desire in the community to open up the issue.

Whenever we got to activating images, that is, to getting the characters in the images to walk and talk, the room froze. We would wait in such long, fear-filled silences. Under the guidance of the support person, we were using talking circles many times a day to debrief. There was a lot happening in the room that was tremendously positive, but, in terms of being able to make the plays that we all kept saying we wanted to make, we were stuck.

Then something happened that gave me an insight that I have carried to this day. The door to the hall opened and a small, elderly Sto:Lo man, wearing a checked shirt, jeans and a baseball hat advertising

---

[20] Sto:Lo Territory is in the Chilliwack, BC, area, about an hour-and-a-half drive east of Vancouver.

farm equipment, walked in and sat down on a chair. Everyone except Kevin and I seemed to know who he was, although no one spoke. Everyone, including us, went and sat with him. We sat in silence for what seemed like a long time. He told us a story:

> He had just returned from a meeting with the Provincial Government and Chiefs from across the province. He was upset because he knew that the Government was trying to divide the Chiefs. There had been a vote. Two Chiefs had spoken. One was a great speaker, he said, whose voice and words filled the room. He had people sitting on the edges of their seats. The other Chief who spoke was not a good speaker. He stumbled in his sentences and was hard to hear and looked at the floor for almost the whole time. When it came time to vote, he had expected that people would vote for what the good speaker had suggested, which was to agree with the Government. But that isn't what happened. They voted for what the other Chief had said, which was to say no to what the Government was suggesting. Voting with the good speaker would have been easy, he said. Voting with the other Chief was going to create a lot of hard work. So why did people vote with the Chief who was not a good speaker, he asked. The room was silent. "Because everyone knew," he said, "that although the Chief had a hard time talking to us, he was telling the truth." He told us, "All you need to do is try your best and tell the truth. The people will understand."

He got up and left the room. The workshop turned a corner at this moment, and improvisation about violence in the community became possible. The man, Kevin and I learned later, was the Grand Chief of the Sto:Lo Nation and somehow he knew we were in trouble. His story was a tremendous gift both to the participants and to me.

Some of the workshop participants, Kevin and I talked at length later in the day about what had happened. There was no question that the workshop participants wanted to continue. They had many issues, however, which included being afraid of losing control of their emotions, of being punished for exposing a secret, of not knowing who from the community would come to see the plays and who would not. We agreed that there were ways to deal, at least to some degree, with these fears. No one was going to be forced to perform. Participants would cast themselves in roles they felt comfortable with and capable of playing; no one would impose a role on them, and within that, we could work with them so that the emotional content was something they could manage. Rehearsal – doing it over and over again – is good for this. It gives the actor an objective standpoint that makes perform-ance easier. Lastly, but very important, no one would play themselves; they would all portray characters. We also asked for more support people for the performance, understanding that this would facilitate some safety for participants afterward. There would be people they could call to talk with, days or weeks after, whose role it would be to help process any tensions or things like disclosures of abuse that might come up.

We made wonderful, courageous plays together. They were theatrically raw, with no lights, sound or complex staging. It was often hard to hear. They told the truth, though, and the Forum Theatre event in the community was very powerful. After all the heaviness of the workshop, it was tremendous to experience the laughter of the public event. Laughter of recognition, laughter of release, laughter because down-right funny things happen when it's all improvisation. Of course a serious investigation of the violence in the community happened in the midst of the laughter. And there were long silences, and there were tears. People were deeply affected and very proud and pleased with what happened. Marcia, the central organizer, remains a friend and a supporter of the theatre work to this day.

At its root, the five-day *Power Play* model worked. Part of my role from then on would be to create as much safety in the workshop room as possible, and to find ways to help participants tell their truth.

During the rest of the tour we adapted the model, played around with moving games and exercises in terms of which ones we used and what order we did them in. The model has evolved over the years and been extended from five to six days, as I recognized the need for extra rehearsal time. New exercises and games have been, and continue to be, created. The core of the model, though, is still intact after all this time.

By 1990, my work started getting press in Canada. This threw me into something of a crisis. Feeling like an imposter doing someone else's work, I wrote to Boal, asking for advice. True to his generous nature, he wrote back that if people were paying attention to my work, it had nothing to do with him – it must be because of what I was doing. Did I think he had invented all of it? No – he had built on the work of Freire, German playwright and theatre director Bertolt Brecht and many others. He told me I should be happy. It was the permission I needed to continue.

THEATRE FOR LIVING AND ITS RELATIONSHIP TO THEATRE OF THE OPPRESSED

Theatre for Living views the world through a systems theory lens. As such it recognizes that the binary poles of the oppressor and oppressed are actually part of the same large organism living in some kind of dysfunction. In order to get to the root causes of a problem, *Theatre for Living* investigates the oppressed, but also makes space to investigate the fears, desires and motivations of the oppressor – with integrity. Why? Because oppressors of the world do not come from outer space. Living communities grow them. The clear boundaries we like to think exist between oppressor and oppressed are very often not clear.

Viewing the world through a systems theory lens, we also confront the reality that we humans are not prisoners of the structures we inhabit. Nature teaches us that structure is created by patterns of behaviour – not the other way round. Working politically to alter the structures in which we live without changing the behaviour that creates those structures is futile. Because *Theatre for Living* approaches the community as a living organism and recognizes the above, when plays are created, they are made to help us investigate ways to change the behaviours that create the structure, not only the structure itself.

Audience members are invited to use Image and Forum Theatre to alter the behaviours that create oppressive structures – not battle against the structure while separating it from the behaviour that created the structure.

What is Forum Theatre?

Forum Theatre is a form of participatory theatre developed by Boal. It is an opportunity for creative, community-based dialogue. The theatre is created and performed by community members who are living the issues under investigation. Workshop participants create a short play, which is performed once all the way through, so the audience can see the situation and the problems presented. The story builds to a crisis and stops there, offering no solutions. In the *Theatre of the Oppressed* the play is then run again, with audience members able to freeze the action at any point where they see an incident of oppression. An audience member yells "Stop!", comes into the playing area, replaces the oppressed character and tries out her idea. The other actors respond in character. This is called an *intervention*.

A new invitation

Theatre for Living broadens out the invitation of who can replace who in a Forum Theatre event.

In *Games for Actors and Non-Actors*,[21] Boal writes: "For a Forum Theatre showing to qualify as true *Theatre of the Oppressed*, only *spect-actors*[22] who are victims of the same oppression as the character (by identity or by analogy) can replace the oppressed protagonist to find new approaches or new forms of liberation."

---

[21] Published by Routledge, Oxford 1992, p. 240.
[22] The word Boal uses to describe the audience member who is a potential actor in the Forum. Not an actor yet, but more than a spectator, she is a spect-actor.

While Boal goes on to describe how this rule can be broken by an audience, he clearly states that breaking the rule is the exception and not the rule.

Humans think in metaphor. When we think about war, peace, joy, sadness, we see those states as symbolic pictures. This is what makes us capable of creating and interpreting art. Living communities also think in metaphor. It is our individual and collective interpretations of metaphor that create our core images of the world and our reactions to it.

In the Forum Theatre experience the metaphorical image of getting rid of what we don't want is very different from the metaphorical image of getting what we do want. For instance, not wanting to get beaten up sets up a very different set of desires, fears and actions in us than wanting to create safety or wanting a healthy family.

The traditional invitation in Forum Theatre is to replace an oppressed character and do battle with an oppressor, to experiment with ways to break the oppression. Because of the direction that my own work had taken by the mid-1980s, and my own interpretation of Boal's *Theatre of the Oppressed*, this had turned into an invitation in my work to enter the stage and get rid of what you don't want.[23] My observation is that this has been at the centre of the invitation of many people doing Forum Theatre.

I believe the oppressor is always in the audience in some manifestation. In some way, he is always part of the living community, whether this is at the micro or the macro level, as an individual human or as an internalized sensibility. When we create a production on family violence, statistics being what they are, it is very likely that there are perpetrators of violence in the audience. This also, of course, can manifest in the form of an internalized perpetrator – in this case, that sensibility may live inside the oppressed and be turned on one's self.

If it is our desire to help end cycles of oppression through the use of theatre, then we have a responsibility to create theatre that rings with authenticity for the diversity of the people in attendance. That is, theatre in which both the oppressed and the oppressors see themselves

---

[23] For an explanation of this 'aha' moment, please see the subsection on *Reclaiming Our Spirits*.

on stage as real people and legitimate members of the community, who are engaged in their own complex struggles. This does not mean that we condone oppressive actions. It does mean, however, that the plays we create must contain as much of the complexity of real life as possible.

In plays that recognize the complexity of life, who can replace who must be wide open. Men replace women, women replace men, youth replace the elderly, rich replace poor and vice versa, and on and on. There is learning for the living community in deep and honest community dialogue. By limiting who can replace who in the Forum Theatre event we put artificial constraints on the dialogue.

Here is a case study example: in 2004, Headlines' production *Practicing Democracy*[24] was created and performed by people living in chronic poverty. In one of the scenes the character Karla is panhandling. She needs 20 dollars so she can have a safe place to sleep that night. She encounters Elaine, who used to be her social services worker. Elaine helped Karla find housing and is surprised and upset to see her back on the street. Elaine is also now unemployed and is struggling with her own personal crisis, which we discover later in the play. She refuses to give Karla any money, saying she has none to give. Karla gets aggressive because she is desperate. Elaine reacts violently, pushes Karla away, berates her and leaves.

One night a woman replaced Elaine in the panhandling scene. This woman was obviously very wealthy. I mention this because it has relevance to what happened on stage, and in some of the discussion throughout the evening.

She took 20 dollars out of her purse and put her arm around Karla, and told her that she would give her money, but only if Karla would "come for coffee and talk about her options." The woman was, I think, in her own way, trying to do development work. She recognized that

---

24 A Legislative Theatre project created and performed by: Lillian Carlson,* Patrick Keating,* Emily Mayne, James Mickelson, Theresa Myles and Sandra Pronteau. Stage Manager: Melissa C. Powell. Designers: Harry Vanderschee, Caitlin Pencarrick, Lincoln Clarkes, Marina Szijarto. Legislative Scribe: Carrie Gallant, BA, LLB. Directed and Joked by: David Diamond.*
*Appeared courtesy of Canadian Actors' Equity Association.
See http://www.headlinestheatre.com/pastwork.htm

there was a larger problem on the stage and this was her well-meaning way to help.

Karla reacted in a very hostile, but not inappropriate manner to the woman, who, from her place of obvious privilege, appeared to be very condescending. Karla's forceful reaction, which grew into yelling and swearing at the woman as the improvisation proceeded, was very shocking for many people in the room. The woman, now also upset, mentioned that she was sorry she had come onto the stage. I asked her to stay, and told her and the audience that I thought what had happened was of great value. I asked her if it was her intention to make Karla upset. "Of course not," she replied.

In deconstructing the moment, we were able to analyze how this impulse from a well-meaning person was perceived to be disrespectful and demeaning by Karla, and, instead of helping to solve the problem, made matters worse. Isn't this part of the larger issue? Of course Karla has immediate need – the 20 dollars – and this must not be forgotten. But isn't what happened on the stage also a mirror of how some social service agencies operate in a demeaning manner to people living in poverty? And how top-down Third World aid operates?

This scene, and the entire play, was structured to have no clear oppressors or oppressed. All the characters were struggling with various aspects of poverty. Inside the world of the play they were all, in different moments, oppressed oppressors. By exploring the issue of the relationship between these two women, and honouring the actions of the woman who replaced Elaine – who could be perceived as an oppressor in the moment of the scene in which the woman intervened – we were able to understand much better not only what was happening to Karla and that she was deeply aware of her situation, but also the role that "Elaines" play in the ecology of this moment.

The actor playing Karla had been very challenged by this intervention. She spoke with me later, though, about how valuable it had been for her in deepening her own understanding of her reaction to "Elaines" in the world. Likewise, feedback from many people in the audience that night was that they had new insights into the dynamics of poverty that will change their relationship to people living in poverty. I believe this will in turn help, even though in a small way, to create the structural change we need to tackle the issue on a systemic level.

The level of dialogue that happened over this five or 10-minute intervention would never have been possible within the rules of: "only spect-actors who are victims of the same oppression as the character (by identity or by analogy) can replace the oppressed protagonist to find new approaches or new forms of liberation."

Theatre for Living, having grown directly out of Boal's *Theatre of the Oppressed*, uses many games, exercises and principles of what has become known as "Boal-based work". Games and exercises in *Theatre for Living* have taken on a new perspective. We are never telling any one person's story, but rather creating the best fictional art we can that tells the true story of the living community. Characters are no longer oppressors or oppressed. Characters have become community members engaged in various struggles with each other and with dysfunction, which is sometimes personal and sometimes systemic. This is the subject matter of the next chapter.

Boal himself has been confronting this in his more recent work, with the evolution of newer techniques like *Rainbow of Desire* and *Cops in the Head*.[25] I will also deal specifically with these techniques in subsequent sections bearing these titles respectively.

The invitation in *Theatre for Living* is to engage in the struggles of the characters, which we recognize as also our own struggles – not to break the oppression (getting rid of what we don't want), but to create healthy community, or safety, or respect (getting what we do want).

---

[25] See Boal's *Rainbow of Desire*, published by Routledge, Oxford 1995.

THE LIVING COMMUNITY

I have witnessed many times through my own experiences of making theatre that a community is made up of individuals that comprise the living organism of the community. Communities need to use symbolic language to express themselves, just like people; if they don't they get sick, just like people. As the use of symbolic language (singing, dancing, theatre-making, etc.) has become more and more commodified, communities have manifested more and more disease.

Autopoiesis

Living systems all have something in common. They have a pattern of organization. In order for that pattern of organization to be present, the living system must have two components: a physical boundary and a metabolic network (a little factory) contained inside the boundary. Nourishment of some kind passes through the boundary, as does the by-product of that nourishment. A living cell is an example of this.

Capra explains the process of autopoiesis very early in his book *The Hidden Connections*,[26] because it is a defining characteristic of life and therefore central to an understanding of systems theory.

---

[26] *The Hidden Connections*, by Fritjof Capra, published by Doubleday, New York 2002.

Principia Cybernetica Web[27] the Web Dictionary of Cybernetics and Systems defines *autopoiesis* as: "a process whereby a system produces its own organization and maintains and constitutes itself in a space; e.g., a biological cell, a living organism and to some extent *a corporation and a society as a whole.*" (Italics are mine.)

Capra refers to the work of sociologist Niklas Luhmann[28] and his theory of "social autopoiesis".[29] Luhmann writes, "Social systems use communication as their particular mode of autopoietic reproduction. Their elements are communications that are recursively produced and reproduced by a network of communications and that cannot exist outside of such a network."[30]

Capra continues:

> "These networks of communications are self-generating. Each communication creates thoughts and meaning, which give rise to further communications, and thus the entire network generates itself – it is autopoietic. As communications recur in multiple feedback loops, they produce a shared system of beliefs, explanations, and values – a common context of meaning – that is continually sustained by further communications. Through this shared context of meaning individuals acquire identities as members of the social network, and in this way the network generates its own boundary. It is not a physical boundary but a boundary of expectations, of confidentiality and loyalty, which is continually maintained and renegotiated by the network itself."[31]

And so, using the work of respected researchers to support his proposition, Capra suggests that social systems may be alive and attain a consciousness. He continues:

> "Social networks are first and foremost networks of communication involving symbolic language, cultural constraints, relationships of power, and so on. To understand the structures of such

---

[27] http://pespmc1.vub.ac.be
[28] I discovered the wonderful work of Luhmann via Capra as I researched this book.
[29] *Social Systems*, by Niklas Luhmann, published by Stanford University Press, Stanford 1990.
[30] Capra, *The Hidden Connections*, p. 83.
[31] Capra, *The Hidden Connections*, p. 83.

networks we need to use insights from social theory, philosophy, cognitive science, anthropology, and other disciplines. A unified systemic framework for the understanding of biological and social phenomena will emerge only when the concepts of nonlinear dynamics are combined with insights from these fields of study."[32]

In other words, we must first be willing to take a step outside the mechanistic Cartesian paradigm and accept that everything around us may be interconnected in nonlinear ways in order to be able to discuss living social systems.

Patterns and structure

Capra defines the *pattern of organization* of a living system as "the configuration of relationships among the system's components that determines the system's essential characteristics." He goes on to describe the *structure* of the living system as "the material embodiment of its pattern of organization," and the *life process* as, "the continual process of this embodiment."[33]

This is difficult to grasp because it goes so against the linear, mechanistic model that most of us went to school in during the 20th century, but please note that it is the *pattern of relationships that creates the structure*, not the other way around. The *structure* is the *material embodiment* of the *pattern*.

Is it then the case that in order to change the local and global structures that seem to control our lives, it is not effective to focus solely on structural change? That we must work to change the *patterns* that create those structures, otherwise the structures will be recreated in their same form again?

Paulo Freire refers to this phenomenon when he writes about the cyclical nature of the deeply oppressed aspiring to become their oppressors. Freire observes that the challenge of revolutionaries does

[32] Capra, *The Hidden Connections*, p. 82.
[33] Capra, *The Hidden Connections*, pp. 70, 71.

not end when they have overthrown an oppressive regime. The challenge continues in trying to not become what the revolutionary movement itself was fighting against. How do we break this cycle, both on an individual, human level, and on the level of structure?

In 1986 I wasn't seeing my own theatre process in these terms of patterns and structure, but in retrospect, when creating the *Power Play* model in the mid and late 1980s, I was developing a considered series of steps contained inside a week-long process. The steps are comprised of games, exercises and spaces for internal feedback that are potential patterns for relationships. The potential patterns become actualized as the group experiences each game or exercise in their own way. The process is not frozen. Quite the opposite. As different participants from various communities work through the patterns, they create structure, in this case, in the form of theatre. The resulting theatre is always different because the life experiences and perspectives that the participants bring to the process are always different.

The focus of the theatre is interpersonal relationships. The experimentation on how to change the patterns of the relationships in a Forum Theatre event is a step along the path to altering the structures that emerge from the patterns.

Understanding how this happens on an organizational level makes it possible to consciously work both with the individual participants in a workshop and also the larger living organism that is in the room: the living community. The larger living organism operates the same way and has the same characteristics as any other living system.

How is a community a living thing?

Community exists when a group of people share geography, values, experiences, expectations or beliefs. Their connection may be voluntary or involuntary. Sometimes we are simply born into a community. A person can be a member of many different communities.

As of 2007, I have lived in a housing co-operative for 23 years. This is a voluntary, geographic community of people who share a common

belief about housing being safe, affordable and not part of a specula-
tive, capitalist structure. Our shared belief about housing does not
mean we share beliefs on everything, like how committees should
function, noise in the courtyard, politics, religion, etc. I am also a
member of non-geographic communities: the theatre community,
which exists locally, nationally and internationally; and the community
of social justice activists which, again, exists on local, national and
international levels. I am also a member of a smaller community
practicing Boal-based theatre. The list goes on.

Children in a school create layers of communities within the structure
of the school: groups of friends, home rooms, grades, teams and
special interest clubs within the community that is the entire school.
The administrative staff and teachers make up yet other communities
in the school, which are linked but separated from each other by
boundaries of power. Canada is full of immigrant communities of
ethnicity: Italians, Scots, Kenyans, Ugandans, Greeks, Chinese,
Japanese, etc. First Nations are also each distinct communities.
Prisoners find themselves in an involuntary community of inmates and
guards. Communities exist within each other, overlapping each other
and seemingly separate from each other.

Capra, in writing about what creates culture, also describes, I believe,
what defines a community:

> "...culture arises from a complex, highly nonlinear dynamic. It is
> created by a social network involving multiple feedback loops
> through which values, beliefs, and rules of conduct are continu-
> ally communicated, modified and sustained. It emerges from a
> network of communications among individuals; and as it
> emerges, it produces constraints on their actions. In other words,
> the social structures, or rules of behaviour, that constrain the ac-
> tions of individuals are produced and continually reinforced by
> their own network of communications."[34]

He goes on to describe the linkages between what we easily perceive as
a living thing (a living cell or animal) and larger, less easily recognizable organisms that exist without readily obvious boundaries:

---

[34] Capra, *The Hidden Connections*, p. 87.

"The analysis of living systems in terms of four interconnected perspectives – form, matter, process and meaning – makes it possible to apply a unified understanding of life to phenomena in the realm of matter, as well as to phenomena in the realm of meaning. For example...metabolic networks in biological systems correspond to networks of communications in social systems; chemical processes producing material structures correspond to thought processes producing semantic structures; and flows of energy and matter correspond to flows of information and ideas."[35]

Capra is describing an entity, larger than a single living organism, that creates a boundary around it. Not a physical boundary, but a boundary of ideas, information, beliefs and behaviour that is distinct to a specific culture or community. The boundary contains a group of people. The group of people function like a metabolic system. A metabolic system surrounded by a boundary is autopoietic. In other words, a living thing.

In the Sto:Lo Nation workshop that was mentioned in the previous chapter – and it is the same in all *Theatre for Living* workshops – the working group and I created our own temporary version of a living cell. We were the metabolic network. We had a common purpose that created a non-physical boundary, but we also established the walls of the community hall in which we were working as another boundary. The Grand Chief, also a community member, brought us much-needed nourishment. When the time was right, other community members transgressed the boundary. The by-products of the metabolic system were a deeper understanding of dynamics in the community and changes in relationships and behaviour, which, in turn, contributed to a process of altering the structures that the community inhabits.

---

[35] Capra, *The Hidden Connections*, p. 261.

entering a living community

A mechanistic view of the universe implies, of course, that a community is a machine.

Machines can be worked on from the outside. It is easy to see this happening all around us. The United States government decided to work on Iraq from the outside, as it has been working on many countries (Guatemala, Colombia, El Salvador, etc.) for decades. US foreign policy is a clear example of what happens when we operate from a mechanistic view. The Government of Canada's relationship to First Nations populations has from the very beginning been based on the same principles. The stated purpose of Canada's Residential Schools[36] was to "take the Indian out of the child." If everything is a machine, it is very easy to dehumanize people.

If however, we embrace the systems view, it becomes impossible to consider that a family, or a community, an organization or a nation, can benefit from being worked on from the outside. Living things change and grow in a healthy way, not because they are made to by outside forces, but because they want to, or because they do so naturally. Even in instances where the impulse to change has come from an outside stimulus, actual behavioural change occurs from within. It cannot be imposed. For this reason, an invitation from the community is essential.

working by invitation

I am not a hunter. However, I grew up with an image of a hunter as someone who armed themselves and then went stomping through the forest, the jungle, the grassland, stalking their prey.

In 1986 I was in Kispiox, in Gitxsan Territory, in Northwestern BC, working on an Agit-prop play[37] (i.e., not Forum Theatre) with the

---

[36] For an explanation of Canadian Residential Schools see the section on *Out of the Silence*.

[37] There is a long history of Agitation Propaganda (Agit-prop) in political, issue-based theatre. In Agit-prop, the play knows the solutions to the issues presented in the play, which gives the audience a strong message that is determined by the creators.

Gitxsan and Wet'suwet'en Hereditary Chiefs that was to become *NO`XYA` (Our Footprints)*. During my research and writing process, Gitxsan Chief Ta'wok (James Morrison) from a Wolf House[38] from Gitanyow came to see me. He wanted to talk about traditional hunting rituals. Chief Ta'wok redefined my image of hunting.

He explained that the traditional and experienced hunter did not stalk prey. The hunter found a place in the forest and calmed himself. Being calm, the other animals of the forest would not feel threatened and would, in time, present themselves to the hunter; he would thank them and respectfully take only as much as he needed to feed the family and the community.

I am not a hunter and neither is Headlines Theatre. But this knowledge from Chief Ta'wok made sense to me in terms of how a theatre company could function in the ecology of many interconnected communities.

One way that theatre companies function is to decide their programming for the public. In most cases the director and/or a programming committee and/or the Board of Directors decide on a season, and then it is the marketing department's job to convince the public to come and see the selected plays.

Another way, I thought, could be that Headlines 'calms' itself; recognizes it is part of the larger community – not an entity that exists separate from our potential audience. Having calmed ourselves, we could wait for project invitations to come to us – to present themselves. We would no longer stomp through the forest.

By 1990, *NO` XYA` (Our Footprints)* had toured BC twice, Canada once and the traditional Maori communities in the northern part of New Zealand. The *Theatre for Living* work was also starting to gain momentum. It made sense that community-based projects would be initiated by community invitation. That is, not initiated by the company. Headlines Theatre took on the properties of a social network. In a hierarchical structure, power is controlled in a linear way. Most theatre companies work that way: a small group gets together, although sometimes it is just one person, and decides what the

---

38 The Gitxsan have four Clans or Houses: Eagle, Wolf, Frog and Fireweed.

company's season of plays will be and then presents it to the public. The theatre company's task is then to convince the public to come see that production or season of plays.

The way Headlines works 90 percent of the time is that the work of the company is determined by communities who are extending invitations. (By contrast, the impulse for a mainstage production[39] comes for the most part, from inside the Headlines company structure, but work does not begin without the active participation of relevant community organizations.) The decision-making process for most of the programming has become nonlinear. It involves multiple feedback loops and the results are impossible to predict. This is the structure of a *network*, with Headlines connected to a myriad of organizations and individuals all over the world who are determining the theatre company's programming.[40]

A *Theatre for Living* project happens because a community *wants something* and has imagined that whatever it is they want can be achieved through theatre. In order to create theatre with community members, the theatre director or *Joker*[41] must pass through the boundary that defines the community.

An invitation from one individual or an organization is not enough to guarantee that the invitation is actually from the community. This lesson has been learned the hard way. A couple of examples follow.

a North American white guy sweats in Namibia

In 1990 the country Namibia was born after years of sometimes bloody struggle. Two years later SWAPO, which had been the prominent revolutionary party and was now the government, decided that it

---

[39] A six-day *Power Play* process happens by invitation. Many of these can happen in a year. Headlines has generally done one mainstage project a year that requires a great deal of fundraising, has a longer creation process and will run in a theatre or community hall for between two and four weeks.
[40] Some of these have included work with Passamaquoddy women in the US on Aboriginal language issues; work with youth on racism and violence throughout BC and Canada; a project on body image in Melbourne, Australia; a project on racism in Italy; and many more.
[41] The term *Joker* comes from Boal and is used to describe the director, animator, facilitator, wild card, in a theatre process that uses Boal-based techniques.

would be a good thing to bring popular educators into Namibia to seed community-based projects in literacy, anti-violence work, etc. I was honoured and excited to be one of the people invited.

Almost 100 popular educators gathered in Windhoek, the capital, for two days of briefings, and then we were sent out to various communities to do our work. I was sent to Rehoboth, in the centre of the country. As it was explained to me, the Basters of Rehoboth, a mostly mixed-race population, had been against the revolution. The Basters, who were lighter skinned than most indigenous South Africans, felt that they would lose power in the social structure if apartheid were abolished. They had lost. I was a peace offering.

The community had extremely high unemployment rates. The most prominent store, right in the middle of the town, was a place called "Boozerama". No one other than the Namibian woman who travelled with me from Windhoek as Ovambo[42] translator knew I was coming. This was a terrible surprise for both of us.

What to do? We started going door to door. Imagine the reaction. 'Hello. We know you have no idea who this white guy that is obviously dying in the heat is, but would you like to come with us and make theatre about the issues in the community?' Slam. Slam. Gales of laughter – slam. Why *wouldn't* they slam their doors?

As we travelled, we started to notice that the children were very curious about what was happening – who was this alien? A parade of children was building behind us. We stopped at a large tree and started playing games with the kids. We had a wonderful time. We asked them if they wanted to come back tomorrow. Yes. Try to bring your parents, OK?

The next day, many of the children came back. Still no adults. We played more games and as the day wore on, the parents started coming out to see what was happening with their kids. Slowly, a group built. By the third day we had a working group of about 20 adults and children. We made a very powerful play about lack of safety because of gangs, drug dealing, alcoholism, unemployment and violence in the community. It

---

[42] An African language with tongue clicks. Time, I am sad to say, has obscured the woman's name in my memory.

was staged beautifully, with characters making entrances over hills, and in a truck that came racing up the road.

A local teacher named Pepsi, who spoke English, got involved. He could see the power of what was happening in the rehearsals – people were talking to each other in a new way, working on something together, co-operating, forging new friendships. Over 100 people came to the performance, which was centred under the large tree. We did Forum Theatre and there was a spirited and creative community dialogue, all of it through translation, about how to create a sense of safety in the community, so that people could go out at night and not fear getting beaten and robbed.

Pepsi and I had been meeting in the evenings and I had been giving him a crash course in theatre. As planned, at the performance, he announced that if they wanted him to, he would try to keep the theatre project going. They did, and he did for at least two years. Beyond that I do not know what happened, as we eventually lost touch.

Going door to door in Namibia, I was in a position of trying to sell people something they didn't want – a travelling 'expert' with services that no one knew anything about – and had every reason to distrust. There was no way out of this role until the games started generating actual relationships with the children. Through the games the power could become more balanced. I would lead a game that they didn't know and they would show me a game I didn't know. It was through this process that we started to get to know each other, to be humans together. The building of trust made it possible for them to engage. It was the children's level of engagement that began my admission through the boundary. This is also what moved the parents to invite me the rest of the way, into the living community. Being in the geographic location does not mean one has entered the community.

In the end, this project turned out quite well, even though we also angered and alienated some people by the way it got started. We were fortunate. The lesson for me was that a workshop does not start on the first day of the workshop. I should have asked far more questions when the invitation came, and taken responsibility for trying to ensure that the invitation really was coming from the community with which I would be working.

is there a time to say no?

When something goes wrong, as it did with the Namibia invitation, it is, of course, an opportunity for reflection and then planning to improve the process for the future. By the late 1990s, Headlines had better thought out material to send to potential organizers in communities. There were some things we insisted on: community organizers would not work alone. If there is a committee of local people organizing the project, there is some assurance that the community is actually making the invitation, and it is not coming from one individual, or perhaps, from outside the community, however well intentioned. The theatre work can be very empowering, but one can't force empowerment on people.

Even though there are many established processes in place at Headlines, in 2003 I found myself at a healing centre in British Columbia facing an extremely difficult situation. I had been invited by someone I knew to create theatre about drug and alcohol addiction with youth in the centre. We had had many meetings both in person and on the telephone that involved me, Headlines' staff and the friend, who represented the Board of Directors of the centre. As is normally part of the contract, we sent a letter from me to be given to all the potential participants, explaining what the workshop structure was and what would be expected of them. This is part of their decision-making process about whether or not they wanted to participate. We also sent a video that documents some of what happens inside a workshop. We had assurances that the youth were very excited about the week-long process and the performance that would follow.

Upon my arrival I discovered that the healing centre was one step away from prison. The youth were there under orders from the Court and under lock and key. Not one of them had any idea I was coming until the day the workshop started. Not even the support person from the centre, who would be with me in the workshop, had been told until that day.

As we went around the circle that first morning, what I heard from the youth was that not only did they not know what the workshop was about, but when they discovered we were supposed to be making theatre about their struggles with alcohol and drug addiction, some of them informed me they had no problems with alcohol and drugs. Of course, under the circumstances we were in I am pretty certain that for some of them these statements were not 100 percent accurate, but what was certainly true was that they had no desire or intention to create theatre about these issues, or to discuss them with me.

I asked them if they wanted to at least do some games and exercises, just so they could see what the work was about. After all, I had driven many hours to get there, I had nowhere else to go, and, if they weren't with me it was probable they were going back to their rooms. We all agreed that we were in a bad situation together and may as well give it a try. I was thinking that they might have fun doing the games and this would kindle a desire which would then make it possible to do some kind of theatre; maybe it would go to performance, maybe not.

I was wrong. It cannot be the workshop facilitator or Joker's role to peel workshop participants off the walls and beg, cajole or try to force them to engage in an activity. I have worked very successfully in prisons. In those instances, of course, the prisoners had no choice about whether or not they were in prison, but they had a choice about whether or not they would work with me. Here, the youth, also prisoners, had not made any choice. They had simply been marched into a room and handed over to me, so I could work on them from the outside, like one works on a car. In this way they had (once again, I imagine) been dehumanized. It was a violation of their human rights.

I told them that if they wanted to work with me I would work with them, but that I wouldn't try to convince them more than I had already. They needed to want to do this work, and if they didn't, that was OK. What did they want to do? They said they wanted to go back to their rooms. I did something that led me into conflict with the organizers. I agreed with the youth and cancelled the workshop.

Forcing people to make theatre together might be possible, but it is the antithesis of *Theatre for Living* and, from everything I know about Boal, of the *Theatre of the Oppressed* as well. The conflict with the organizers had to do with my contractual responsibilities to them to run a workshop. I felt strongly, and still do, that my responsibilities to the participants to not dehumanize them took precedence, even though the organizers were paying the bill.

a constant evolution

The manner in which a *Theatre for Living* project enters a community is constantly evolving. Since the experience with the healing centre, part of the contractual obligation with the project organizers is to have at least one of the theatre workshop participants on the organizing committee.

It is also important that the organizing committee, through discussions with other community members, decide on the general subject matter *before participant recruitment starts.* What the organizers are doing is creating a container, a space, in which the living organism that is the workshop group is going to gather and work. They are extending an invitation and, like any invitation, it needs to be clear what people are being invited to do.

This makes it possible for the workshop participants to make a choice. If there is no predetermined focus, how can individuals decide if they want to participate or not? Coming together to look at community issues or oppression is not focused enough. If the sense from community conversations is that there is a desire to look at issues of violence, for instance, or intergenerational conflict, then people can choose to involve themselves in it or not. If the workshop is left open, with the subject matter determined by the participants after they arrive, inevitably there will be some people who are alienated from the process because they end up working on issues that they would not have chosen. Either that, or, because they didn't have enough information, they may leave the process feeling angry, defeated and disempowered, having agreed to participate in something that turned out to be very different from what they were imagining.

Most often, organizational processes like these will help pave the way for an entry into the community and a start to the workshop process that feels safe for everyone. Of course there are never guarantees. In the same way that all individuals have their own history that shapes their reactions to events, all communities also have their own histories that shape their reactions to events.

Is it theatre or therapy?

A *Theatre for Living* workshop that goes to public performance is not a therapy session for participants and must not be organized as such. It is an opportunity for the workshop participants to articulate interactive theatre about relevant issues and to create something that is of great service to their community. It is this that is the empowering nature of the process.

Part of creating a safe environment in which people can work is being very clear about what the event is and what it is not. A *Theatre for Living* workshop is a theatre workshop, not a group or individual therapy session. Like any good theatre, it can and often does have therapeutic value. If the community organizers want to create an event where, very specifically, a therapy session takes place, they have a responsibility to be clear and honest with potential participants about that desire. Again, the participant must be able to make a choice about whether or not she attends. The decision to participate in a theatre project that will make plays about personal, community issues is very different than the decision to enter group therapy. This is also important from the Joker's perspective. People enter the room with very different expectations when they come for theatre than when they come for therapy.

Why does a theatre company choose to produce Shakespeare's *Romeo and Juliet*? Because there is a hope that the audience, regardless of age, orientation, origin, etc., will identify with the young lovers and, through this identification, have some kind of transformational experience in the theatre, leaving different than when they arrived. Is *Romeo and Juliet* individual or group therapy?

Theatre that grows out of community process and issues has the same goals as any other theatre, with other goals attached. There is a desire that voices will be heard that are most often not heard in the mainstream theatre; that issues will be discussed that are very seldom discussed; that through the interactive Forum Theatre process, the community will have a dialogue about solutions to the issues with which it is struggling. Like a production of *Romeo and Juliet*, though, it is theatre. Like all good theatre, it has therapeutic value.

when and how to have project support people

A *Theatre for Living* process will usually start with individuals' stories in some manner, offered as silent images or as gestures. In the making of the theatre, though, we are not creating a play about one person's life. We are not there to serve any individual. We might use one person's story to attract people who have similar experiences, like in the *Magnetic Image* or *Song of the Mermaid* exercises,43 but from those exercises we are then creating a theatrical fiction that tells the truth of the community's experience. We are always moving from the singular to the plural and using theatrical language to make art.

The theatre process then continues to pluralize when the larger community comes to participate in the interactive event. Once this happens, the focus is no longer on the workshop participants. The Forum Theatre is not designed to serve only the participants, but the community members who have gathered to see the theatre and engage in a theatrical dialogue about the issues under investigation. We go from the singular to the plural in the workshop, to the meta-plural at the public event.

Of course, there are times when the subject matter that the community wants to make theatre about is going to be emotionally and psychologically volatile (violence, abuse, racism, addiction, etc.). In these situations a counsellor or support person from the local community is needed. Situations may arise where participants want to engage in one-on-one counselling or need referrals to counselling in a way that the supportive nature of the group work itself cannot provide.

The support person could be an Elder (I mean this in both Native and non-Native contexts), a social worker, a teacher or a peer, etc. The important thing is that the community recognizes the person and accepts him or her in the support role.

The Joker has many functions, all of them theatrical. Of course the Joker can and should be a compassionate human being, but cannot, I believe, be in the role of a social worker, therapist or counsellor. One person cannot fill both functions, as each has a very different focus.

---

43 For a detailed explanation of both of these exercises see the *Creating plays* section of the chapter *In the Workshop Room.*

The Joker being both theatre director and support person also puts far too much power in the hands of one person, a person who is in many instances leaving the community once the process is finished.

The support person (or people) needs to be in place before the workshop starts; needs to live in the community, be *part of* the community. The support person needs to be a partial participant in the workshop – playing all the group-building and trust games, so as to become an integral and trusted part of the group – but not participate in the exercises. Her experiences of the issue are not material for the play creation or part of the group investigation.

It is my preference that if there are support people in a workshop, that they not be proactive. This means that they make themselves available to participants who have the opportunity to come to them if they want. The support person does not constantly check in privately with participants if and when they perceive one or more of them are struggling with an issue. This has the potential to rob the participants of reflective experiences during the process. The participants know that this person is there, what his or her role is, and that they can go to the support person if they want to, during and after the workshop. The support person should be a supportive resource for the group. Not a therapeutic obligation.

the 'why question'

In 1985 I attended an international *Theatre of the Oppressed* workshop with Boal in Orvelte, Holland. It was at this workshop that something central about being a Joker became apparent to me. People kept asking Boal the same question over and over again: "If 'x' happens, what do I do?" It was as if there were supposed to be a formula.

Of course, there isn't one. Practitioners of community-based work can and do evolve guidelines and ethical codes in which they work. But once one adopts a formula, one is no longer present inside the moment with the people in the room. The notion that a formula can exist is a manifestation of the idea that a process with a community can be mechanical. Functioning inside that paradigm makes it extremely difficult to recognize the living properties of the community. If we relate to the community as a machine that will always react the same way to the same game or exercise, we lose our ability to really listen, to really see. We lose our ability to direct the creation of *this theatre project* because we are no longer in a real dialogue with *this living community*.

There is a question to ask other than "what", and that is "why": "Why are we making this investigation?" By investigation I mean to include the facilitation of a game or exercise, an activation of an image, the creation and Joking of a Forum play. The answer to the question leads to a solution regarding what to do in any given moment.

We are making this investigation: "to learn how to deal with violence in the schools"; "to understand how not to criminalize poverty"; "to help doctors understand how to provide health care to First Nations patients in a culturally appropriate way." If that is why we are here, then what can I do as a Joker right now to take a step in that direction that is relevant to this moment? What kind of exercise or game can I suggest? What kind of direction can I give the actor? What kind of question can I ask the group or the audience? Moment-specific answers flow from the "why" question.

So far we have discussed in basic terms what Forum Theatre is and how *Power Plays* got started. We have investigated through science and anecdote how a community is a living organism and have looked at some guidelines to ensure that communication is clear. Before we get into theatre workshop process, I want to spend some time investigating the mechanistic model.

FEEDBACK LOOPS

In nature we can see that any organism, from a single cell to a human being to a nation, has patterns of behaviour. The patterns of behaviour set up actions that are experienced by the organism's immediate world and, in turn, produce a reaction. These reactions become the organism's experiences, which either reinforce the behaviour, or create within the organism an adaptation of the behaviour. The organism either behaves the same way again, or it behaves in a different way. This same or different behaviour is again reacted to by the immediate world, which itself is made up of organisms that are constantly adapting behaviour in the same manner. Every living thing (single cell, human, vegetable, organization, community, nation) is in a complex network of overlapping feedback loops, or dialogues with the world around it, and these dialogues are part of what shapes the world. Capra refers to this complex network as "the web of life". As discussed earlier, out of these patterns structure emerges, including but not limited to: institutions, laws, architecture, patterned ways of being.

In the mechanistic model it is easy to see people as disconnected from each other, their immediate community and their environment. Within this context it is also possible to live within a fabrication of highly delineated Good and Evil; to create an artificial and tightly defined construct of oppressor and oppressed.

Oppressors and oppressed emerge from, and are sustained in their roles by, living communities, through this complex interplay of feedback loops. The disparities and various forms of destructive behaviour in the world, one might argue, are a sign of dysfunction in the living organism as a result of an extended period of time in feedback loops that are detrimental to the organism's health.

In the *Pedagogy of the Oppressed*, Freire writes about how the oppressed aspire to become the oppressor:

> "But almost always, during the initial stage of the struggle, the oppressed, instead of striving for liberation, tend themselves to become oppressors, or 'sub-oppressors'....Their ideal is to be men; but for them, to be a 'man' is to be an oppressor. This is their model of humanity....It is a rare peasant who, once 'promoted' to overseer, does not become more of a tyrant towards his former comrades than the owner himself.

> To surmount the situation of oppression, men must first critically recognize its causes, so that through transforming action they can create a new situation – one that makes possible the pursuit of a fuller humanity. But the struggle to be more fully human has already begun in the authentic struggle to transform the situation. Although the situation of oppression is a dehumanized and dehumanizing totality affecting both the oppressors and those whom they oppress, it is the latter who must, from their stifled humanity, wage for both the struggle for a fuller humanity; the oppressor, who is himself dehumanized because he dehumanizes others, is unable to lead the struggle."[44]

Freire recognizes that there is a complex relationship between the oppressor and the oppressed, and that they are inextricably linked to each other, because each is, inescapably, part of humanity.

If we embrace the ideas inherent in systems theory, it becomes apparent that the oppressor and the oppressed are not only linked, but they are an inseparable part of the same network and sometimes the same organism. In theatrical terms, sometimes the same character. If we want to end cycles of oppression, the empowerment of the oppressed

---

[44] Freire, *Pedagogy of the Oppressed*, pp. 22, 23 and 24.

is only one necessary step along a path of numerous steps that lead to a healing of the larger network or organism. Empowerment cannot be an end unto itself without working to change the patterns of behaviour that create structure.

Capra reiterates this idea of interconnectedness from a very technological perspective:

> "As this new century unfolds, there are two developments that will have major impacts on the well-being and ways of life of humanity. Both have to do with networks, and both involve radically new technologies. One is the rise of global capitalism; the other is the creation of sustainable communities (ecodesign)...the goal of the global economy is to maximize the wealth and power of its elites; the goal of ecodesign is to maximize the sustainability of the web of life.
>
> These two scenarios – each involving complex networks and special advanced technologies – are currently on a collision course. We have seen that the current form of global capitalism is ecologically and socially unsustainable. The so-called "global market" is really a network of machines programmed according to the fundamental principle that money-making should take precedence over human rights, democracy, environmental protection, or any other value. *However, human values can change; they are not natural laws."*[45]

Capra is urging us through all of his work to step out of the paradigm of the mechanistic model. Those of us who are interested in civil society, social justice, human rights, the survival of humanity and the creation of community-based art that works towards any of these must seriously consider the historical lessons of continuing to operate in the mechanistic paradigm.

---

[45] Capra, *The Hidden Connections*, p. 262. The italics are mine.

The oppressed leader of the death squad

Referred to earlier, Headlines' 1989 production ¿SANCTUARY?, created and performed by people who were refugees, was an attempt to help Canadians understand the situations of refugees at a time when there was increasing public tension over Canada's refugee policy.

The play was in two scenes, the first in Guatemala, and the second in a Canadian refugee interview room. In the first scene, a student is leafletting the town square (our audience), trying to get people to come to a demonstration. Two men with guns come through the audience, showing a picture of her, asking where she is. She sees them and runs away, entering the house of some friends (onstage), where she can hide. The men interrogate members of the audience until someone tells them where she has gone. They enter the house, bursting through the door, find the student, beat her, put a bag over her head, drag her outside and shoot her. The leader of the death squad knows the woman and man who live in the house. He is very surprised that he has found the student in their home. He asks the woman if she knows what can happen to her for hiding rebels. She is silent. The death squad leader's partner wants to take them in for questioning. Instead, the leader warns the woman to behave herself and leaves. His warning is a clear message. The wife and husband, terrified, leave their home that night and begin a very long journey to Canada. When they get to Canada, they are interviewed by two Canadian bureaucrats who process refugees. They are treated very badly and are sent back to the US, the country from which they entered Canada. The wife and husband are certain that from there they will be sent back to Guatemala, where their lives will be in extreme danger. This scenario is all based in factual information from the lives of the original workshop participants and cast (all refugees).

¿SANCTUARY? was performed 22 times in Vancouver and also toured to 27 communities around BC. It was also the first live, interactive telecast we did on community television.[46]

In 1989 I was still using the classic language of the *Theatre of the Oppressed*. My invitation to the audience was to come onto the stage to replace a character who was oppressed, and to try an idea to break the

---

[46] See the section *Television and the World Wide Web* in the *Appendix*.

oppression. One night, in the middle of the tour, a woman from the audience who was originally from somewhere in Central or South America yelled "Stop!" and wanted to replace the leader of the death squad, Victor. (I did not ask this woman about her country of origin on stage and did not get a chance to speak with her afterwards.) I told the woman that we didn't want audience members to replace characters who were *causing the problem* and turn them into a nicer person by magic. "Magic" is Boal's term to describe this kind of intervention. Inside me, I have to admit, I was thinking she had either misunderstood the rules of the event, or was sympathetic to the agenda of the death squads. No one had ever asked to replace the death squad leader. It seemed preposterous, and I could feel the tension in the cast rising onstage.

She told me again that she needed to replace Victor, the leader. I didn't want to get into an argument with her in front of about 150 people and so I said OK, thinking we were about to waste a lot of precious time, and enter a situation that might lead to an argument between her and some of the cast members.

She started the scene at the point just before she and her death squad partner burst into the house where the student is hiding:

Woman	I can't do this anymore
Partner (laughing)	Right
Woman	I mean it. I don't know what it is about this girl, but she reminds me of me.

The woman then told her partner a very emotional story of how, as a child, she had stolen some bread because her family was hungry. The police had caught her. They told her that unless she did 'an errand' for them, they would arrest her for theft. She did as she was told. Having done the errand, they said, "OK, now you have done this, so you will do a bigger errand for us and if you don't we will hurt your family." She did as she was told. This cycle continued until years later, and here she is about to break down a door and murder a young woman who is fighting the very forces that turned her into who she is today, a person she despises. The room was very silent. I had no idea what to do. I turned to the actor, Victor Porter, who was playing the death squad leader and who had himself spent almost three and a half years as a political prisoner in Argentina, some of that in solitary confinement, for his work against the death squads. I asked him if he thought this was real. "Yes, this is real," he said, and talked about the jail guards who he got to know, some of whom came from extreme poverty to the point that their first pair of shoes were those issued by the Corrections Service.

The audience in the small, rural community hall that night was, I believe, mostly people born in Canada. Their knowledge of the issues of refugees and death squads, like many people's, was mostly what they got from 30-second items on the news. They had a profound experience that night, as did all of us. This brave intervention from a woman who understood things that most of us did not, didn't excuse the actions of the men in the death squad, or solve a problem for the characters who were about to become refugees. It did, however, present the death squad leader as a real person – not some evil guy who had dropped in from outer space to impose his will on people. The death squad leader was part of us, and if this was the case, it changed the way we could approach the issue. The moment was both visceral and symbolic; it was lived in the theatre and it was transformational for many of us, myself included.

For me, it threw into question, for the first time, whether or not it was appropriate to be creating characters who were so clearly either oppressor or oppressed. ¿SANCTUARY? was a very successful and popular project. But were the characters too one-dimensional? In retrospect, the answer to this question is yes. The characters were mostly either the "good oppressed" or the "bad oppressor". By making such clearly defined and unrealistic distinctions, we were making the situation too simple and therefore, ironically, harder than it needed to be to dig deeper into the root causes of the problems we were presenting on stage. As a result, we were creating theatre that, as powerful as it was, did not accessibly represent the complexities of life; something I believe all good theatre should do.

This is one example from my own work. In order to further and deepen this idea, I want to give another example, from other people's research.

Suicide bombers[47]

In her book *Dying to Kill: The Allure of Suicide Terror*,[48] professor Mia Bloom points out that the idea of suicide bombing is not new. It goes back to Judeo-Christian biblical times. We see it throughout the 19th century, including in the Second World War Japanese kamikaze pilots. It is, she says, "a tactic of last resort." Suicide bombing has historically been aimed at military and political targets. She claims that the new development at the turn of the century was the bombing of youth in shopping malls and dance clubs by Hamas and of the Twin Towers in the United States. (More recently, the 2005 incidents in London and Spain and the ongoing suicide bombings in Iraq and Afghanistan.)

However horrific the image, the dichotomy remains the same. I believe it is fair to say that for the people experiencing the terror of the bombings, the suicide bomber is an oppressor. A terrorist. For the movement that the bomber represents – which I also think it is fair to say, in the examples given above, is not a small cell of fanatics but a manifestation of a broad-based movement – the bombers are heroes, fighting oppression. Which version is true? Historically, answers to this question have been one of perspective. It is the victors who write the history books.

Dr. Eyad El-Sarraj is a psychiatrist and founding chairman of the Gaza Community Mental Health Programme.[49] As a psychiatrist, he started seeing young patients coming to him in 1987, who wanted help with plans to be suicide bombers. Dr. El-Sarraj, being a non-violent man, refused to assist with their plans, but started a study of the youth.

He studied 3,000 children in Intifada and found 55 percent had experienced extreme ongoing violence from childhood, been victimized by traumatic events and had witnessed humiliation and beating of their parents at the hands of the occupying Israeli military. He found that the youth were not insane, contrary to the way they are often

---

47 Professor Mia Bloom, former professor of Middle East politics at Cornell University, and Dr. Eyad El-Sarraj, founder and chairman of the Gaza Community Mental Health Programme and a human rights activist, were interviewed on Canadian Broadcasting Corporation (CBC) Radio's *The Current*, July 7, 2003. This information is taken from a recording of that interview.
48 Published by Columbia University Press, New York 2005.
49 For more information see http://www.gcmhp.net/eyad/

portrayed in the Western press. They were, however, deeply affected by the violence and loss of control that they witnessed in their own and their parents' lives.

Dr. El-Sarraj has witnessed the escalation of what violence is imaginable in the Middle East – from stone-throwing to suicide bombing – and wonders, if the current situation vis-à-vis vis the Israeli occupation persists, what will be next?

The work of these two individuals, one a Jew and the other an Arab, begs the question: how does the cycle of violence end? Of course the land issue must be resolved if an end to the violence is to be imagined. Retaliation after retaliation is obviously not the answer. Criminalizing the oppressed oppressor, from whichever angle of the conflict one attaches those labels, is not the answer, just as it is not the answer in the ever-escalating issue of violence in North America and other parts of the world. Suicide bombers are the product of a complex network of feedback loops deeply embedded in lived realities.

This is true also when the lived reality is in a country other than where a conflict is centrally located. On July 7, 2005, four bombs went off in London, England. Much to the distress of UK citizens and many people around the world, police investigations discovered that the suicide bombers were not Islamic radicals imported into the UK. They were young men, born and raised in Leeds, who had embraced Islam as their legitimate faith and were outraged by the imbalance of the value of lives in the conflict in Iraq. Britain, along with the US, Spain and Australia, had declared war on Iraq for, it became obvious, illegitimate reasons. There were never weapons of mass destruction. The rationale for the war had been an intricate web of lies. Thousands of innocent Iraqis – men, women and children – were murdered and continued to be murdered long after the war was officially declared over by the US. Although "Allied Forces" were also experiencing their men and women coming home in body bags, it wasn't until 2007 that visible outrage in the West over this ongoing atrocity was anything more than minimal. In a world that had so successfully created the "other", these young men in the UK, who everyone saw as "normal and kind lads", strapped explosives to their bodies and entered the London Underground and a bus and committed an appalling act. They blew themselves up and sent many other innocent people to their deaths. These four young men will go down in Western history books as terrorists. It is certainly the truth that in their own minds and hearts, and in the minds and hearts of many, they were fighting terror.

It is impossible to stop these kinds of acts with more and more laws or increasingly tighter surveillance, regardless of where in the world they may occur. We must step out of the reductionist, mechanistic paradigm that allows us to create the image of everything being disconnected from everything else. It is only when we start to focus on the living organism of the entire community – be it a family unit, or two nations in tight geographic quarters, or the diverse family that inhabits Earth – when we understand that the boundary we draw between oppressor and oppressed is artificial, that we will have a chance of confronting the root causes of these actions instead of the symptoms, which are the actions themselves.

Many of my own insights from which *Theatre for Living* emerged were made while working in collaboration with various First Nations communities in Canada during times when they were working to re-establish healthy communities, after the trauma of colonial atrocities such as the imposition of Residential Schools.

The chapters *Out of the Silence* and *Reclaiming Our Spirits* explain in detail two of these projects, both of them pivotal in the evolution of *Theatre for Living*. First, I want to go back into the workshop room and ask the age-old question: "Yes, but is it art?"

THE ART OF INTERACTIVE

THEATRE

Art is process

A Canadian theatre director once told me that she thought I should be stopped from doing what I am doing because "ordinary people cannot make theatre that is art," and further, that my work was undermining Canadian theatre.

I am very pleased to be able to write that on June 14, 2004, the Vancouver professional theatre community honoured *Practicing Democracy*,[50] Headlines' community-based Forum Theatre play created and performed by people living in chronic poverty (two of the cast of six were homeless at the time) with two Jessie Richardson Awards in the small theatre category. The first was a Special Artistic Achievement Award for "demonstrating the power of theatre in the community". The second was for "outstanding production".

---

[50] See chapter titled *Theatre for Living and Its Relationship to Theatre of the Oppressed* for production details.

After years of arguing that theatre created and performed by community members who do not self-identify as actors can aspire, like any other theatre, to be art, for me this was a wonderful moment. I know, though, that the need to put forward the argument is not over yet.

On page one of the *Theatre of the Oppressed*,[51] Boal writes about art and Aristotle:

> "The first difficulty that we face in order to understand correctly the workings of tragedy according to Aristotle stems from the very definition which that philosopher gives to art. What is art, any art? For him, it is an imitation of nature. For us, the word 'imitate' means to make a more or less perfect copy of an original model. Art would, then, be a copy of nature. And 'nature' means the whole of created things. Art would, therefore, be a copy of created things.
>
> But this has nothing to do with Aristotle. For him, to imitate (mimesis) has nothing to do with copying an exterior model. 'Mimesis' means rather a 're-creation'. And nature is not the whole of created things but rather the creative principle itself. Thus when Aristotle says that art imitates nature, we must understand that this statement, which can be found in any modern version of the *Poetics*, is due to a bad translation, which in turn stems from an isolated interpretation of that text. 'Art imitates nature' actually means: 'Art re-creates the creative principle of created things'."

Art is process, not product, although I will suggest that art often is regarded as product because it suits our consumer society. I say this knowing that a painting, a finished product, is art, or rather part of the artistic equation. Perhaps it is not truly art until a viewer engages in a process of viewing and interpreting the painting. If the painting elicits a response from the viewer, the viewer might decide the painting is art.

Art can be the result of an individual or a group in a room, creating. Art can also be an image of the serendipitous juxtaposition of the struggle between capitalism, or subsistence economies, or human life

---

[51] Originally published in Spanish as *Teatro de Oprimido* by Augusto Boal, 1974; subsequently in North America by Theatre Communications Group Inc., New York 1974; and outside North America by Pluto Press, London 1992.

that happens in the street every day, if that image is captured by, for example, an astute photographer.

Theatre for Living (and other processes like *Theatre of the Oppressed* and Community Play[52] creation) employs a *social artistry*. This artistry is conducted, in an improvisational way, by the Joker, or director. The process engages the living community at a deeply creative level. Both the process itself and the result of the process, experienced by the community itself and possibly by people from outside, can be as transformational as any great art.

All people, even those with whom we disagree, are part of nature. This means that when we practice this social artistry that "re-creates the creative principle of created things," we must make a point of putting all characters on the stage as real, complex representations of humanity. Humanity is, of course, also a part of nature.

How does an audience factor into the process of theatre art? An audience member's way to experience traditional, presentational theatre (i.e., theatre that does not invite the audience to intervene in the action of the play) is most often to see it from a distance, separate from the performance. Even when a director stages a play so that the audience is sitting on the stage, and the actors are mingled with the audience, the audience is expected to respect the artificial boundary that has been created between actor and spectator.

This a is a wonderful thing to do sometimes. I enjoy experiencing and creating this kind of theatre.[53] The art of this theatre includes playing extensively with light, sound, costumes and the poetry of the language. It can be a feast for the senses and the soul – transporting and transformative.

In a Forum Theatre production, the art is similar, but the production must be designed in every way to encourage the audience to transgress the sacred theatre space. The audience member has to find the

---

[52] In a Community Play an artist or theatre group in residence will work with community members and organizations over a long time period to create a play, the sets, costumes, props, etc. The process often transfers skills and also creates working relationships between people and organizations.
[53] See *No ` Xya ` (Our Footprints)* (1987), *Mamu* (1994) and *Thir$ty* (2002) at http://www.headlinestheatre.com/pastwork.htm

problematic situation so compelling that they feel they have no choice but *to do something*. Because of this, the actual words that the actors say, which have come from an improvisational process, are sometimes not as specifically important as they are in a traditional play. What is of the utmost importance is the clarity of the action, the clarity of motivation of the characters, their desires and fears – in other words, all the layers of *subtext* under what the characters say.

In order to be clear, I want to point out that sometimes the words the characters say in Forum Theatre are *very important*, and must be very precise when, for instance, there are entrances or other cues attached to them. When the scene is about a legal matter, this is especially important. In this case the creators must work very hard to get the legal detail right, and also to understand all the background material so that improvising can happen about the subject matter with integrity.

In a Forum Theatre project, except in very exceptional circumstances, the actors and I never put pen to paper to create a script. What the characters say to each other, and the story they tell, *emerges* through an interaction between the Joker and the actors who are members of the community. The script is not created outside and brought in; neither is the script meant to be transported to another community or situation and replicated by another cast. This would negate it being a true voice of the performers, who come from the community.

Written scripts of Headlines' mainstage Forum Theatre projects are created, usually after the final performance, for archival purposes.

The structure of an interactive Forum play

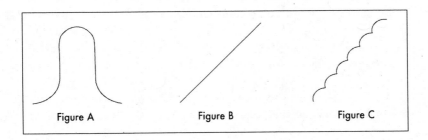

A traditional play very often has a structure that looks like Figure A. The play builds to a crisis, which resolves nicely. Often the audience members leave the theatre relieved and happy that the onstage characters solved the problem so that now the audience members don't have to. How many of us have enjoyed experiencing this "whew"?

When I started doing Forum Theatre I structured plays to look like Figure B. A play would build inexorably into a crisis and stop there. This "one straight line building into a crisis" is effective, certainly, but it is not the richest possibility for interactive theatre. Inside this structure, every aspect of the play tends to move in the straight line; a character is most often either oppressor or oppressed. Life, however, does not move in straight lines. It is filled with twists and turns, irony, double standards and all the complexity that makes us human. The play in the straight-line model does not, by the very nature of the model, contain a great deal of complexity.

As I dug deeper into how theatrical moments for Forum are best constructed, I understood that if I took a fragment of the line of Figure B and magnified it, I could imagine that, although it appeared to be one straight line, it really looked like Figure C – a series of unresolved arcs. Like in life, a crisis is created not in one straight line, but in many interconnected moments, some of them obvious and some hidden, some of them directly connected to a central character and some affecting that character because they have affected other characters.

The model becomes a series of unresolved arcs, some of them obviously connected, some appearing not to be connected, which, like Figure C, build to a crisis with no resolution. If you take a single arc of Figure C and magnify it, each arc (each dramatic unit) will also be a series of unfinished arcs, some obviously connected, some appearing not to be, building to a crisis with no resolution. The unresolved arc between two people is made up of internalized unresolved arcs. Think of it as a fractal, a mathematical equation represented in a computer graphic. The complexity keeps appearing the more you zoom in.[54]

Much of the work for the actors and Joker in creation and rehearsal is below the surface of the play, which is designed to ask questions, but give no answers. Once the audience interventions start and ideas for problem-solving start coming onto the stage, doors of understanding start to open, which lead to other doors and other doors; layers of complexity are revealed to both the audience and the actors. The Forum Theatre event tonight will be different than the one tomorrow night because the ecology of the audience tonight, and therefore the interventions they offer, will be different than tomorrow night – although the play itself has remained the same.

In order to create a play that invites this kind of scrutiny, the Joker must work with the actors to help them *not resolve* the little moments that together create the arc of the whole play. Often it will feel good for the actors to complete the moments – it is human nature to want to do that – but one is creating a structure that invites audience intervention. It is the build-up of small unresolved moments that makes the audience so 'itchy' that they just have to jump onto the stage.

Working without a preplanned resolution also applies to the very early stages of setting up a project of this nature. If the community organizers already know the answers to the issues they want to look at, why do Forum Theatre? Perhaps it is better to make a play that communicates the answers to the audience that the organizers already know. In this case, the decision should be to create a purely presentational play that delivers the answers. There is a fine and worthwhile tradition of this kind of theatre, and I engage in it myself sometimes, as mentioned previously. Forum Theatre is the most valuable, when the desire is really to create a community dialogue, about issues the community is truly struggling to resolve. It is an invitation to seek solutions, or at least a deeper understanding of the issues, *together*.

---

54 If you are interested in fractals, see http://www.softsource.com/fractal.html

Authenticity and a true voice

In my own work I have insisted, under some circumstances, that 'a real person' must play a certain character. In *The Dying Game*,[55] for instance one of the characters was a doctor and so the role was played by a real doctor. Without the character being able to respond with the knowledge of a doctor, the production would simply have been pretending to be a truthful investigation of the interface between people who are dying, their families and the medical profession.

This brings me to authenticity. Part of the power of *Theatre for Living* is its authentic voice. The people from the community who are living the issues under investigation and who are the experts in their own lives, create and perform the theatre. *Squeegee* is a good example.[56]

A mainstream theatre company producing a play about issues of street youth would very likely have hired young professional actors who would have hung out with street kids to study them, been costumed as street kids by a professional designer, and then learned a script that was written by someone – hopefully a street kid, but most likely not – and then been on stage pretending to be street kids, to the best of their ability. This kind of theatre can be very successful. It can also, in my experience, be quite painful to watch 20-something-year-old (or older!) actors pretend they are disenfranchised teens living in the street.

When we did *Squeegee*, our purpose was to engage the public in a dialogue about criminalization of youth using the structure of Forum Theatre to both stimulate and contain the dialogue. Could professional

---

55 *The Dying Game* (1998) is the only one of Headlines' projects (so far) in which a script was written for Forum. The play was about my experiences and frustrations with the medical profession during the time I was supporting my mother in her process of dying. I wrote the script based on these experiences, and then cast and directed the play. Cast: Pat Armstrong, Angelo Moroni and Fraser Black, MD. Stage Manager: Claire Nicol. Technical Director, Set and Light Designer: Adrian Muir. Costume and Props Designer: Barbara Clayden. Conceived, Directed and Joked by David Diamond (with help from the late Edna Diamond). See http://www.headlinestheatre.com/pastwork.htm

56 Forum Theatre with street youth about criminalization of youth (1999). During production cast members asked that they be identified by first name only so some of them could not be tracked down by family members. Cast: Lisa, Matt, Michael, Rachel, Elizabeth and Yoshi. Live Sound: Matt Deacon Evans. Stage Manager: Bree Wellwood. Support Person: Sam Bob. Directed and Joked by: David Diamond. See http://www.headlinestheatre.com/pastwork.htm

actors (who had never been kids living in the street) accept interventions from audience members and improvise truthfully about the realities of living in the street, accessing the dynamics of their relationships with other youth and the police, using years of lived experience as the basis for making decisions on stage? No, they could not, regardless of how much work we had done in the rehearsal hall, or how talented they were. It would have been a fantasy. It would have meant that the dialogue we were having, while it might have been entertaining, was not authentic, and therefore of little value to our understanding of the complexities of the issues at hand. The lived knowledge of the street youth was as important in this instance as the knowledge of the real doctor in *The Dying Game*.

It is essential, if the cast are going to be able to do the hard work that is involved in creating authentic art, that they work in an environment where they will be safe and can focus. We provided the youth working on *Squeegee* with housing (a safe hotel) from one week before the start of the project to at least two weeks after we finished – in some instances this was longer. We also paid them above union-scale wages and made certain they were eating nutritious meals by having one hot meal a day catered. We ensured that these meals were not fast food and had a good balance of complex carbohydrate and protein. We hired both a community liaison person (a young man who had been in the street himself) and a counsellor to be on the project full-time, in case issues arose for the cast. We offered to open bank accounts for them and facilitated introductions, when possible, with potential future employers and/or training programs.

authenticity vs. 'acting'

In Forum Theatre there is most often not a written script, and never a predetermined outcome for the audience-interactive part of the event. We have the original play that builds to a crisis and stops, that the cast is capable of performing the same way over and over again, but when the audience member enters the stage and replaces a character, no one, not even the audience member, knows what is going to happen. The challenge for the actors remaining onstage in this moment is to let the audience member be in the driver's seat – to steer the improvisation.

The actor must be in a *reactive* mode. He must not control the improvisation, and must also remain true to his character. He must really listen, observe and have no exterior agenda, like trying to make the improvisation entertaining, going for a laugh, or creating a happy or sad ending. His main focus is to tell the truth of the character in that moment, however convenient or inconvenient that truth may be. In order to do this he must be centred. He must allow his responses to emerge from the situation, not create them from a preconception of who the audience member is, or what she is going to do. If the actor is going to initiate an action, it must never be in order to show the audience something. We are not there to teach them lessons. *Theatre for Living* is not prescriptive in that way. We are there to explore this moment, this idea that has come from the community.

This is one of the most difficult challenges for an actor, whether professional or community member, trained or never been on the stage before. The actor might be deeply invested in the issue and have a strong desire for the audience to learn certain lessons or come to certain conclusions about the issue under investigation. In order to be authentic, he must set this desire aside. It is his authenticity and honesty that will create the environment in which the community will understand new perspectives on the issue. In the same way that a person experiences deeper learning by making their own discoveries, so too does the living community.

This is a difference between role playing as one would do in psychodrama, which has an overtly therapeutic purpose and may be highly directed, and being authentic in a *Theatre for Living* performance, the purpose of which is the creation of true dialogue.

In order to accomplish this authenticity, the director must work with the actors so that they will be comfortable on stage inside their characters. There are many improvisational techniques to help them build histories, understand their relationships with each other, and be clear about their desires and fears.

Following are a couple of techniques that I use very often in rehearsal.

complete the character[57]

> I first came across this technique in the early '70s in theatre school as a Stanislavski[58] exercise. The Joker should help the actors discover the depth of their characters. They are going to be called upon to respond in character in the interactive Forum Theatre event. In order to accomplish this, they have to develop a history of the character and also a history of the character's relationships to the other characters.

The Joker interviews each character in the play and asks them questions about who they are, and about their relationships to each other. The questions can be like a dialogue, each one being a response to the previous answer. This helps the actor go down a path of self-discovery. The actor's answers can also often lead to new moments in scenes in the plays, as the hidden reasons for events come to the surface.

improvise a memory[59]

> We cannot lose something we have never had. This is a good technique to give characters memories of good times together, so that they can feel the resonance of the crisis they are now in together.

Put the characters in different situations with each other and explore their relationship before the crisis. Explore the moment a couple who are in conflict met and fell in love; a moment that two co-workers worked together very well; a moment when a parent and child had the

---

57 This technique is called *Interrogation* by Boal in *Games for Actors and Non-Actors*, p. 212.
58 Konstantin Stanislavski (1863-1938). As founder of the first acting 'system', co-founder of the Moscow Art Theatre in 1897 (it is still running in 2007) and an eminent practitioner of the naturalist school of thought, Stanislavski challenged traditional notions of the dramatic process, establishing himself as a leading pioneer in modern theatre.
59 There are other sense memory exercises in Boal's *Games for Actors and Non-Actors*, p. 161, which deal with individual participants' memories.

most fun together; anything that will help the actors know what is at stake in the crisis in the play.

the desire to instruct

Something happened during *Squeegee* that is a good example of one way that the desire to instruct can manifest.[60]

The first public performance was very exciting. The audience had been really engaged in the Forum and it had been lively, but there had also been an odd edge to it that I couldn't put my finger on. After the performance, I was surprised to find the cast was furious. Why? Because they thought that some of the interventions from the audience had been 'cheesy' – in other words, naïve. They wanted me to control the kinds of interventions that came from the audience.

I asked them what they were really upset about. They answered that they wanted people to know what it is really like in the street and wanted them to try to find answers to how to make the street safe for kids in the street.

"Right. Of course, this is why we are all here. People, though, are going to come up with ideas that you know don't work."

"But what are we supposed to do with that?" they asked. "We are trying not to be rude to them; you won't like that!"

I agreed that I wouldn't like it if the actual actors got into fights with audience members, but reminded them that they were playing characters, and their greatest power on the stage was to *respond authentically as their characters*. If someone from the audience was doing something that they thought was 'cheesy' on the stage, they had the ability to react to that in character as truthfully as possible. Their frustration was real and well founded. Some audience members' naïveté was also honest. Their task was to turn their frustration into character authenticity, not the actor frustration of wanting to teach the audience member something. "We can tell them their idea is stupid?!" "Of course! In character!"

---

[60] Excerpted from my daily journal.

The Forums on the following nights were spectacular. The cast was very centred, and found a way to give themselves permission to just *be* on the stage.

it's all theatre, and the Joker, while not an instructor, can be a provocateur

Whatever story comes onto the stage is, in some way, the living community trying to express itself. Important dialogue can come from unexpected moments.

One night, in Prince George, a community in the north of BC, a group of young offenders (youth who were in trouble with the law) who had made plays were now in performance, taking interventions from an audience of about 150 people.[61] One of the plays was about family violence. An abusive father was being played by one of the young women in the group. A young man in the audience (let's name him Mike) yelled "Stop!" and wanted to replace the son.

Mike was about 16, tall and lanky. He had been sitting with a group of friends near the back of the hall. He came on to the stage laughing. At first, I thought it was that he was nervous, but it soon became obvious that he was performing for his friends, who were cheering him on. As sometimes happens in a Forum, he had come on to the stage to entertain.

Mike replaced the son, turned to the father and said, "Dad, I have a present for you." He then turned his hand into a gun, pulled the trigger and made a loud gun sound with his mouth. The audience and cast burst into laughter. The woman playing the father looked at me and shrugged her shoulders, not knowing how to respond. I waited for the laughter to die down and then said to her, "Lie down. You're dead." She did.

Now the room was very quiet. "Mike," I said, "I understand why you want to shoot the father, and guns are easy enough to get. So, OK. He's dead. Now what?" We stood together in the silence, and this young

---

[61] This workshop gave birth to a theatre group in Prince George, BC, called Street Spirits. See www.streetspirits.com.

man's demeanor transformed. The plays were made by young offenders. Most of them had been in youth detention or prison, some for violent crimes. His 'funny solution' to the violence in the home was real. It was playing out in this community and communities all over the world. It was the reason we were together there creating theatre. "I guess," he said, "I have to get out of town. I'm in deep shit."

The Joker is a provocateur. I asked the audience why it was so funny when Mike shot the father. Silence. "Who thinks this is a true response?" Many hands in the air. "Who thinks shooting the father solves the problem?" No hands in the air. "So, what do we do?"

I asked Mike if there was anything he wanted to say. He acknowledged that when he came on stage he thought it would be funny. This was a courageous moment from him. I thanked him for his intervention and acknowledged that without the intervention we could not have explored the truth of the impulse. "Are there any other ideas for this moment?" Of course there were. And, spurred on, I believe, by Mike's intervention, the audience dug underneath the surface of what was happening to the family, and tried and (some) succeeded in creating safety in the household.

It would have been possible, when Mike first started his intervention onstage, to tell him to stop fooling around. "Mikes" come onto the stage often, in one form or another. If we are honest in our request for the living community to express itself, then we must accept whatever comes onto the stage and treat it with respect.

production value and authenticity

Production value, which is the quality of the set, lights, costumes, sound design, etc., enhances the theatrical experience in wonderful ways, but it is not, I believe, the core of theatre. Interactions among the actors and between the actors and the audience is the core of the theatrical experience.

For a *Power Play* (a six-day *Theatre for Living* process that culminates in a Forum Theatre performance in a local hall), we do not generally concern ourselves with light, sound, sets, etc. We don't have time, for one thing, and they are not essential.

This is not to say production elements don't have their place in Forum Theatre. Theatre is a metaphoric language, and this is one of the reasons it reaches easily and deeply into the living community. We must, however, find a balance between how we create those metaphors, and having them so 'produced' that the audience can do nothing but remain in their seats in awe.

Headlines' mainstage Forum plays (projects that have a three or four-week creation process) do have set, lighting and sound designers. The designs are always relatively simple, by choice.

Whatever the set is, it must include easy access from the audience area to the stage area. When chairs go out in a large hall, they need to have a centre aisle. The physical space must be designed for traffic flow to and from the stage.

Lighting helps the audience see the actors and also has emotional, psychological meaning. The lighting in Forum Theatre must not be such that it blinds the actors on the stage, creating a dark void out in the house. I experienced this kind of lighting many times as an actor in the mainstream theatre. The actors and the Joker need to be able to see the audience.

Headlines' 2004 production *Practicing Democracy* was very beautifully produced with wonderful lighting by designer Caitlin Pencarrick. It also featured a backdrop of slide images by photographer Lincoln Clarkes. My choice in this instance was to darken the house (audience) lights and to use quite high production value in the first run of the 22-minute play, and then to raise light levels in the house for the Forum. This brought the audience fully into the artistry of the production the first time they saw the play, and then, during the Forum, removed any impediments to participation created by the lighting.

It is also possible to use *real places* to stage productions. In 2003, *Don't Say a Word*[62] was staged on and around the main stairwell of Sir Charles Tupper Secondary School in Vancouver. We created a theatre in the school's foyer that could accommodate 100 seats and, for three

[62] Forum Theatre on violence in the schools created and performed by Iliana Bonilla, Derek Kwon, Shaun Omaid, Patricia Alducin, John Walker and Qing Jian Zeng. Stage Manager: Melissa C. Powell. Directed and Joked by: David Diamond. Performed at Sir Charles Tupper Secondary School in February 2004.

weeks, invited the public to participate in this Forum project about violence in the schools.

The location was a very strong artistic choice. We were able to transform it into two of the characters' homes, a subway station, a bridge and, of course, school hallways and stairs. The location created a level of authenticity in the storytelling that we could never have achieved with this particular project in a theatre. The audience interventions were also affected by the reality of being in an actual high school where the unwritten but universally understood codes of behaviour permeate the hallways.

All the actors in this production were high school students ranging from grades 8 to 12. They had all developed very complex and believable characters. A theatre colleague of mine came to see a performance and made a comment later that has relevance to the question of whether or not she was witnessing art.

She was very impressed with the cast and the honesty that they were capable of in both the play and the interactive Forum. It wasn't until after the event was over, though, and she saw them offstage talking to some friends, that she realized they were not playing themselves in the two-hour event. They had been in character all that time! These youth were not the characters she had seen on the stage.

There is a very rich and complex art practice in the creation of interactive theatre. Professional artists have a place in this work if they have the desire and the ability to engage at a true grassroots level. The practice has to be flexible in order to respond to the situations in which the living community is functioning, and is richest when it recognizes that the community itself is alive and has a story to tell. Given safe space in which to work and create, the story will emerge from the living community.

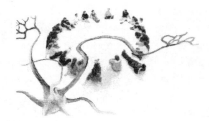

IN THE WORKSHOP ROOM

The workshop

An invitation has come from someone who wants to use theatre to explore community issues. Through a consultation process an organizing committee has been formed and a broad topic for investigation has been decided. The organizing committee has done the recruitment of participants.

setting up the workshop environment

The space for the workshop must be safe in various ways: safe means free of judgment; a place where it is safe to take risks, or not. Safe space means somewhere where it is safe to fail. Space where failure is impossible is not safe space; it is very tightly controlled space that contains no risk. Safe space is somewhere where it is possible to think new thoughts, feel new emotions; and to think and feel deeply, alone and in groups; in private and in public. Safe space is private; space in which strangers are not going to be coming and going to visit or to observe. Safe space also means space free of physical obstructions (such as pillars, excessive furniture, etc.), open, clean (I spend lots of time on the floor with participants) and warm. The participants need room in which to run around.

What creates emotionally safe space? In a workshop with Boal in 1987, I witnessed something that had a profound effect on my development as a Joker. A woman in the workshop started to cry. Boal did not draw attention to her tears. Some of the other participants were very angered by this and challenged him on his seeming lack of caring. He looked around the room and asked a question.

"If she was laughing," he said "would you go to her and say, there, there, it's not so funny, stop laughing!?" Many people in the room started to laugh, including the woman who had been crying. Boal crystallized something very profound for me in this moment.

Emotions are not good or bad. They are just emotions. We humans feel hate as well as love, sorrow as well as joy, emotional pain as well as emotional pleasure. What we do with those emotions, of course, has consequence. We must be responsible for the actions we take from feeling emotions, but the act of feeling them is human.

We are in a theatre workshop and theatre is an emotional language. People are almost certainly going to laugh during the workshop and they are going to cry, they are going to get angry and they are going to get joyous. Part of the Joker's job is to try to create an environment where it is safe for the participants to be fully human.

starting the workshop

This is a very theatrical moment. In the same way that the first scene of a play or a movie sets the tone for the whole play or movie, the first moments of a workshop set the tone for the workshop.

There are some ways that the Joker who has come from somewhere else will always be set apart, but there are ways to bridge the gap. Whenever possible, I enter the room on the first day with one or more members of the organizing committee – people the other community members already know. The best scenario is that we are all already there when the first participants start to arrive. Refreshments are ready.

We sit in a circle. We all introduce ourselves in as equal a way as possible. The participants get to talk about what they want from the process and why they are there, as well as anything else they want to say about themselves. I get to listen. We establish very early that their expertise is *equal in importance* to mine. In some ways the community expertise is *more* important; without the participation of the community, there is nothing.

After the introductory circle I will spend a short time giving the participants the history of where the work we are about to do comes from. I will speak briefly about Freire and Boal and the evolution of *Theatre for Living*. I will also deal with the practical issues of beginning and end times each day and also approximate when the lunch break will be, depending on what we are doing at the time. It is very quickly the moment to get onto our feet and start the physical work.

I start every day with games. I am including some games, for illustration purposes in this chapter. Other games and exercises are included in the *Appendix*. When writing about the games and exercises here and later in the book, I will be addressing "you", the reader, as if you were a workshop participant in the room and I was Joking the activity. The activity descriptions will be indented. Sometimes there will also be "Joker Tips", in which I take you 'backstage', into some of the reasons I choose to do the particular game or exercise, or share insights I have had doing it in a particular workshop. These will be indented further than the directions.

balancing[63]

pushing

> Take a partner – any partner will do. Stand facing each other and place your hands on each other's shoulders, and push. Really push. Use your muscles. One of you is going to be stronger than the other. That's life. The person who is less strong, push harder. The person who is stronger, push less hard. Don't try to push each other over. This isn't about winning or losing. The idea is to find the balance of strength between the two of you. Do this without speaking. Have the

---

[63] This game is in the *Feel all that we touch* category. The game categories are explained at the beginning of the *Games and Exercises* section of the *Appendix*. There is a version of this game called *Pushing against each other* in Boal's *Games for Actors and Non-Actors*, p. 65.

conversation with your bodies. You should always be moving. Don't just lean against each other, push!

Use different parts of your bodies. And again. And again.

pulling

Facing each other, take each other by the wrists. Now lean out, taking each other's weight, so that if one of you let go, the other would fall. Now, without talking, continuing to lean out, sit down. Bums to the floor. Now, pulling against each other, stand up. Repeat this a few times. Now in circles of four, then in circles of eight, and 16, etc.

> **Joker Tip:** I choose to do this game first, in every workshop, regardless of the community. We come back to the core concept of the pushing aspect of the balancing game many times during the workshop. The participants might all be people with physical disabilities – still, we adapt and do this game. It contains the essence of theatre and also the skill required to accept interventions in Forum.
>
> The essence of drama is conflict. One character wants one thing, the other character wants something else. Those two desires are in opposition to each other. This creates drama. You don't see movies, TV shows or plays about people just 'getting along'.
>
> We are going to make plays where the characters are struggling with each other about the issues we are investigating. They are all, regardless of how symbolic the play might get, pushing against each other. If they don't do this, there can be no drama.
>
> Often, participants will cast themselves as characters who are doing things that they themselves disagree with or would not do; consequently, they have a high level of discomfort performing. It is very helpful for them to see that, in this instance of theatre-making, pushing against

the other character is not a hateful or negative act – it is an act of love. If they don't push, the other character has nothing with which to work.

This is also a very important concept in the interactive Forum. It is not the actor's job to be onstage saying "no, no, no, no" to every person who comes onto the stage – pushing them over. Nor is it the actor's job to be overly agreeable and do whatever the audience member asks – letting the audience member push them over. It is the actor's job to push against the audience member – to make him work – to give him the opportunity to engage in the struggle and in this way really try his idea.

Inside the struggle, the actor must be listening and seeing and sensing in every way. If she is, she will be able to respond truthfully – saying "yes" if the intervener moves her character to do so, and saying "no" when he does not. It is all contained in the balancing game.

Group building

A process in which people come together to make plays about issues that they share is bound to begin from a place of apprehension for at least some of the participants. If we understand that the people in the room are going to be nervous and wary, then the first thing we need to do is try to build comfort and trust in the room.

Most of the first day of a week-long process is games. These games are designed to start the group thinking about what the essence of theatre is, what experiences are common in the room, and what power relationships and layers of complexity exist in the issue we are investigating.

all games are symbolic

People often get trapped into thinking that the games are warm-ups and the real work is in the exercises and Image/Forum Theatre. This shortchanges every aspect of the process. The games are integral to the investigation. Make time every day for them. You never know who is in the workshop, even if the workshop participants are people you know. The games are themselves images – each person will experience them privately, filtering the game through their own life experiences. They are creating links in the working group, building group awareness and trust, but they can also, in surprising ways, unlock access to the issues that the group wants to investigate.

How are the games the work? In 1989 when we were creating ¿Sanctuary?,[64] Headlines' Forum Theatre production with the refugee community, something happened in a blind game called *Effective Hand* that is a wonderful example.

effective hand[65]

Stand on your own in the room, eyes closed. Without talking, when you encounter someone, feel their hands for a moment and then move on. Do this for a while. Then, after a while, when you find a hand, keep it. Each person should have at least one hand being held. It's OK to have both being held, but no three hands or more together.

Keeping your eyes closed, get to know the hand or hands you are holding. Is it a dry hand, or a moist hand? A bony hand, or a fleshy hand? A warm hand, or a cold hand? If you are feeling adventurous, remember you have senses other than touch. Really get to know the hand(s). (Give this some time.)

---

64 Vancouver creators and cast: Saeideh Nessar Ali, Victor Porter, Nora Patrich, Daniel McLeod, Eduardo Aragon, Paul Kriz, Jose Morales. Touring cast: Saeideh Nessar Ali, Victor Porter, Nora Strejilevich, Daniel McLeod, Jose Morales. Directed by: David Diamond. Joked by: David Diamond and Sherri-Lee Guilbert. Stage Manager: Borja Brown.
65 This game is in the *Feel all that we touch* category. There is a version called *Find the hand* in Boal's *Games for Actors and Non-Actors*, p. 114.

Without talking, open your eyes, look to see whose hand(s) you are holding and close your eyes again. Without talking, say goodbye and, keeping your eyes closed, start to walk. (Give this some time.) Now, *keeping your eyes closed and without talking*, find the same hand(s) again.

> **Joker Tip:** It's a good idea to ask participants to remove finger and wrist jewelry for this game.

I had done this game many times with various groups and nothing dramatic had ever happened. This time, Saeideh,[66] one of the women in the group, burst into very deep crying in the middle of the game. Everyone stopped. We all sat together in a circle for a long time.

The game had been very symbolic for her. The story emerged that the game had triggered her own experiences of needing to get out of Iran with her husband, having been caught hiding students when the Ayatollah was in power. The game took her back to a place of wandering around in the dark (blind) and trying to find a friendly hand, but not being able to talk (everything was in secrecy) and not knowing who she could trust or if she would ever find any help. Most of the people in the room (all refugees) knew exactly what she was talking about.

We all knew, on this second day of a three-week process, that we had surprisingly found something that would be at the very core of the play we were making. It had not come from Image Theatre or any of the other activities I had expected would yield core images. It had come from something we considered to be a warm-up and group-building game.

Making images

Freeze life in any moment. That is an image. Freeze a play, movie or TV show in any moment. That is an image. Images are in magazines, on billboards. Images are everywhere we look. In *Theatre for Living* and also *Theatre of the Oppressed*, an image is a frozen tableau, made by a workshop participant using their own and other participants'

---

[66] Saeideh Nessar Ali was to become both a Joker and outreach coordinator for Headlines Theatre for eight years, and a close friend. (Identified with permission.)

bodies. The tableau is like a living photograph of *a moment of struggle* in the participant's life. Images can also be made by groups of participants working together. Because the image is silent, it is also highly symbolic and can be interpreted in various ways.

Images are the core building block of theatre. Often a director is creating images from his or her vision on the stage by manipulating actors' bodies, light, set, etc. Working with the living community, it is essential to discover that images can emerge in an organic way, and that this process can be fun, even when the images are about very serious topics. It is possible, even on the first day of a workshop, to create an environment in which the group consciousness can express itself, sometimes at a subconscious level, using the language of image.

complete the image[67]

Let's get into a large circle, please. I am going to make a shape, here in the centre of the circle. It could be anything, just a shape, frozen in space. What do you see? Yell it out. "A bear." "A man looking in a window." "Someone up against a wall." "Someone jumping off a building." Etc. OK. Good. You are correct. All of you. Because it's what you see, and what you see is correct.

But if I would have come into the circle and said, "Here I am (making the shape), rock climbing for the first time in my life, and, I am stuck" – this is the only thing, I believe, you would have seen. No other imaginative things would ever have entered your minds. It would have been as if I had come into the circle and said, "I am the one here with imagination, the artist. None of you have any imagination. Man Rock Climbing." I would have named the image, and in doing that, I would have shut down your creativity.

This is exactly what I will ask that we *not* do as we work. We are going to be making images, and their power is in the

---

[67] This game is in the *See all we look at* category. There is a version (same name) in Boal's *Games for Actors and Non-Actors*, p. 130.

different ways we all see them, so please do not name your images, just offer them. It is OK to disagree.

In preparation for this, could someone come into the circle and offer a shape. It doesn't have to mean anything. It's just a shape in space. Good. Now, someone else come in and, without speaking or explaining in any way (no miming, please), just by offering another frozen shape, complete the image so it tells a story. Good. First person, go back into the circle. What do you see now? Another person complete the image. Good. First person go. Another. Remember there is no way to do this wrong; whatever you see is correct, so please try not to censor yourselves. (Let this go for a while.)

Now a third person. Good. First person go. What do you see? Someone else complete the image. (Do it in threes for a while.)

OK. Good. From now on, we are making images about (the subject matter of the workshop). What do you see? Someone add themselves. Good. First person go. Another. Good. (After a while, when a very dramatic moment presents itself.) A fourth person. A fifth. A sixth...seventh...eighth...and so on, until whoever is able to add themselves is in the image.

> **Joker Tip:** It is then possible to walk around inside this frozen image (the first image that the workshop has created) and ask the characters to speak *internal monologues*.[68] Voilà – they have made an image that can also speak.
>
> The Joker is always trying to create an environment where *content can emerge* from the group. This is different from giving them direction and *telling them to do something*.
>
> Language is very important in setting up the game. Say something like: "Someone come in and make a shape. It doesn't have to mean anything – just a shape in space. *It doesn't have to mean anything.*" If you are patient, the

---

[68] See section in this chapter titled *Image activation*.

group will start to make images of the subject matter that they have come together to investigate *without you telling them to do so*. This might take some time, but in my experience it will always happen. After it has happened, ask them to start making images of the subject matter, as above. This will enable you to point out to the group that they have done this on their own, even though you were very specifically not telling them they should do so. This kind of realization of their own collective power and collective consciousness is an important step in building the group's ability to trust that they can work together.

sculpting partners/build an image[69]

It is important that the group also get to make personal images somehow on the first day. They should leave the room having a sense of what the rest of the workshop is going to entail, and a sense that the image work that reflects their own life experiences is central to the workshop. In order for them to do this, they need some skills in sculpting.

Stand facing your partner. You are both going to do both parts of this. For now, decide who is going to be the sculptor and who is going to be *intelligent clay*.

What is intelligent clay? Your partner is intelligent clay. You can shape your partner into any position (within reason) and the clay will stay in that shape. Because your partner is intelligent clay, he will fill the shape with thought and emotion that is indicated by the body position in which he is placed.

Sculptors – you are responsible for all limbs, facial expressions, etc. Don't be afraid to touch, but be respectful. It is not necessary to sculpt a story at this point, just to make a shape. The clay, as he is put into shapes, should be trying to understand and feel the emotional messages of that shape. Sculptors,

---

[69] This game is in the *See all we look at* category. There are various *sculpting* exercises in Boal's *Games for Actors and Non-Actors*, p. 127.

once you have made one image, erase it and make a second. (This is to get people used to manipulating each other's bodies.) Clay, once you are in your second shape, remember what it is, and then relax.

Now, sculptors. One at a time, bring your second 'sculpture' into the centre of the room. It's as if we have an art gallery. Place your sculptures in relation to each other to try to build a larger sculpture that tells a story.

Sculptors, come out of the gallery now so we can all look at the larger sculpture. What do you see?

The group discusses what they see in this randomly made image. Are there stories? There always are.

Now the sculptor becomes the clay and the clay becomes the sculptor. Again, sculptors, make one shape and when you are happy with it, erase it and make a second. Clays, when you are in your second shape, remember what it is, and then relax.

And once again we are going to make an image in a gallery, by each sculptor bringing their clay into the centre of the room and placing them in relation to each other. This time, though, let's do it on the theme that we are investigating in the workshop.

Joker Tip: This can be an important exercise in helping the group demystify the process of making theatre and start to access the larger consciousness in the group. They may see that simply by bringing shapes together it is possible to develop a coherent story. This works because each individual in the group brings her entire life into sculpting a partner – even on a subconscious level. The hands of the sculptor are conveyors of the sculptor's subconscious. When the whole group is engaged, the sculptures cannot help but reflect the subconscious of the group. Very often you will find that the core issues of the group are present in their very first group-sculpted images.

groups of 4 (or 5...)[70]

I like to use this exercise on the first day of a week-long workshop, and I like to start it by making the working groups myself, in order to create a situation where individuals are working with other participants that they might not work with normally. If there are 25 participants, say, and I am going to create five groups of five, I will assign everyone a number. "Remember your numbers! 1, 2, 3, 4, 5, 1, 2, 3, 4, 5, 1, 2, 3, 4, 5, 1...ones over here, twos over here, threes over here...

> In these small groups, each of you is going to make an image, using yourself and other people in the group, of a moment from your own life, when you were struggling with (the issue under investigation). This must be your own moment, not a friend's or a relative's, not Hollywood. Each image *must* contain a minimum of two characters – you, and the person with whom you were struggling. Images can have more characters, but only as many as there are people in your group. If the image is only two people, the others in the group are not in that image. You are yourself in your image. This means a group of five people will create five images.

> You must make the image without speaking. Sculpt your partners with as much detail as possible. Part of your job in this exercise is also to remember what you are doing in each other's images, because we are going to see all of them. (Give the group 15 or 20 minutes to work.)

Because time is always an issue, I tend to have the participants *look at* all of the images, but *animate* just one from each group. Facilitate the whole group deciding which images to activate. I like to do this through voting, once we have seen all of one group's images.

> We're going to vote. The reason to vote for one image over another is not that it is the most entertaining image, or the best-made image, but that it affects you the deepest. It has the strongest connection to your own life. You can vote twice. Don't vote for everything. Make a choice and *vote.*

---

70 There is a different version of this exercise called *Sculpture with four or five people* in Boal's *Games for Actors and Non-Actors*, p. 129.

This means that one of the images of the group is going to get activated and the others will not. It is important that you not take this personally. It doesn't mean your lives are boring, or that your experiences are not valid. It does mean that some-one from the group offered a moment that many others in the room have also experienced in some way.

The power of not naming images

By not naming images we start to break down the artificial barriers between the individual consciousness and that of the group. In doing so we bridge the mind/body gap and start to awaken the group consciousness.

An image in *Groups of 4* originates from the experience of one person. That person makes a very specific image. She knows who the characters are, what they are thinking, doing, feeling. Her only way to convey this to her clay, though, is to sculpt them in detail. She might create an image that has characters who are real people in it, or she might create something highly symbolic, in which the characters are representations of ideas.

Once the participant puts her very specific but unnamed image in front of the group, it ceases to be her sole property. It starts to become an image of the living community's experience. The sculpted character who is standing over her in a threatening way may be her father in her reality, but the man or woman playing the part may believe he or she is her boss, or her angry lover, or a human embodiment of consumerism, etc. Each individual participant is going to view the unnamed image from their own perspective, informed by their own life experience. They may see and feel the image differently, but what they experience will very often be linked by emotional content to the central experience of the original image creator. The image may evoke as many responses as there are people in the room. This is the power of images.

We can have a dialogue about the image through image activation. We place ourselves in the image as characters we believe we understand; and we do understand them from our own perspective. When we speak sentences as the characters, we start to name both the character and the image. The questions that arise from this are, invariably, about what the connections are between our various perceptions of the original image: how is the father linked to the boss, the lover, to consumerism or our struggles with the environment or addiction? Do they, as symbols, have metaphorical links?

In order to facilitate the actors being able to speak in the image, it is very useful to encourage them to decide who they are – to portray people, not things. The actor can play a bank manager who supports the concepts of capitalism, but he cannot play capitalism. We are working towards creating theatre that invites audience members to intervene in the action and try to find real solutions to the problems presented. In order to accomplish this, all the characters on the stage must be flesh and blood with desires, fears, hopes, histories. The actor, almost certainly, isn't the image maker's bank manager, but her own image of a bank manager. If all the actors in the image are doing this, we are getting a very broad-based expression of the contents of this still unnamed image.

Having frozen the image in time, we have the opportunity to walk around this 'frozen moment', to view it from different angles, perspectives; in a symbolic sense, to unpack it. The characters in the image, frozen in physical relationships to each other, have their own knowledge. Asked questions, they can help us look into the past, understand the present and rehearse the future. Even though the image is about something specific, having not named it, it is a broad metaphor. Humans think in metaphor,[71] and so the image can resonate deep inside the consciousness of the group, and be a catalyst to investigate the psyche of the living community. We have engaged a group consciousness, which now owns the image.

---

[71] Capra, *The Hidden Connections*, pp. 63, 64.

the group and the individual

It is important in *Theatre for Living* that, while the images are created by individuals about their own lives, the images are accepted and worked on as symbols. The realistic detail of the story is not as important as the perception in the room of the many possible variations of the story that the specific image portrays.

Likewise, it is very important that, when groups make plays, the plays are not any one person's story, but a fiction that the group creates together, telling the truth of some aspect of the living community's struggle with the issue. The play is a symbol in the same way the image is a symbol.

This is an opportunity for the living community to use primal language to tell its stories. And it demonstrates one of the many ways that *Theatre for Living* is not individual-based therapy. It is not a therapy session for any one person or group of people in the room.

Image activation

Activating the images is a deepening of the community dialogue. Each activation is really a question that the workshop participants answer through action. Integral to image activation is the *internal monologue.*

internal monologue

This is a technique that I teach to all workshop groups on the first day as part of *Complete the Image,* and that I use in image activation throughout a workshop.

> If I am in a shape like this (curled up in a little ball), my thoughts and feelings will, of course, be very different than if I am in a shape like this (standing upright with arms extended over my head and my mouth wide open). My internal monologue, which is my thoughts and feelings *as the character,* will

be very different depending on whether I am in a ball shape or an arms-extended shape.

An internal monologue is like an onion. It has layers. The way to get down beneath the first layer is not to say the same thing over and over again. Depending on the shape, the first layer of monologue for a character might be, "I hate you." But let's not say "I hate you, I hate you, I hate you, I hate you." What is underneath that? Perhaps, "I hate you, you intimidate me so much, I am frightened, what am I afraid of..." And so on and so on.

An internal monologue is not a dialogue. Two people standing next to each other cannot hear each other and converse. It is a monologue – the character's thoughts and feelings, spoken out loud. Everyone does it at the same time.

Don't stop until I ask you to. Go! (Let this go for at least 30 seconds; more if the group can sustain it.)

Stop! Stay frozen! I am going to come and touch you. When I do, please say one sentence as the character, loud enough for everyone to hear. I want that sentence to begin with the words "I want..." Speak as the character... Here we go.

identifying fears and desires

Why does an actor cross the stage? He is either moving towards something – a physical thing or an idea – that he believes will give him pleasure, or moving away from something that he believes will give him pain. Sometimes pain and pleasure get confused, and this makes life complicated. We are motivated by our fears and desires. They are central to our lives both on and off the stage.

"What do you (the character) want?" and "What are you (the character) afraid of?" are key questions that a theatre director can ask an actor, whether the actor is a professional or someone who is in a theatre workshop for the first time in their lives.

Ask each character to begin their sentence with "I want..." Giving the participant a prefix for a sentence is not determining the content of the sentence. It is a tool to help them focus and to discover motivations of the character they are portraying.

What happens from this request? Each character wants something. It is human nature. The *want* is a motivator for action. The request helps the participant clarify what he wants. Sometimes the participant will say something like:

"I want him to behave." "I want her to go away." "I want him to succeed."

This is what the participant wants the other person to do, not what the participant wants for himself. What do *you* want?

"I want to feel safe." "I want to be alone." "I want to feel useful."

Other possible prefixes are "I wish," which is different than "I want." "I hope," "I wonder," etc. The Joker can use these to great effect to help peel the layers of complexity away from the frozen image.

Here are a couple of image activation techniques. More are in the *Appendix*.

stand with a character

This is a great technique for gauging the relevance of an image to the rest of the participants.

> If any of you looking at this image have ever been one of these characters – either realistically or symbolically – come and stand with the character, taking on the same shape. You can all do this at the same time. Come. Now, internal monologue. Now, when I touch you, say a sentence that begins with the words (I want...I wish...etc.).

wide shot

> If we think of this image as a close-up in a movie, and we pull back into a wider angle shot, is this the entire image or are there other people you think should be in the image? The entire community (or the world, if desired) is in our lens. If you see other people, come and be them. Internal monologue. Say a sentence as the character, etc.

secret thought

I thought of doing this for the first time during a public Rainbow of Desire event. I had a sense in the moment that the internal monologues and sentences that were being spoken by the characters on the stage were superficial. And so, with the people frozen in their shapes, I asked them for their "secret thought":

> I am going to come and touch you. When I do, speak your secret thought – the thing your character is really thinking deep inside right now but would never actually say out loud in the situation. Your *secret* thought. Admit to yourself what it is, as the character, and commit to it. Don't change it when you hear the other characters' secret thoughts.

group discussion

After an image activation, group discussion is very important in order to continue to stimulate the awakening of the group consciousness. Different participants feel comfortable communicating differently, some with their bodies and some verbally. Because it is important not to name the image for as long as possible, it is good practice to do the physical work first. It is the most symbolic.

In discussion, the Joker asks questions that are as open ended as possible. "What do you see?" "What do you hear?" Everything is accepted. Nothing is challenged. The participants will answer from their own life experiences. An image is like a blank screen. In an image of violence, one will see a teacher hitting a student, another a father hitting a daughter, or a brother and sister, an inter-gender wrestling match, a sales clerk fighting back a robber. At this stage, the image could mean many different things. It is important to accept and validate whatever anyone sees.

The Joker might also at this point comment on what she sees, but objectively, not editorially. For instance, no one in the image might be touching, certain characters might be looking at others, and others might be looking at no one. These may be things that no one else has talked about. The Joker's observations encourage the group to exercise their ability to 'see' and to awaken their senses.

As mentioned previously, the Joker is more than likely outside her own community in some way. Each living community has its own vocabulary that it has developed through the combined life experiences of the individuals that make up the community. The Joker may interpret an image as being something very different than the community with which she is working. The workshop participants will project their own understanding onto the images that they see. While I believe it is perfectly acceptable for a Joker to share what she sees in an image, it is not the Joker's role to try to convince participants of the validity of what the Joker sees.

In image activation it often isn't so important *what* direction the Joker gives to an actor or workshop participant, as it is to give very certain and clear direction. The process really is a dialogue. If the Joker gives clear direction, the actor will feel more secure and be able to experiment or improvise with more clarity. *Something* will come from this, some kind of discovery. It may be different than we expect – these surprises are often wonderful – but it will be *something*. Sometimes roadblocks occur because the Joker is unclear, or because she is uncertain and does not commit to her idea of what facilitation is needed in this moment. When this happens, the participant/actor will also be unclear and then, in this lack of clarity, it is harder to improvise, harder to experiment.

In order to take the risk of committing to her idea, the Joker must remember that she really is engaged in a process, along with the individual participants, of stimulating the larger consciousness that is in the room. Each has a role to play of equal value. The Joker does not have to have all the answers – the participants contain the living community's knowledge of the issues. In any investigation, we get the answers to the questions we are asking. The Joker needs to ask clear questions and then wait for the participants to do their part.

The power of gesture

Before the evolution of spoken language, humans communicated through gesture. The gesture is primal.

Philosophy in the Flesh[72] begins by laying down three major findings of cognitive science: (1) that the mind is inherently embodied; (2) that thought is mostly unconscious; and (3) that abstract concepts are largely metaphorical.

> "We are neural beings," writes cognitive scientist George Lakoff (Berkeley University). "Our brains take their input from the rest of our bodies. What our bodies are like and how they function in the world thus structures the very concepts we can use to think. We cannot think just anything – only what our embodied brains permit."[73]

an example in Iqaluit, Nunavut

Very often I work with people who have been silenced, in one way or another. One girl, in Iqaluit, Nunavut, in a workshop on suicide prevention called Shutting Down,[74] in 2003, didn't speak at all for the first three days of an eight-day process. Her school kept checking in to see if she was still in the workshop, because knowing her and her life experience, they didn't believe that she would finish a process in which she would become an actor who had to play a character with words to say in a play about 'shutting down'. She became a central character and did wonderful improvisational work in front of audiences of over 100 people.

---

72 By George Lakoff and Mark Johnson, published by Basic Books, New York 1999.
73 From The Third Culture "Philosophy in the Flesh" at
http://www.edge.org/3rd_culture/lakoff/lakoff_p1.html
74 For a full report on this project see
http://www.headlinestheatre.com/pastwork.htm

My process with her and the rest of the participants in this workshop was not therapy. It was theatre creation, but, as always, it met them and her where they were living, in a world where the response to never being heard was to become silent. How was this 'opening up' accomplished? By concentrating on the language of physical gesture for longer than usual, and then slowly moving into gesture and sound, before taking the leap to dialogue. This girl's own courageous will to persevere should not be underestimated; without that the rest was impossible.

I believe the reason this works in such situations is that language *originates* from physical gesture. Capra writes about the work of George Lakoff (see footnotes 72 and 73) and anthropologist Gordon Hewes, who proposed that early hominids communicated through hand gestures.[75] As gestures became more precise and hands became more articulate through the use of tools, gesture patterns became more complex. Capra writes that neurologist Doreen Kimura advanced Hewes' work by discovering that the same region of the brain controls speech and hand movement. Psychologist Roger Fouts, first through his revolutionary work with chimpanzees and sign language, and then with autistic children, confirmed that autism in children is not a problem of language, but of spoken language. He used sign language to help children break through the barrier of autism. In some cases, these children began to speak after several weeks of signing. Speculation is that the signing triggered the capacity for speech, as both functions are controlled by the same part of the brain.

The girl in Iqaluit was not autistic. I watched her, though, struggle with her desire and inability to communicate. I also marvelled at the courage she showed by not leaving the workshop, something she always had the permission to do if she so desired. Here are excerpts from my workshop report journal.[76]

> Day 2   Something is appearing with one of the girls: Ida really wants to be here, but whenever the work comes to her, even in a game, if she has to do *anything* – make a sound, or a gesture – she just freezes. Once she freezes, attention gets focused on her, and I can see her vanish, vanish, vanish. Her

---

75 Capra, *The Hidden Connections*, p. 58.
76 None of the references to workshop participants use their real names.

eyes glaze over. She shuts down. What happens to Ida is what we are here to investigate and make plays about for a national suicide prevention conference.

I am trying various things – giving her space, letting her know she can pass – to take the pressure off her, hoping this will make it possible for her to participate. I am concerned, though, that once in performance (if she stays with us, and I hope she does), she is going to have to respond by herself. Ending up in front of an audience and shutting down will be the worst possible thing for her. I have asked the support people to keep an eye on her.

Day 4   I always do a lot of gesture work in every workshop, but in this one, because of Ida's presence and some others who are having a problem similar to hers, but not as extreme, I used a game that I started to develop a few years earlier. My reasoning was that we use gestures all the time, hundreds of times a day, often unconsciously. If spoken language originated from gesture, then it should be possible to re-create this process and help potential actors in a workshop find their ability to use spoken language in public.

speed gestures[77]

I use this exercise to bring a group of 'non-actors' very gently into improvising. This game begins with an *open-ended gesture*, one that can be interpreted in various ways. This might, for instance, be extending an arm and waving a finger, it might be looking up at the sky and raising one's arms, or turning one's back. All of these gestures can be interpreted in a variety of ways. An open-ended gesture is *not miming an object*, like miming looking through a pair of binoculars. While the person looking through the binoculars might be looking at a variety of things, he will always be looking through binoculars.

Everyone line up at one end of the room, along a wall, please. Does someone have an open-ended gesture they could offer?

---

[77] This exercise evolved from an exercise of Boal's called *Ritual gestures* on p. 182 of *Games for Actors and Non-Actors*.

OK. Come and face the rest of the group. (This is person 'A'.) Let's see the gesture three times, each time starting from a neutral position, so we can really see it. Fill the gesture with emotion.

Now, one at a time, starting on this end of the line (pick an end to be the front of the line), each person ('B' for purposes of explanation), will run into the centre and stop facing 'A'. Come, please. OK.

'A' make the gesture. 'B' very quickly respond with another gesture, so it's a short exchange, with no words. Good. 'B' runs to the other the end of the line.

Another 'B' from the front of the line. 'A' make the gesture. 'B' very quickly respond with another *different* gesture (the 'B's cannot repeat!). It's a short exchange, with no words. Good. 'B' runs to the end of the line. Another 'B' from the front of the line. Do this quickly please. (Each person does this, always inventing something new. It is important to make it clear that there is no way to do this wrong, as long as the gestures are a response to each other.)

Good. Thank you, 'A'. Join the line again. Another 'A' who has a different gesture, please. Let's see the gesture three times, each time starting from a neutral position, so we can really see it. Fill the gesture with emotion.

(Repeat the above.)

Good. Thank you, 'A'. Join the line again. Another 'A' who has a different gesture, please. Let's see the gesture three times, each time starting from a neutral position, so we can really see it. Fill the gesture with emotion.

This time, 'B' run in to the centre, face the group and stop. 'A' will make the gesture. 'B', very quickly respond with another gesture *and a word or phrase that grows directly out of the gesture*, to which 'A' will respond with another, new gesture *and a word or phrase*, creating a short exchange that has *spoken and gestural language*. 'A' must accept the reality that 'B' creates. 'B', then run out and join the line. Good. Another 'B'. (As above) Each person does this, always inventing something new. Again, it is important to make it clear that there is no way to do this wrong, as long as the gestures and words are a response to each other. Repeat with yet another new 'A' and gesture.

Now, the final layer: a new 'A' and a new gesture, please. Let's see the gesture three times, each time starting from a neutral position, so we can really see it. Fill the gesture with emotion. Now, 'B', run in, stop. 'A', make the gesture. 'B', very quickly respond with another gesture and a word or phrase that grows directly out of the gesture, to which 'A' will respond with another new gesture and a word or phrase. Now 'A' and 'B' will continue, without gestures, just with dialogue. Keep going, listen and respond to each other in an improvisation that walks and talks. Just see where it goes. Don't stop until I say stop, please. OK, good. Stop.

'B' runs out. A new 'B' comes in, always inventing something new, until everyone has done this.

Let's do it again with another 'A' and a new gesture.

> **Joker Tip:** A key to this exercise is to keep it moving very quickly. Encourage the participants not to censor themselves, not to think too much, to go with their first impulse. There is no way to do it wrong.

"yes, and" – "yes, but"[78]

In order to accomplish speed gestures, 'A' must really be attentive. He must see and listen carefully to the different offerings of each 'B', and respond authentically. In order to help the group understand how to do this, I will most often use the following improvisation technique.

---

[78] I encountered this simple but very valuable improvisation tool for the first time in 1971, when I entered acting classes, and have been using it in *Theatre for Living* workshops since 1986. It is a central rule of any improvisation class.

Ask a participant to stand beside you and, for example, to look up and say:

Participant	O, what a lovely moon.[79]
Joker	It's daytime.
Participant	(Will respond somehow. Let's imagine she says...) OK, it's daytime... What a great sun.
Joker	This is a nice restaurant.

This is an example of *blocking* in improvisation. It is impossible to create any coherent reality, because one of the actors is not accepting what the other is offering. Start again:

Participant	O, what a lovely moon.
Joker	I've seen nicer moons.
Participant	(Will respond somehow, let's imagine she says...) But it's so full.
Joker	What about that night we were camping in the mountains...

In this second example, anything is possible. In the first exchange, the Joker has internalized a "YES, I see the moon, BUT, I've seen nicer moons." In the second exchange the Joker has internalized a "YES, it is full, AND I am going to remind you about that night."

Here are some more of the Iqaluit journal entries.

(Still Day 4) Ida sweated a lot in this game. She had been virtually silent for the first three days and up until this moment. No one forced her to participate now, except, I suppose, the fact that it was a group activity and she was there in it. Running in each time was Ida's decision. The first time she did, she stopped and stared at me – frozen. "It could be anything," I said to her. She gave the person ('A') the "fuck you" finger and ran off. "YES!" The room howled in appreciation.

The next time Ida ran in, the gesture was more subtle and 10 or 15 minutes later she was very quietly speaking a sentence when it came her turn.

---

[79] The Joker has fed the participant this first line.

Day 5   Ida joined a play-making group and is in one of the plays. Up until yesterday, she was saying she would not perform on stage. The workshop group made three plays. One was about being used by friends and another, very complex, about alcohol, drugs and betrayal. I am going to detail only the play Ida's group made.

Here is the scenario: A group of girls are sitting in the library of the school, talking about how disgusting the girls' washroom is. A girl who is new to the school enters. She tries to join the conversation. The girls reject her, except for Ida, who makes a small attempt to reach out, but is stopped by the other girls. The new girl goes off to the other side of the library and sits alone.

The girls start to ask one another if they are going to the dance that is coming up. It turns out that one of them is going with a boy that another had just broken up with two days earlier. This is really bad. A fight starts, but it is broken up by the leader of the group, who says that they will get the girl who is seeing the boyfriend later, after school. Ida doesn't like what's happening with her friends and goes across the room to see if she can make friends with the new girl. Her friends yell abuse after her, but she ignores them. The new girl is very hurt and angry, and when Ida approaches her, the girl rejects her and walks away. Ida is now alone and alienated. End of play.

Day 7   There were over 100 people in the audience today. One of the great joys in the first play was Ida. She came forward with ideas in the Forum, and improvised! And when I asked her why she had done what she did as the character, she answered me! In a loud voice!!! It's hard to describe what an amazing moment this was. Members of the group talked about it in the final circle.

Day 8   Ida has really bloomed in the last few days. From so quiet to a leader in the play. Many of the audience members know her and know her silence – she got tremendous applause today for her improvisational abilities.

Postscript: Many of the people on the plane out of Iqaluit had seen the performances at the conference. I had long talks with suicide prevention people from Quebec; also with a doctor and an Inuit police officer who had been very moved by the Forum Theatre event and the group's plays. They talked about how revealing and practical it was, and that it changed them and their perceptions about the issue of suicide.

An Inuk man said something that really struck me. We were talking about why kids (Inuit kids in particular at this moment) commit suicide. I understood him to say, "Because when children are born, they are pure and that means they are born 'traditional' – and they see at a very young age that their parents and grandparents are trying to be white. And they know something is very wrong, and that it is in their lives, and they don't know how to fix it. This play you made, and how it works with the audience, helps us all understand how to fix it."

He has made me wonder how what he is talking about might translate into other cultures and situations. About the purity of all children who are not born to be global consumers, but having been born into a consumer culture, struggle at a very young age to learn and fit into an unnatural value system that is based on what we can be perceived to possess, instead of who we are, what we think, feel and do.

Post-postscript: Jonathan (the central organizer) has told me that Ida approached him and has asked to be part of the theatre group that is forming out of the workshop.

Creating plays

When a group of individuals starts a *Theatre for Living* workshop they are very often people who have never met before. A week later, when they are performing the plays they have made, they are working together in very complex ways, displaying the qualities of an ensemble, having allowed the identity of the living organism to emerge. In very simple terms, what happens during the course of the workshop, from the Joker's perspective, looks as follows.

Different individuals become ready to communicate, to trust, to improvise, to make plays, at different times in the process. For some it happens early, maybe even by the end of the first day. These participants gather in a metaphoric area and become somewhat impatient. Their impatience energizes others in the group. Each day, more of the group gathers in this energized place, and the more of them there are, the more urgent the organism's impulse to make the plays. They are not allowed to do this. Critical mass has to build; more of the group needs to arrive into this place of readiness, until, on the fourth or fifth day, as many of the group as possible are straining against the constraints of Image Theatre.

The Joker has been holding them back in a way – looking deeper and deeper into the issues with them, finding ways to excite, activate, invite, awaken the whole organism. This is not about convincing any individual in any way to join the group, or to agree with a point of view. Disagreements are valuable, forming part of the necessary and valid tension in both the process and the actual play. But finally, on day four or five, it is time to release the energy of the room, and let the group make their plays. Often it is like letting go of a big elastic band. There is an urgency now to articulate the complexity of the issues in more than frozen images. The plays, having incubated in the group, emerge now as very layered articulations of the larger organism's story. This does not mean they are not also very raw and need a lot of work.

A week-long *Theatre for Living* process that is creating plays for public performance will generally have three or four days of Image Theatre work using the above and other techniques. During this time we are engaging in a process of accumulation. I am asking the participants to consciously allow the images to accumulate inside them, allowing one day's work to affect the choices they make in focusing on a moment of struggle the next day.

In order to complete this process I will generally use one of two lovely group exercises: *Song of the Mermaid* or *Magnetic Image*.

before doing song of the mermaid

Before embarking on *Song of the Mermaid*, I sit down with the participants and show them a diagram of opposing forces (see next page) and make a list with them. The list is of all the issues that we have seen come up in the course of the workshop. Having asked the participants to actively engage in a process of accumulation, this is usually an easy task to accomplish.

In order for a play to be successful as Forum Theatre, it must have a certain structure. We must be able to see the characters travel into the crisis that is the heart of the issue, engage in a struggle with each other, and be unable to resolve the crisis. In the audience interactive part of the event, if the cast members in the scene don't push, the intervening audience member loses the opportunity to gain any knowledge out of the theatrical struggle. The cast members must truly understand the character they are playing. This is why it is essential that the actors are members of the community doing the investigating – not actors brought in from outside who have no knowledge of the issues.

As we have already discussed, the balancing game contains the very heart of theatre. In the pushing part of that game, there are two characters. Character 'A' (the Protagonist in the diagram) wants something, and character 'B' (the Antagonist in the diagram) wants something else. These two forces push in opposition to each other and that is what creates drama.

The task of a group is to find the crisis of their play and work backwards, moving their characters out of the crisis. The play is the story through which the audience follows the characters' journey into the crisis.

opposing forces[80]

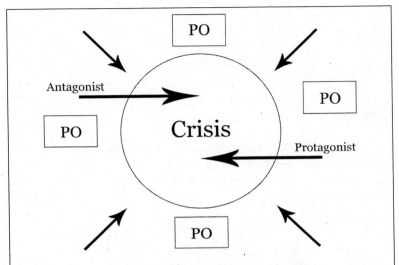

What creates layers in a Forum Theatre play is not only seeing the Antagonist and the Protagonist travel into the crisis, but characters adjacent to them and aligned with or against them also travelling into the same crisis (the other arrows).

In many Forum plays we also have characters who are "powerless observers" (PO).

powerless observer

What I call the "powerless observer" first emerged from Headlines' anti-racism work in the schools in the early 1990s. Often, Caucasian participants had not been direct victims of racism, but were very concerned about the issues. How could they do this work if they sensed that, within the working rules of oppressor and oppressed that we were articulating at that time, they had never been directly oppressed? Taking these young people into a discussion of white privilege and an analysis of how, through their silence or seemingly inconsequential acts in the school hallways, they may be oppressors themselves, would have been far more "instructive" than I believe this work should be. The learning is in the moment of an individual's discovery.

---

[80] This diagram, in its original format (without PO), is from Boal during a workshop in Paris in 1994.

The answer came from the students themselves. Many times, participants had been present in a moment of racism and for any number of reasons (peer pressure and fear being big ones), did nothing, although they knew that what was happening was wrong. They said often that they "felt powerless." I started to recognize that it was possible for them to understand this powerless state as, itself, a form of oppression that they were experiencing. We found that including their experiences was of great value in opening the issue up in what was very often an atmosphere of silence.

Having the investigation meet them in their comfort zone, also, in many instances, provided the kind of safe space necessary for these same participants to recognize how their own behaviour was contributing to the problem.

Some people don't like the name "powerless observer". I experimented for a while with changing it to "witness". I find, though, that in the moment of crisis, these characters *want to act* but *feel powerless*. They really are "powerless" "observers". Self-identifying as a witness may, in and of itself, be a powerful act that comes after the powerless observer is activated.

In structuring a Forum, try to help the participants resist their natural urge to resolve the problems in the play. By doing this they rob the audience of its role as intervener. The plays that the participants make only have to show the problem. In fact, the best time to do a Forum play is when the participants really don't know the answer to the problems they are facing.

song of the mermaid[81]

> Everyone lie down on the floor, with as much space between you and the others as possible, eyes closed. Notice your breath. Breathing is something your body will do all by itself, like your heart beating. Please, everyone – exhale. Push all the air out of you. Keep going. Push more out – more – and more!

---

[81] There is a version of this exercise called *The siren's song* in Boal's *Games for Actors and Non-Actors*, p. 115. When I first encountered this exercise with Boal in 1984, he called it *Song of the mermaid*.

And then, when you can't push any more – push more! Now – allow the air to fill your lungs, and from now on, allow your body to breathe without trying to control it.

We have seen many images over the last few days; powerful images and improvisations, discussions. Many of you have, I imagine, had insights and learned things that you haven't talked with anyone about. That's OK. In this exercise, we are going to bring as many of those things together, in an organic way, as we can. But once again, you will only tell personal stories in your group if you *want* to tell them. So, please, for now, let the images and insights parade through your mind. And breathe.

I am going to read you the list – of kinds of struggles – that we made before we started this exercise. As you listen to the list, I want you to allow yourself to see whatever images are attached to the words. Eventually, I will want you to focus on what is, for you, the one most important kind of struggle. I want you to only focus now on images that came out of the workshop. Nothing new. Perhaps it was something you offered in the workshop, perhaps someone else offered something that connected to your experience deeply. (The list is read, slowly.)

You are the person who is struggling with the issue in this moment. You do not have to live the moment again, you can observe it from a distance, but observe it clearly. Where does it take place? Who are the players? What time is it? What is the temperature? What happens? And most important, what do you feel in the moment? Be specific. Understand that there is a difference between anger and rage, for instance. Focus on the strongest emotion.

Now, I want you – just inside yourself, do not do this out loud – to turn that emotion into a sound. Not a mechanical sound – no clapping or stamping your feet. Not language – no words. But, a sound that you can make with your breath. If there was only one way to express the emotion and it was by making a sound, this would be the sound to make. When you can hear the sound inside you, raise your hand, resting your elbow on the floor. I will wait for a number of hands to be in the air.

Lower your hands. I am going to take one person. Everyone, including the person I am taking, please keep your eyes closed. (Help the person onto her feet and guide her to one corner of the room.) I am going to ask this person to make her sound three times, loud enough for everyone to hear. Do that now, please. If anyone did not hear that sound, please raise your hand. (Ask the person to repeat the sound if there are hands raised.)

If your sound was anything like that sound, please do not offer it. I only want you to offer a sound now if it is different from this one. Who has one that is different? Raise your hands, please. OK, lower them, I am taking another person.

> **Joker Tip:** Repeat the process above, until there are at least three sounds. Depending on the size of the group there may be four or five. The math of it? If there are 20 or more people, do at least three, but balance off how much time you will have to rehearse each of the plays that will get made based on a sound type.

In a moment, I am going to ask the people who have offered sounds to start making their sounds and to keep going until I ask them to stop. This might take a while, so find a way to do it without hurting your throats. When the sounds start, I want the rest of you, *keeping your eyes closed*, to go to the sound that is either the most like your own sound or is the sound you relate to the strongest. It is very important, if you know who is making the sounds, to divorce the person from the sound. Do not go into a group to be with your friend(s). Go because of the sound.

To the people making sounds: it could happen that no one comes to your sound. A group of two is fine for this exercise, but a group of one is not. If it happens that you open your eyes and are alone, try not to take that personally. There are many possible reasons – it might have scared people, or it might be abstract, or someone else may have offered something that many others understood more easily, or felt more comfortable going to. Just in case this does happen, know which sound you would go to other than your own.

Is anyone confused? OK, if everything is clear, begin.

So – now we have four (or three or five) groups. I want each group to sit in a circle, please, as far away from the other groups as possible. The people who made the sounds – you are not responsible in any way for leading your group. If you have specific stories to tell, that's OK, but you do not have to share your stories if you don't want to. I do want you, though, to share the emotion that went into your own sound. As you do this, you are going to find that there is something that you all share. Actively seek this out. It is some form of struggle that links you together. There is some reason you are in this group, with this sound, and not another group. Find out what you have in common. Name it.

Once you have done that, I want you to use the tools you have from this workshop. Start with frozen images and then make an improvisation that walks and talks, about the struggle that you share. The improvisation could last 30 seconds; it doesn't have to be long. It must contain at least two characters, who are engaged in the central struggle with each other. Remember the structure of the opposing forces diagram. Decide on the final crisis of the play and walk your characters backwards in time, out of the crisis. Your play is the characters' journey into the crisis.

Obviously, your play can have more than two characters. Be true to the play. Not all of you have to be in the play, especially if some of you don't want to. If someone *does* want to, let them. Cast yourselves. Do not volunteer each other for roles. If you have questions, or get stuck, ask and I will come and talk with you.

(I usually give the groups about 90 minutes to accomplish this task.)

Joker Tip: the Joker should resist the temptation to help the participants too much at this stage in the making of their plays. The group needs to own the play. The only way for them to own the play, is to make it themselves. Part of their creation process may be sorting out how to work together. The play can be 30 seconds long, literally, and very rough. After the group has presented what they have made, the Joker can and should work intimately with the group to help them make the play the best it can be.

magnetic image

This exercise came out of an emergency. In 1994 I was in a week-long workshop that was to create Forum Theatre plays, but the workshop had started two days late, because of a death in the community. I needed to come up with an exercise that combined two days' work into one. I use *Magnetic Image* very often now, as it creates the potential for improvisations to come very fast.

Everyone sit on one side of the room. Think of a moment when you were struggling with (the issue we are investigating). Again, it has to be something from your own life. It can be something you already offered, or something new. Let your choice be affected by the work we have been doing so far.

The way the moment will be offered, is by making a shape, using your own body, that will convey the strongest emotion that you felt inside this moment of struggle. All you have to work with is your own body, in a frozen shape. Who has a shape they could offer? OK, come. Make the shape, so everyone can see it.

This is the first shape. If the shape you were going to offer is anything like this shape, don't offer it. Is there a different shape? OK, come. Make the shape, so everyone can see it. Is there a third, different shape?

(Depending on the size of the group, you might want from three to five shapes. The people making the shapes should not speak.)

To the people who are offering shapes: it is possible that no one will come to your shape. This happens sometimes. If it does, try not to take it personally. You might have offered something that scared people, or accessed a moment that is very specific to you. There are many reasons why no one might have come. If this happens, know which other shape you would go to. A group of two is fine, but a group of one is not – you cannot work alone in this exercise.

Those of you still sitting, please divorce the person from the shape. Be careful not to go to a friend, just because you want to be in his group. And, likewise, if someone you perhaps don't like is making a shape that you relate to very strongly – get over it – go there. Divorce the person from the shape. Please, in silence, go to the shape that is either the most like the shape you would have made, or is the shape that you relate to the strongest.

Now we have groups. Sit in circles, please. The person who made the shape – you have no leadership responsibility in your group. I do, though, want you to speak first. If you have a story to tell, you can tell it if you want to. You don't have to. But I do want you to talk about the emotion that went into making your shape. The rest of the people in the group, listen actively. Think about what it is in your own life, and in your relationship to the issues we are looking at, that connects with what the person who made the shape is saying. When it is your time to talk, you can tell a personal story if you want to, but you don't have to. I do want you to talk about the emotion connected to your own struggle that brought you to the shape.

As you talk, you are going to find that a sense of something you share starts to appear in the middle of the circle. Seek it out, this struggle that you share. Name it. It is the core struggle of your image or play.

using magnetic image to create an image

Once you have identified what it is that links you together, work together to make a frozen image that shows characters engaged in the struggle that you share. Each of you will know who you are and what you are doing in the image. Create a fiction that tells the truth of the group; do not make an image of one person's story.

using magnetic image to create a play

To use *Magnetic Image* to create plays, ask the groups to make images as above and then animate the images (using the animation techniques like *internal monologue, stand with the character, wide shot* and others) one by one in front of the whole workshop group. Use the image animations and the feedback from the others in the room to help the group deepen their understanding of the characters they are making and the story they are telling. Then ask the *Magnetic Image* groups to continue their small-group work together.

Now that you have feedback on your image from the other workshop participants, work together to make an improvisation that walks and talks, that shows us the characters engaged in the struggle. The frozen image may be the crisis. If it is, back the characters away from the crisis and let their journey into the crisis be the play. Create a fiction that tells the truth of the group; do not make a play of one person's story.

Joker Tip: In both *Song of the Mermaid* and *Magnetic Image* it is sometimes important to help the participants get over the difficult transition from sitting and talking to standing up and making their plays. Remind them that they can use image-making techniques that they have learned in the workshop as a starting point. Once they have the core image of the central struggle, and the crisis that the struggle leads to, they have the core moment in the play. Beyond this, *the Joker must not help them make the play.* They have to make the play themselves, even if it is a great, terrible, awful, ugly struggle for the group. And on rare occasions, it is. The first incarnation of the play does not have to be long. It could be 20 or 30 seconds and extremely raw. This is the only way for them to own it. Once they have made the play, the Joker can and should get inside it with them and direct it for the theatre.

The Joker transforms from a workshop facilitator into a theatre director

Once the plays are made, it is the Joker's responsibility to get inside the plays with the cast and make the best theatre possible under the circumstances in which the group is working. There are people who disagree with this approach. They have told me that the workshop participants are not professional actors and it is, after all, community-based theatre, so the group's plays should go to performance exactly as they manifested from the group process – as a true, unfiltered voice.

I believe it is the Joker's responsibility to both the working group and the larger, living community to make the best theatre with them that is possible under the circumstances under which they are working. What is it that creates a deep connection for the community to the plays? Is it watching one's neighbour or child or spouse on the stage, in and of itself? Certainly, seeing someone you know telling a story that is about your own community is powerful, but it is only part of the equation. Is it that the play reflects real issues in the community? Again, this is only a part of the larger picture.

Two essential ingredients are emotional engagement and metaphorical engagement. Theatre is an emotional and symbolic language. There is a difference between watching people on stage *pretending to feel emotions* and witnessing them *feeling authentic emotions*. It is the authenticity of the storytelling that grabs the audience. Also, because we humans think in metaphor, creating strong theatrical symbols that grow out of community experience reaches deep inside the conscious-ness of the community. It is these artistic elements, as well as who the cast is and what story they are telling, that compels members of the living community to have the courage to transgress the sanctity of the theatre, to enter the playing area and make interventions in the play, and to work, in their own authentic ways, to resolve the issues or create safety in the world of the play.

This is why it is so important that the workshop groups create the plays by themselves initially, without the Joker's help. They must own the plays. But having been in the workshop with them, the Joker must now exercise his or her artistry and work on the plays with the group. There are different areas of expertise in this working relationship. The Joker has an expertise in theatre: he can function as an outside eye and ear, be a traffic cop, dramaturge, set designer, stage manager, whatever is necessary. Theatre needs to have one director, and, for this time period, this is the Joker's primary role. The workshop participants have expertise in knowing their collective stories. The Joker and participants can create something together that it is likely neither can create alone; that is, relevant *art* that is a true voice of the living community.

The workshop has, up until this point, been very collaborative. It must now change gears. From this point on, workshop participants must be responsible for their own roles. They must try to avoid directing each other, or answering questions for each other. The actor playing the father is not going to be able to turn to another cast member in performance and ask what he should do. He is going to have to figure it out himself, in a way that is real for his character. Now is the time to start.

Likewise, if the actor is taking direction from the Joker as well as other cast members, these directions may often be contradictory. There can be only one director in theatre, one person who is responsible for orchestrating the larger picture. She does not need to be a dictator; she can take input from everyone, but the final decisions need to be the Joker's. To proceed otherwise is to risk confusing the actors and creating space that is very unsafe for them in performance.

I generally see the play(s) created by the small groups, give them some feedback, and then go into a final circle and finish the day. This gives me the opportunity to process the plays overnight and come back with ideas that I will work on with each group the next day. My preference is to move through each play quite slowly, sometimes in five or 10-second segments, getting those to work, then going back to the beginning, running another segment, running that from the beginning, etc. When we are finished, the cast knows all their lines backwards and forwards, without pen ever going to paper, and can usually start playing from anywhere in the play, which will be essential in the Forum.

basic stagecraft

There are some basic technical requirements. The characters have to be seen and heard. The theatre we make is about real life, but it is theatre, it is not real life. In real life many people talk at once. We generally don't concern ourselves with needing to be seen by others, which way we are facing, or reaching the back of the room with our voices. For anyone with knowledge of the theatre, these things will seem elementary, but when working with people who are new to the theatre, they are not elementary at all. They are learned skills that we must do consciously in performance. If the audience cannot see and/or hear, all the wonderful work of the group will be lost.

Following are just a few very simple techniques.

voice projection

People spend their lifetimes studying voice. The Joker may have 30 minutes to resolve sound issues. I have never met anyone who could speak, who, when they wanted to, could not call to their friend from across a large room or a playing field and be heard. Do this with the cast. Make it a game. It is a skill they all have and use naturally in their lives outside the workshop. Let them experience it, and then translate it from the moment of calling a friend to the moment of performance. This is not the same as years of voice classes, but it will help them 'on the night'.

> I am going to the back of the audience area, to the furthest point away from the stage an audience member might be. Everyone line up at the back of the stage, please. Now, one by one (start at the left or right and work across), answer my questions. What kind of day are you having? Louder please... What did you have for dinner? Good – you are reaching me. Whenever you speak, it needs to be at least that loud. Next.

sight lines

There are rare occasions when it is appropriate for an actor to have his back to an audience. It is even more rare to block the audience's view of another actor. Sometimes, with people who have never been on stage before, the Joker must not be afraid to get inside the scene during rehearsals and gently move the actors around. Sometimes telling them is not enough – they have a lot on their minds and hearts during this time period – they need to feel it physically. Their bodies will sometimes remember this better than their minds.

making thought visible

It is easy for actors to get trapped in their heads. Once the play is worked out, and the actors know the sequences of lines and of entrances and exits, the following is a wonderful exercise to bring physicality back into the play.

> Play the scene as you would normally, keeping all the lines the same, but whatever you are thinking about, *do – make thought visible*. For example, if you are talking in a seemingly calm way to another character in the scene, but are really thinking about how you want to be pounding on his chest, *do that* (gently, of course), but keep playing the scene. If you want to be hiding under the table, wishing you could disappear, *do that – make thought visible,* but keep playing the scene.

Wild and insightful things can happen. The actors and the Joker make discoveries, some that they can keep.

acting is not acting [82]

When a community wants to make theatre, one of the reasons is almost always the hope that the process will help create some kind of transformation in the community. A person's behaviour does not change based only on what they think. Our thoughts are only one layer of consciousness. Our feelings motivate us. This exercise becomes very important in this context, because, if the actors' performances

---

[82] I encountered this exercise for the first time in theatre school. The first time I did it with Boal in 1984, he called it *Acting without words*, but I notice it is now called *Play to the deaf* in *Games for Actors and Non-Actors*, p. 211. For many years I have been calling it *Acting Is Not Acting* – taken from the most basic but important thing an acting teacher (Bernie Segal) ever said to me when I was an acting student in 1972: "Acting is not acting – acting is being."

are to activate the audience, the actors must engage the audience on a physical, emotional and psychological level. They must transmit all this to the audience. The only way to do this is give themselves the permission to feel the physicality, the emotion and the psychology of the characters they are playing.

> Play the scene as we have rehearsed it, but you cannot speak. All of your intentions, desires, fears, subtext must be communicated, but without words. This is not a mime exercise. Convey the physicality, the emotion, the psychology of the moment, so that an audience could understand everything in the scene.

analytical rehearsal of emotion[83]

One's emotions are often, if not always, a complex 'stew'. Thankfully, the theatre is a laboratory. Sometimes, even though we are trying to step outside of the paradigm that reduces the world into mechanized, disconnected components, it can be very helpful to distill complexity into its component parts. After understanding the individual components, we may be able to put them back together again and understand the total complexity.

> Play the scene (or segment of a scene) focusing on one emotion only. For instance, play a love scene through the emotion of 'pure love', but then also play it again through 'pure hate'. Everyone plays the scene as created, but only feels one emotion as strongly and purely as possible. Now, choose another emotion and repeat, only focusing into that emotion. Now another. Now play the scene again, having talked about the discoveries made, and try to integrate the complexity.

> **Joker Tip:** The emotion can be an obvious part of the emotional content of the scene, or it may be useful to try something that seems very contrary to the content of the scene. Be careful not to do too many emotions, as the cast will overload. Be selective.

---

[83] There is a version of this exercise (same name) in Boal's *Games for Actors and Non-Actors*, p. 214.

faster – louder

The wonderful professional actress Pat Armstrong told me a story, when we were in rehearsal for *The Dying Game*, about the Canadian theatre director John Hirsch. Evidently, late in the rehearsal process, he would sit in the darkened theatre and yell only two directions at his actors: "Faster – louder! Faster – louder!"

Rehearsal exercises and the exploration that happens through them can fragment theatrical moments. The actors are taking in large amounts of emotional, psychological and physical information and trying to integrate that information into an authentic performance. This will very often slow them down. There they are, onstage, thinking their way through each moment. This is fine for a while in rehearsal, but eventually it has to stop, because one thing theatre should not be is boring for the audience.

> Run the play (or the scene) at double (or triple) the speed we have just done it. Don't miss anything, feel what you are feeling, move where you should be moving, pay attention, just do it all very, very fast – and also very loud.

> How did that feel? (As is most often the case...) Yes, it looked and sounded great, too. Do it just like that from now on, please.

Forum Theatre rehearsal

It is impossible to second-guess what members of an audience will do in an interactive Forum Theatre event. It is, however, possible and necessary to help the actors know what it is going to be like for strangers to invade their play with radical, problem-solving ideas. This does not mean telling them what to do or how to react. It is a revisiting of the pushing part of the game, *Balancing*,[84] but now in a context of interventions. This can be accomplished during rehearsal by having workshop participants make interventions in each other's plays.

---

[84] See the *starting the workshop* section of the chapter *In the Workshop Room*.

Whenever an audience member enters the play, he is coming to push against one or more of the actors. The actors must push back in such a way as to make the audience member work; not so hard so as to defeat him immediately, and not so agreeably so as to give in, either. The actor must listen with every faculty and, if the intervener convinces him in some way, the actor should go with that. If not convinced, the actor must stay true to his character's position. In either case, the Joker will hold the actor accountable for the character's actions on the stage. The actors must be able to justify their actions, as their characters.

This also applies to the other actors in the play. The intervener might replace a mother, playing a scene with a father at a kitchen table, while children are in the living room. The actors playing the children are 'alive'. They must not become audience members, sitting onstage watching the 'parents' play a scene. If something happens in the kitchen that they can legitimately see or hear and that affects them – maybe it draws them into the kitchen, or expels them from the living room – then they must allow that to take place.

These are some of the kinds of things that the actors might discover, for the first time, in Forum rehearsal. This is also the only opportunity for the Joker to investigate ways to Joke these particular plays before she gets out in front of an audience.

For the Joker who is not a direct community member, this is extremely important. The plays that the Joker and community members have created are the 'tip of the iceberg' in relation to the issues that the group is investigating.[85] It is a wonderful opportunity for the Joker to have the time to try to understand some of the complexity of what lies underneath the plays. This will help her ask more probing questions in the Forum – one of her jobs being to challenge the living community to see the issues from unfamiliar perspectives, and to be as creative in its discussion and problem-solving as possible.

I hope it is starting to become apparent that the Joker is in a very fluid position in this theatre model. The Joker is an animator, an activist, a

---

[85] Boal has referred to this phenomenon as the "Loch Ness". People only ever see the very tip of the legendary Scottish monster above the surface of the water. Most of the beast is invisible to our eyes, yet we know it is there, lurking underneath the surface.

conductor, a mirror, a character, a traffic cop, a "difficultator" (as Boal would say), an improviser, a channel for energy, a wild card, an artist on a tightrope.

The Joker, having been invited to transgress the boundary of the living community, meets individual members of the community and, with them, forms a metabolic structure that is the workshop group. Speaking the symbolic language of the theatre, the community and the Joker work together to discover and then to tell a story of the living community.

Two case studies of how this happens are presented in the next chapter.

PIVOTAL FIRST NATIONS
COLLABORATIONS

As I mentioned in *Reader Tips and Acknowledgements*, many of the insights that led to the movement away from the oppressor/oppressed model and towards *Theatre for Living* happened while I was working with First Nations communities. I want to detail two of these projects.

Before doing so, it is important to note that I am invited to work on issues of violence often, and with a diversity of communities. While the two projects outlined in this chapter, *Out of the Silence* and *Reclaiming Our Spirits*, are both on issues of violence and both with First Nations communities, I want to state that violence is something that permeates our overarching culture. It is not a problem of any specific community.

Out of the Silence

In 1989, as a response to the ¿SANCTUARY? audience member's courageous intervention to replace the leader of the death squad,[86] I started saying to audience members: "who is oppressed in any moment in the play is up to you to decide." Beyond that, I didn't have any answers.

Then, in 1990, Ron George, who at that time was president of United Native Nations (UNN), called me. He wanted to know if it would be possible for Headlines to do a production with the urban First Nations community. He felt that with all the important activity throughout Canada on land claims and Native self-government, the issues of the urban sector, made up of individuals from so many different First Nations across the country, was getting left out of the discussion. These conversations with Ron led to a meeting between Headlines and the Urban Representative Body of Aboriginal Nations (URBAN), during which we agreed to do a co-production. We left it up to URBAN and UNN to decide what the project should focus on, and they chose issues of family violence.

The boards of directors of the organizations had one request. We all knew that because of the subject matter, there would be an abuser in the play. They wanted an assurance that, while the production would not condone the actions of the character, she or he would be portrayed as someone who needed healing, not as a criminal who needed to be locked up and have the key thrown away.

This tied directly into the ¿SANCTUARY? experience a few years previous and should have been easy to implement. I had my own challenge, though. I found myself very resistant to this request. The death squad situation in ¿SANCTUARY? wasn't personal. This was. I had, myself, come from a childhood filled with alcohol, drugs and violence. The more we talked about it, though, the more I began to understand that our prisons were full of abusers who were coming out of prison and reoffending. The criminalization of these people was not solving the problem and, in some instances, was making the situation worse by locking up the family's main or only source of income, often

---

[86] See the section *The oppressed leader of the death squad* in the chapter *Feedback Loops.*

throwing the family into a cycle of welfare. I was being presented with a different image of the problem by the members of the UNN and URBAN boards. While they understood that the symptom of family violence was a 'justice issue', they also knew that at the root-cause level it was a 'health issue'. They were asking for a project that would investigate ways to end the cycles of violence.

This project went into performance in 1991/92 and was called *Out of the Silence*.[87] The boards of directors of UNN and URBAN were correct. Their direction helped create a very powerful Forum Theatre project that performed in Vancouver and toured to 27 communities throughout BC, and that enhanced the evolution of *Theatre for Living*.

The language of oppressor and oppressed was still very present in my work at the time, but the manner in which we constructed the characters changed. We incorporated the abusing father's experiences in Residential School (see below) into the play, giving him a very symbolic sequence in which he was tormented by the internalized voices of the nuns and priests who abused him as a child. We did not condone his actions. We did, however place them in a context that helped us understand why he would do such things.

Although the Canadian government has recently announced a financial compensation package for remaining survivors of Residential Schools, the story remains an unresolved part of Canada's history.

In the early 1900s, the Canadian Government asked the Christian churches to open schools that would assimilate First Nations children into the Eurocentric Canadian culture. The goal was, in the government's words, to "take the Indian out of the child."

It became law that First Nations children had to attend these schools. If their parents did not give them up, the parents faced prison. Many times, children were abducted from their homes in the middle of the night. Most often the schools were far away from the children's home communities. At the schools they were not allowed to wear their

---

[87] *Out of the Silence* was first created and performed by: Dolores Dallas, Evan Adams, Sam Bob, Sophie Merasty, Sylvia-Anne George, Valerie Roberts. Director: David Diamond. Assistant Director: Patti Fraser. Choreographer: Denise Brillon. Joked by: David Diamond, Saeideh Nessar Ali and Levana Ray. Designers: Paul Williams and Mia Hunt. Rehearsal Stage Manager: Dena Klashinsky. Project Support: Donna Lee Johnson and Susan Elaine Martin.

traditional clothing, had their long hair cut and were severely punished for practicing their culture (singing their songs, speaking their language, etc.).

Sometimes children would enter a school at seven or eight years old and not leave, except for short family visits, until they were 18. Brothers and sisters were separated by fences and not allowed to speak to each other. Incidences of abuse at the hands of nuns and priests (rape of girls and boys, beatings, starvation, psychological and emotional violence) were extremely high. One man told me he was raped so many times as a child that he used to go behind the curtains in the gym and check his belly, because he worried he might get pregnant. Another told me that he tried to escape when he was 12 years old and was caught while crossing a frozen lake, trying to get home. He was taken back to the school, tied to a bed frame and horsewhipped. There are many stories like these.

The following is taken from the Indian Residential School Survivors Society website:[88]

> "Psychological and emotional abuses were constant: shaming by public beatings of naked children, vilification of native culture, constant racism, public strip and genital searches, withholding presents and letters from family, locking children in closets and cages, segregation of sexes, separation of brothers and sisters, proscription of native languages and spirituality. In addition, the schools were places of profound physical and sexual violence: sexual assaults, forced abortions of staff-impregnated girls, needles inserted into tongues for speaking a native language, burning, scalding, beating until unconscious and/or inflicting permanent injury.
>
> They also endured electrical shock, force-feeding of their own vomit when sick, exposure to freezing outside temperatures, withholding of medical attention, shaved heads (a cultural and social violation), starvation (as punishment), forced labour in unsafe work situations, intentional contamination with diseased blankets, insufficient food for basic nutrition and/or spoilt food. Estimates suggest that as many as 60 percent of the students died

---

[88] http://www.irsss.ca

(due to illness, beatings, attempts to escape or suicide) while in the schools.

Despite having signed the United Nations genocide convention 40 years before the last residential school closed, Canada continued to commit acts of genocide:

'With the intent to destroy in whole or part, a national, ethnical, racial or religious group, as such: ...(e) forcibly transferring children of the group to another group.' (*Convention on the Prevention and Punishment of the Crime of Genocide*, 1948)"[89]

And so, three generations of entire Nations of people were subjected to Residential School. The last school in Canada closed in the mid 1970s. First Nations communities across Canada have been deeply affected by this attempted genocide. Children would come out of these 'concentration camps' having learned how to 'parent' by the nuns and priests who raised them. The results are still being felt in First Nations communities today (in 2007), although very courageous progress and healing has been made and continues to be made.

The way *Out of the Silence* came together vis-à-vis the community involvement and the way the play was structured broke new ground for me as a theatre director and producer. The systems developed at that time – for partnering with communities, outreach, workshop recruitment, casting, having full-time support people attached, the process during creation and rehearsals and at the Forum Theatre events – all helped form the basis of my way to work with the living community.[90] One of the most visible changes was that we started to make an overt invitation to audience members to replace that character we would consider the central oppressor, if they understood the struggle in which he was engaged, and had an idea to solve the problems presented in the play. More about that soon, but first, more on building the infrastructure of the project.

---

[89] http://www.unhchr.ch/html/menu3/b/p_genoci.htm
[90] For a very detailed account of this project see the chapter on *Out of the Silence* in *Playing Boal: Theatre, therapy and activism*, edited by Mady Schutzman and Jan Cohen-Cruz, published by Routledge, Oxford 1994.

building the project infrastructure

We wanted to have one person at URBAN who would be our permanent liaison with the community. All decisions regarding the project were going to have to be made jointly and it would be too confusing to always be dealing with different people. Levana Ray, an URBAN volunteer, took on this role. Her immediate tasks were to pull together the workshop participants from the urban First Nations community and to raise the 28 percent of the project budget that had been committed by URBAN. Headlines would raise the rest of the money and deal with theatre and rehearsal space, publicity, project administration and drawing in all other personnel. Levana came onto full-time salary at Headlines.

It was also decided at this time that Levana would co-Joke the Forum Theatre event along with two of us from Headlines (Saeideh Nessar Ali and me). It was essential that there be a First Nations Joker, both because of the subject matter and how the project was developed.

I wanted to incorporate movement into the Forum and experiment with taking interventions in dance. I wanted to see if we could invite non-verbal interventions that used movement to investigate internalized moments of oppression, particularly internalized moments that explode into violence. This was appropriate, because many First Nations communities have strong traditions of communication through dance.

Spiritsong, a Native theatre training school in Vancouver at the time, connected me up with Denise Brillon, a First Nations choreographer who worked with non-dancers creating issue-based dance. Denise agreed to collaborate. I imagined the choreography 'exploding' a moment of violence in the play into sound and gesture – possibly using the repetition of language as 'music' for the dance. If we were going to try to take interventions in the dance, it could not be attached to a treadmill of recorded music.

Paul Williams had been the technical director/stage manager for the creation and first tour of *NO` XYA ` (Our Footprints)*, Headlines' 1987 to 1990 co-production with the Gitxsan and Wet'suwet'en Hereditary

Chiefs on ancestral land.[91] Paul agreed to become technical director, stage manager and part of the design team. Mia Hunt, the co-designer, was a First Nations artist, at that time working primarily in cloth and leather. She and Paul participated in the community workshop in the first week and then created the set and costumes together. As is often the case with collaborations like this, there was a two-way skills transfer.

Poster design was done in the same collaborative manner. Levana found Richard Thorne, a First Nations artist. He created the graphic signature of the project – a Native bird design with a tear, containing the figure of a woman, falling from the eye. Doug Simpson, an accomplished creator of posters in the theatre/music community, incorporated Richard's graphic as the central image of a very effective poster.

We also had two full-time First Nations counsellors attached to the project as support people. They were in the community workshop, attended all rehearsals and were present for all performances. They were available to all project personnel and audience members – to anyone who needed to talk or who needed referral to an agency to deal with issues that had been triggered through participation in the project. The counsellors were Donna Lee Johnson and Susan Elaine Martin.

finding the workshop participants and cast

Levana informed the 55 organizations in the URBAN network that we were looking for people to participate in a workshop that would draw on their life experiences as the basis of a healing-centred play on family violence. She and I interviewed all the applicants. Anyone who wanted to be in the workshop, up to our financial limit of 30 people, would be in it. The only criteria were their ability to commit to the time and their willingness to be open and honest about personal life experiences, knowing that we would not use any of that material directly; that is, would not attribute it directly to any one individual. We stressed that no acting experience was necessary. We gathered 17 participants,

---

[91] See http://www.headlinestheatre.com/pastwork.htm

including two counsellors. Everyone was paid above union (Canadian Actors' Equity) minimums to attend the workshop.

While the money was important to people, I know it was not their main reason for participating. Even at this early stage, the community recognized the potential this project had for bringing the family violence issue out into the open in a creative and positive way, and how healthy that would be for the community.

I wanted to decide on who the cast would be *before* the workshop, so the workshop itself would not be a competition. It would have been awful to set up a dynamic in which the workshop was a contest, the prize being becoming a cast member. Anyone who wanted to be considered for the cast did an improvisational audition with me. I looked for an ability to play, not technical expertise. I wanted to find people who could be 'in the moment'. After the interviews, Levana and I put the acting company together from the workshop group based on the auditions and people's availability. We cast four women and two men, without knowing exactly what roles they were going to play.

the community gathers

The workshop and all rehearsals were at the Vancouver Aboriginal Friendship Centre, where the participants would feel somewhat at home. This was a great place to develop the piece, and everyone there was very supportive. We were given a carpeted room that was ours alone for a three-week period, and another space, where the centre's carvers also worked, in which to build and paint the set.

Every day of both the workshop and the rehearsal process began with a traditional smudge (burning of sweet grass or other herbs as a spiritual cleansing and balancing ritual) and ended with a traditional talking circle.

In this formal circle we used an eagle feather brought into the hall by Donna Lee, one of the project support people. The feather was placed in the middle of the circle. Whoever wanted to start would reach in and take it. Whoever held the feather had everyone's absolute and undivided attention. This was a time for monologue, not dialogue; a time to say whatever was necessary to finish the day. The feather passed from one person to another, to the left. If a person did not want to speak, they passed the feather along when it got to them. This sacred ritual became extremely important to all of us as we moved deeper and deeper into the creation process. I now use stones given to me by people from all over the world instead of a feather. But every day of every workshop finishes with this ritual.

Smudging is not part of the customs of every First Nation. A daily smudge was, though, a desire of this workshop group. It became part of our daily ritual, which we carried through to the Vancouver run and BC tour, cleansing the theatre with sweet grass before every perform-ance. The primarily First Nations audiences were very struck by this, commenting often at how it created safety for them immediately upon entering the hall. They were also aware that, although Headlines is obviously not a First Nations theatre company, this First Nations tradition was a valued part of the process.

the workshop

The images that came out of the first day were exceptionally strong. We photographed the images with a Polaroid camera and named all of them as we worked. This gave us the ability to surround ourselves with the images (we put them on the walls) in order to refer back to them later. Many of the themes of these first images appear as references or character traits in the play. Some of the titles of these images were: 'don't worry, be happy', 'what is a family?', 'don't take my baby away', and 'assault in residential school'.

As usually happens during a workshop with a community outside my own cultural background, I found myself in an intense learning situation. The questions I chose to ask and the directions I chose to pursue as a facilitator were aimed partially at increasing my own understanding of the issue. I found that if I was honest about things I didn't understand and kept asking questions, the participants were able to explain things to me in a manner that also helped them clarify issues for themselves and each other, in an atmosphere of real dialogue and exploration.

This must happen as part of the process of making a play that articu-lates a clear story. I was reminded of a poster I once saw in an adult education centre: "The stupidest question is the one that is not asked." Good advice.

At the end of the community workshop (the fifth day), we made very short plays and did a mini-Forum inside the group to close off the process. As was always going to be the case, the participants who were not the cast were leaving us at this point and we wanted them to have a sense of closure.[92] The Forum also helped everyone understand the kind of play we were going to be making – how it had to be different from normal presentational theatre and build to a crisis without ever offering solutions. There had been some resistance to this concept throughout the workshop. Why do the play, people asked, if all we were going to show was the problem? In the end, the participants were able to see the value of solutions coming from the audience, and how powerful a vehicle for change Forum Theatre could be.

Then the cast and production team and I had a couple of days to discuss the bases the play had to touch and to distill our discoveries from the workshop. It was decided who would play which character. I left this up to the cast members themselves, having asked them to think about what kinds of characters they wanted to play both for themselves and for the good of the project. The roles they chose to take on were: Sam (the father, Bill); Dolores (the mother, Emily); Sylvia-Anne (Bill and Emily's 13-year-old daughter, Kelly); Evan (Emily's 16-year-old son, Dylan); Sophie (Emily's sister who is living with the family, Theresa); and Valerie (a friend of Emily and Sophie who the kids think of as an aunt, Rose).

Sam, a very gentle man who chose to play the abuser, Bill, did a wonderful job of helping us all understand this character who is himself in crisis, isolated inside his family and haunted by his past. Bill is acting out behaviour learned in Residential School and in other colonized situations where his power as a male in his own society had been taken away from him by the dominant non-Native culture.

We all knew it was important to put this play in a context, to indicate that the abuse in the modern, urban First Nations home was rooted in historical elements. It was for this reason that we chose to precede the

---

92 Workshop participants did, however, have an open invitation to drop into rehearsals any time they wanted.

play with a series of tableaux (frozen images) that were created in the community workshop. They depicted:

- a Nun and Indian Agent[93] taking a First Nations child away from her family and into residential school
- a Nun beating a First Nations child while his friends are forced to look on
- a Priest sexually abusing a First Nations child in a dormitory while the Indian Agent silences (shhhhh) the other waking children
- a broken circle of people, one chanting and being interrupted by the Indian Agent who yells "Stupid Indian!" while a Nun and another person look on

rehearsal and play creation

Because the workshop experience was so rich in generating a base of material and a possible cast of characters, we were able to make an easy transition into the two-week rehearsal and play creation process. The play fell together relatively easily in terms of content. We considered the first week of rehearsal a chance to come up with a 'first draft'. I put this in quotation marks because, in fact, other than making a list of general events that we thought needed to occur in the play, as a result of the input from the workshop, pen was never put to paper. We just started improvising based on the characters and situations we knew we wanted to portray.

Characters were deepened with the *Complete the Character*[94] exercise. A particular scene in which Bill apologizes to Dylan came directly out of images we explored about the cycle of beating and apology. Some cast members had experienced this with their parents. An exercise that made the performances stronger had the actors switch roles – Evan played the apologizing father and Sam played the beaten son. Once Sam understood what the character Dylan needed in the scene in order to make it authentic, he could provide it as Bill.

---

93 The historical representative of the government. The Indian Agent (a non-Native) would, in reality, not have been physically present in some of these moments – except the first – but symbolically present in all.
94 See the section *authenticity vs. 'acting'* in the chapter *The Art of Interactive Theatre*.

During these very intense and courageous emotional investigations, there were lots of tears from us all. In order to tell the truth in the play, we were all having to confront the truths in our lives. Many times each day we would take breaks to clear the air, and to breathe. We participated in a lot of circles in the middle of the day, in order to process the strong emotions in the room. Everyone had everyone else's phone numbers, and in the evenings, the phone lines were busy.

Our intent with the choreography was to explore the moments of violence. Using gesture and sound that came from each actor's character, we developed a vocabulary of movements and phrases that we had seen or heard during the workshop: "stupid Indian", "you deserve it", "loser", "drunk" and "good for nothing". We found that although these gestures and phrases came both from Residential School and from members of the abuser's family in the past, they also existed inside the mind of the abuser in the present – for example, in the moment he is beating his son. We were able to create a movement bubble – a moment when the play warps and we look inside the psyche of Bill and hear these voices that torment him and push him into the abuse. None of this was intended to condone the actions, of the character, but rather to shed light on how all our actions, regardless how repulsive, are a product of the lives we are living. Denise, our choreographer, helped the cast develop simple gestures that grew out of these phrases.

During the second week of rehearsal we clarified action and intent; pared down the play, removing anything we felt was unnecessary in the telling of this specific story; and clarified action and intent some more. We were getting ready for Forum Theatre.

The clearer, the more crystalline and specific a play can be, the more universal it will become. This clarity is what gives an audience the opportunity to see their own lives reflected back to them. The more a play tries to be everything to everyone, and tries to touch all the issues of a community out of some sense of duty, the more unfocused it will be. Part of the Joker's job is to make choices.

the community performances

Although by the third week of performance we were playing to at least 150 people a night, and invitations were coming in for a tour of British Columbia, it took time for audiences to build for this project. The opening night was, of course, packed with friends and colleagues who were somehow attached to the process. The theatre event did not exist, though, inside a traditional theatre world, although the mainstream press reviewed it and raved (see below). Audience-interactive theatre about family violence was, and still is, a hard sell in the theatre community.

> "...incredibly powerful. I left with a feeling of hope and a belief that this technique has the potential for affecting significant, long-lasting change in individuals, families and communities."
> Suzan Denis, *The Observer*, Queen Charlotte Islands, 1992

> "...coherent and complex. I can recall few times when I have been so moved in the theatre...electric moments... *Out of the Silence* offers comfort and acceptance."
> Colin Thomas, *Georgia Straight*, 1992

What built the audiences was word of mouth. A very high percentage of people attending the play were from First Nations communities. Regardless of their community of origin, however, audience members had such strong experiences in the theatre that they could not help but talk about it to others. These experiences sent ripples through their own families and larger communities. But this took time.

The resulting British Columbia tour went into 27 communities across the province and culminated with a live, interactive satellite broadcast that covered all of BC and parts of the State of Washington.[95] These performances outside Vancouver were collaborations between Headlines, the BC Association of Indian Friendship Centres and many organizations in each community. Attendance was very high.

---

95 The live television and Web broadcasts are discussed in the section *Television and the World Wide Web* in the *Appendix*.

The feeling in the room would shift each night; it was palpable, as the group consciousness moved through anger, sometimes rage, into sadness and then into action. Individuals were coming onto the stage, but it was evident that something much larger than a single individual was thinking, feeling, experimenting.

Of special interest is the audience's relationship to the character, Bill. In the early parts of the interactive Forum, people would come onto the stage to replace the daughter or the mother and try both to do battle with, and to reason with, Bill. Often their actions were played through tears. Many of them described later that what they had done in the theatre was what they had always wished they had done in their own real-life situations, but couldn't.

Also of particular interest is the choreographed part of the play, when Bill beats his stepson Dylan. The scripted scene[96] follows:

> The adults have been partying throughout the play. They are all drunk. Bill gets upset when he realizes it's past the time he told Dylan and (his daughter) Kelly to be home from the movie they went to see. Emily (his wife) and Theresa (her sister) downplay the lateness, make light talk, and ask Bill to tell them a story about when he was 13:

> | | |
> |---|---|
> | Bill | You want to hear a story about when I was 13? I don't want to tell this story. |
> | Emily | Come on, Bill. Come on. |
> | Bill | I was in residential school when I was 13. It was late. I was supposed to be asleep, but I wasn't. 'Cause I got hungry. I went for a little walk. I was walking down the hallway. Past the junior boys' dormitory. I heard something. I didn't know what it was, so I went to take a look. |

> (Kelly and Dylan come sneaking into the house. Theresa is the first to see them.)

---

96 Once the project was over, a script was transcribed from the telecast.

Theresa	(To Bill) Just a minute, I'll get you some more wine.
Bill	You wanna hear this story?!
Theresa	Yes, I want to hear the story.

(Theresa has diverted Bill's attention and has forced him to move in his chair so that his back is facing where the kids are sneaking in.)

Bill	So I get to the doorway. I can see my cousin, Kenny. His bed is against the wall. Next to the bed is a window. Through the light of the window I can see that Kenny is still awake. Do you know why he's still awake? Because he's not alone. I can hear him crying. Brother McIntyre is laying there with him. I don't know what to do. But there's this piece of wood holding the door open. I pick it up.

(Dylan and Kelly have by this time reached the stairs leading up to the bedrooms. Dylan trips on a stair.)

	Dylan! What are you doing sneaking in? What time is it?
Dylan	We missed the bus, Bill.
Bill	What time did I say to be home? Huh? What time is it?
Kelly	Dad, we missed our bus!
Dylan	Bill, don't!
Bill	What time did I say to be home?

(Bill grabs Dylan and throws him onto the floor in the middle of the room and starts hitting him.)

Kelly	No!

Bill	Huh?! You never listen to me!
Emily	No, Bill!
Bill	It's for his own good!

(The lights change to a tight pool around the actors. Dylan rolls out from under Bill. The next section is accompanied by choreo-graphed movement/gestures in which the other cast members become voices from Bill's past.)

Bill	You never listen to me!
Theresa	Stupid Indian.
All	Stupid Indian.
Bill	You stupid Indian!
Kelly	You deserve it.
All	You deserve it.
Theresa	Loser.
All	Loser.
Emily	Good for nothing.
All	Good for nothing.
Dylan	Drunk.
All	Drunk.

(Bill is now huddled on the floor and starts to chant as these voices repeat two more times. Bill then rises out of his chanting. As he stands, Dylan slips back under his legs to the position he was in when he was getting beaten. The lights go back to normal.)

When we first started performing *Out of the Silence*, we asked for interventions from the audience for this movement section in the same way as in the rest of the play. I soon realized, however, that the theatrical language of the movement section was different from the theatrical language of the rest of the play. There was dialogue in the rest of the play, but here the exchange was designed to be more physical – that was why I had worked with a choreographer. It made sense to change the invitation.

We found that if we asked specifically for non-verbal interventions during the movement segment this freed the audience up. They were able to offer wonderful, non-verbal insights into the healing process that were very valuable to explore. One First Nations man, for instance, intervening to replace Bill, rose up from his knees and acknowledged the Four Directions, part of a traditional Native ceremony. What he was showing us was the way he had overcome his own 'voices' through reconnecting with the spirituality of his culture. He was willing to share with us and the audience that, while this had not been an easy thing to do, it was possible and had been a solution for him in his personal life, ending his own cycle of being an abuser. This type of intervention happened on more that one occasion.

Other interventions in this section sometimes involved Bill pleading for forgiveness (which the other characters were always very slow to give – saying that they wouldn't believe that Bill meant he was sorry until they saw his behaviour change), or Bill yelling out "I am not a stupid Indian," "I am not a loser," etc. The response to this from the other characters tended to be that this recognition was a good first step, but that it, too, had to be followed by action.

During rehearsals the actor playing Bill was very concerned that he would be hated by people who could not separate him from the character. Exactly the opposite occurred. Women and men, Native and non-Native would line up after performances to thank him for the honesty of the character portrayal. They saw a human who they knew on the stage. We didn't shy away from showing the atrocity of his actions, including a drunken rape of his own daughter later in the play, but we (and, in particular, this courageous actor) managed to portray a man who embodied all the complexities and contradictions of life. We could condemn this man's actions and know that he must be held accountable for them and still understand that he was a product of his history – one that had been imposed on him in the same way he was

now imposing on his wife and children. I believe that this was the heart
of the power of the play.

legacy

Many years later, when I travel throughout British Columbia doing
Theatre for Living work in various communities, many, many people
still come to me and tell stories about how when *Out of the Silence*
came to their community it altered their lives.

On January 6, 2006, Headlines Theatre was invited to a meeting on
the Skwah Reserve (near Chilliwack, BC), organized by Marion
Robinson of the Fraser Basin Council. Skwah First Nation Band
Councillor Lester Mussell and other community leaders of the Sto:Lo
Nation, including Band Councillor and Elder Violet George and Grand
Chief and Elder Dr. Elizabeth Rose Charlie, were in attendance.

This meeting requested the creation of the province-wide *Theatre for
Living* project called *Meth* (see the *Epilogue*).[97]

Crystal meth was described as "the new plague." There is a great deal
of pain, people said, and many things are not being talked about. At
the same time, they explained, community presentations from various
authorities are telling them what they already know. Something else is
needed, they said.

A story was told in the Skwah meeting about the issue of battering and
sexual assault – of a time when communities across the province found
it extremely difficult to discuss those issues. Then, it was said, something happened in 1992 that was a pivot point – something that Elders
in many First Nations communities across BC evidently still talk about
as having brought the issues into the open: the BC tour of Headlines'
Out of the Silence.

Why was *Out of the Silence* so powerful? From the very first spark of
the idea, a conversation with Ron George from United Native Nations,
through the community workshop, and all the performances, it was a
collaboration with the living community. Every aspect of fundraising,

[97] See http://www.headlinestheatre.com/pastwork.htm

administration, artistic creation, tour management and reporting back was affected by the collaborative nature of the project. *Out of the Silence* was a true voice of the living community. It broke the pattern of projects before it, in that while it did not condone the actions of the abuser(s) in the play, it did present that material with humanity. That is why I believe it became a catalyst for real community dialogue, which led to real change in living communities.

> "It is an enormous task to give 'voice' to issues and topics which are usually not discussed openly and honestly. The performance and treatment of the difficult topic of family violence had the clarity, focus and brilliance that comes from direct experience."
> Lorna Williams, First Nations Education Specialist, Vancouver School Board, 1992

> "*Out of the Silence* will add immeasurably to the new pool of knowledge and understanding about the root causes and results of abusive behaviour, however dramatic or however subtle."
> Blair Harvey, Vancouver Aboriginal Friendship Centre, 1992

> "I felt more electricity discharging around this small stage than I've felt in any of the black-tie openings I've attended in glitzy big city theatres. The play's cathartic power springs from its ability not simply to let light into the dark corners of the soul, but to give constructive voice to people struggling with demons. *Out of the Silence* offers the redemptive hope of self-directed solutions."
> Stephen Hume, *Vancouver Sun*, 1992

Reclaiming Our Spirits

a breakthrough question

When *Out of the Silence* toured, in late 1992 it played for one night in a community called Port Alberni on Vancouver Island. It was there that a woman named Lisa Charleson attended a performance of something she had never seen before: Forum Theatre. Lisa and Mary Martin, both Nuu-Chah-Nulth[98] women, had started a group called Native Families in Crisis in an attempt to look at issues arising from the Residential School experiences in their own community. In 1995, Lisa contacted Headlines with a request to have the theatre techniques she had witnessed at the performance in Port Alberni used on Residential School issues in Nuu-Chah-Nulth communities.

The first workshop, during which we developed a model that was to become a province-wide initiative, was organized out of Tofino and Ucluelet, BC, in Nuu-Chah-Nulth Territory. Eventually, the *Reclaiming Our Spirits* project involved 10 First Nations across British Columbia and was a collaboration between Headlines and the Nuu-Chah-Nulth Tribal Council. The Jokers for the project were Jacquie Brown, Saeideh Nessar Ali and me, in rotation. Excerpts from my report on the first workshop (indented text) follow:

> Day 1   There are 17 participants – three men, 14 women. A broad range of ages and experience, from mid-twenties to late eighties. One woman is an Elder. All of the participants are struggling with issues in their present lives that originate in Residential School experience. Some of the participants were students at the Christie Residential School. We are working in the old gym of that school, on Meares Island, just north of To-fino, BC.
>
> We did an introductory circle today that took two hours. In the afternoon we did group-building work and introduced the

---

98 For information on the Nuu-Chah-Nulth Nation go to
http://www.nuuchahnulth.org

participants to sculpting. The images at the end of the day were strong and very emotional for many of us.

The organizers and participants wanted to return to the site of the Residential School to do the workshop. This seemed like a very intense decision to Jacquie and me, who were Joking the process. There were the emotional issues, of course, but the school, being on Meares Island, can also only be reached by boat, and supplies had to be brought in. The school had been abandoned for years, although the Nuu-Chah-Nulth had recently opened a healing centre adjacent to the school. But the living community knew what it was doing. There was an intrinsic knowledge that the power of what we were about to create was rooted in a geographical spot. In a self-regulating way, the living community was ready for this risk.

Day 2   We did trust work in the morning. The group, while finding this difficult, loves making their way through the games, finding ways to trust each other. They are making personal breakthroughs, often in private, and only expressing themselves about it hours later.

At the end of the morning, we asked if there were any images from the previous day that they wanted to explore. The group chose one that represented a boy being whipped on the hand for not coming on time when the school bell rang. Many people joined the image, all of them standing in the same position as the boy. They had all had this same experience. When we activated the image and asked them to say sentences as the characters, there was so much silence. Of course, talking back got more whipping. Crying got more whipping. These were childhood lessons in being silent.

The second was an image of a girl being whipped by a nun. They were the only two people in this emotionally very 'naked' image. The girl, now an old woman, presented her bum to the nun for whipping. During the activation of the image, the woman who made it cried bitter tears, many of the group cried with her, and when the tears were done, they held each other and laughed.

Humans are emotional organisms, and theatre, a primal language of humans, is an emotional language. We were making images of real events. They were not the real events, but they were images of truth.

The images the group chose to work on were the two that resonated with most of the group. No longer individuals' images, they were now images that belonged to everyone. *The group* was working its way through its silence to being able to create and perform plays.

There are as many different kinds of tears as there are different kinds of snow. (I grew up in Winnipeg, Manitoba, so I know something about snow.) Snow can fall in beautiful, large, pillowy flakes that reveal intricate crystal structures. Snow can also fall in hard, biting pellets, whipped up by the wind. One knows when one is in a storm that could contain danger. Sometimes crying in a safe space is an intense and beautiful luxury.

Is there such a thing as a bad emotion? Mustn't we have the capacity to feel all emotions in order to be truly human? This is one of the wonderful things about theatre: it creates a container in which we have the permission to feel. Sometimes individuals need to cry, and sometimes they need to do that in public. There is a primal ritual in giving one's tears, and having the others who are present accept those tears without judgment. Sometimes, a whole group needs to cry. Is this a group of individuals crying? Or is it a larger entity in tears? Does a community weep? Absolutely. This microcosm of the Nuu-Chah-Nulth community wept and laughed that day, in preparation for giving a larger gift (the plays) to the macrocosm – the larger living community.

> Day 3   We did more games and trust work in the morning. A genuine sense of play has emerged in the group, with many of them saying that they have hated being asked to do games in other workshops, games children might play – have been afraid and resentful. But here they are really enjoying it and having insights about themselves in the bargain.
>
> The group, while finding the trust games difficult, is making its way through. Today, every participant, including Jacquie and I, fell backwards off stairs into the group's arms. Some of the participants are in their late eighties. One woman was so frightened. Of course, no one forced her to fall. She waited

until everyone else had gone, and she had seen everyone caught. Then, trembling like a leaf, she fell off the first stair into the group's arms. We all were crying.

After the games we did the *Magnetic Image* and created three groups. Out of the exercise came images and discussions about:

- how children 'hide' and then sometimes stay hidden all their lives
- how people who want to help sometimes suffocate those they are trying to help
- how some moments that are based in Residential School can easily be translated to current domestic violence moments as well: Nun becomes Mother, Priest becomes Father or Uncle, for instance

We used Cops in the Head,[99] often on day three, as part of the *Reclaiming Our Spirits* process. I want to tell a story about this from a subsequent workshop – not the one we are currently discussing.

The story offered was from a woman who had not been to Residential School herself, but whose parents had been. They had raised her with the strictness they had been taught as children. Now, when her own son didn't clean his room, this mother would go into a rage and beat him. The group chose this woman's story unanimously as the one that they related to the strongest.

The Cops – the voices in her head in this moment – were saying terrible things like: "He is a savage who only understands beatings" and "He will be cleansed through his suffering" and "He is a dirty Indian." People from the workshop group became these voices and portrayed them.

At one point in the exercise, the woman whose story was the centre of the animation exclaimed "Oh my God – it's the nuns!" The nuns had done all these things to her parents who

---

[99] See *Cops in the Head* in the chapter *Awakening the Group Consciousness.*

had internalized the phrases, the actions and the nuns themselves. Her parents had handed the voices down to her during
her own childhood beatings. Even though she had not been to
Residential School, the nuns were in her head. Years ago, she
told us, she had originally thought they were her own voices.
During the course of her own therapy on herself over many
years, she had come to realize they were her parents' voices. In
the Cops in the Head exercise, she understood that the voices
originated beyond her parents.

The group became very, very quiet. What seemed like a pa-
ralysis set in. It became impossible to continue the exercise.
We had a break and then a talking circle, having decided to
finish the day. At the hotel that night, Jacquie and I talked at
length, and decided that we should not do Cops in these workshops any more. We went in the next day ready to explain and
apologize.

We didn't get very far. When they realized what we were suggesting, many people in the room stopped us and made us
promise that we would continue to do Cops in all the upcoming *Reclaiming Our Spirits* workshops. They told us that
many of them had not slept all night – but that the revelation
of the origin of the voices had altered their relationships with
their parents, some of whom were no longer living.

They said themselves that it was not about condoning their
parents' behaviour towards them as children, but about putting a perspective on it that they could now understand.
Forgiveness lay in this understanding – and through forgiveness, the ability to let go of the voices within themselves so
that they would not hand them down again, to their own children. Jacquie and I listened to the group. She, Saeideh and I
did do Cops in the Head in all the *Reclaiming Our Spirits*
workshops.

Day 4   We adapted *Song of the Mermaid*[100] to fit the needs
of this workshop.

---

[100] See *Song of the Mermaid* in the *Creating plays* section of the chapter *In the Workshop Room*.

We already knew that there were going to be two plays. One would be historical and the other about how Residential Schools affect people's lives today. So, instead of having the *Mermaid* exercise create groups, we needed the participants to self-select into two play groups. Then, after the groups were made, we asked the participants of each group to go back into a moment of struggle from Residential School – to focus into the strongest emotion, and to turn that emotion into a sound. Then, working with each group, we asked everyone to make their sounds and, with their eyes closed, to move towards another sound (in their group) with which they felt they belonged. One play group became two subgroups and the other group became three.

Then we asked the subgroups to sit and talk so they could find out which emotions they shared and from there to try to discover one central desire that they could name. These emotional desires were the core of the scenes. The subgroups came back together. Having discovered and named the emotions and desires, they were able to discover who the characters were and the action of the play. From this point on, they could make short plays in which the characters tried to achieve their desires.

There are now two strong plays which we will rehearse tomorrow. We had a two-hour-long circle at the end of the day. Many of the participants spoke about how wonderful they were feeling. Jacquie is directing the historical scene and I am directing the one in the present.

Day 5   We rehearsed all day. Our work was to make the plays as clear as possible, and, because they have such strong emotional content, to find ways for the actors to be authentic but also safe.

When is a community workshop participant an actor? Very powerful and emotional scenes get played out in *Theatre for Living* workshops all the time. The first time a scene is done, there is almost always an 'in the moment' reality to it because the workshop participants are drawing on their own life experiences. This first time a scene is played is not a moment of "acting". The participant is not yet an actor.

It is when the participant is called upon to do the scene again, and again, and again – to work the craft of the moments, to create the same rhythms of speech, to say lines in a set order because another participant (who is also becoming an actor) has to make an entrance on a line, to move across the stage the same way each time, to throw a punch that is not a real punch but looks like a real punch, to reach an emotional reality again and again, and to keep it all visible, audible and authentic – it is at this juncture that the participant becomes an actor.

In developing the *Reclaiming Our Spirits* project across the province, we always made each organizing community aware that they had choices regarding attendance at the Forum Theatre event. It could be private, in that the audience could be made up of specifically invited people; it could be open to members of the First Nation only; it could be open to the local, geographic Native and non-Native community; it could be wide open, including the media. Different communities made different choices. Some wanted the event to be wide open, combining the community's work on Residential School issues with public education. Others chose the First Nation-only option, as they saw the project as a private, community-healing event. In this case, the Nuu-Chah-Nulth wanted it to be wide open, including inviting the media. This was typical of the role they were taking in British Columbia in opening up the issue of Residential Schools.

> *Play 1*   The first, or historical, play takes place in the Christie Residential School.[101] It begins with a class of First Nations students joking around in their own language – Nuu-Chah-Nulth. All the characters are played by elderly participants ranging in age from 60s to 80s. They are laughing. A nun comes into the room and starts yelling at them to not 'speak Indian'. One of them insists that they weren't. He is pulled up out of his chair by the nun.[102] They struggle. She calls for assistance from another nun, who holds him in a bent-over position in front of the class while the other beats him with a broom handle, yelling at him to not 'speak Indian'.

---

[101]All the characters' names have been changed from people's real names for purposes of anonymity.
[102] We played a little with historical truth here, in that boys and girls were segregated, but the cast decided that, rather than limit what they could portray, or who could be in the play, they would put a mixed class on the stage.

The nun then goes to a girl in the class and starts to interrogate her about 'speaking Indian'. The girl does not respond. She goes to another girl, a new girl who speaks no English, and tells her to answer yes to the question about having spoken Indian. "Say yes!" the nun keeps yelling. The girl does not understand, but thinks that the nun is speaking a Nuu-Chah-Nulth word that sounds like "say yes" but means "to crawl". The girl very excitedly gets down on all fours and starts to crawl, sending the rest of the class into gales of laughter. The nun yells at her, pulls her up off the floor, and forces her to stand in a corner. The girl doesn't understand what is happening. The nun pulls 'Anne', a different girl, over and tells her to explain that she wants the girl to stand in this corner and not move. She gives no reason. Anne explains in Nuu-Chah-Nulth.

The nun then yells at Anne, telling her to stop 'talking Indian'. Anne protests, telling the nun to make up her mind. The nun tells Anne that as punishment for talking back she is going to take her to the principal's (priest's) office. Anne panics and begs not to go. The nun drags her there.

At the principal's office, the nun explains that Anne has been talking back to her and 'speaking Indian' and needs to be punished. The principal tells the nun to leave Anne with him. He launches into an angry tirade about her speaking 'the Devil's language' and needing to be punished. She begs to be let go, saying she will not do it again. He tells her to take off her dress and put it on his desk, calling her by her number '62' and not by her name.[103] She cries. He yells the command at her again, slamming his desk with his hand, and says she is a sinner and has to be punished. She takes off her dress, and puts it on his desk. He orders her to place her hands on his desk and leave them there. She does. He walks out from behind his desk, telling her that the punishment she is about to receive is for her own good. She is weeping. He rapes her.

When he is finished, he tells her to put her dress back on and to leave. Out in the hall, she cries. One of the nuns comes to

---

[103] This was standard practice in Residential Schools. The children lost their names and were given numbers.

her and puts her arm around her, telling her again that this was for her own good, and that she should go wash herself. Anne walks past the whole class to go and wash. This is the end of the play.

Every incident in this play had manifested somehow in the participants' life experiences. We did not do Forum on this play. We all understood that one cannot travel back into the past and change what has happened. We created and performed this first play to set the second, modern-day play in the proper context.

In creating this historical play, something became apparent to us all. Our task was not to 'do battle' with the priests and nuns. The schools were no longer open, although the culture of silence regarding these issues was very much alive. We couldn't change history. The urgent issue at hand was that the historical oppressors had taken up residence in the psyches of the children who grew up in the schools, and who were now adults. It was these adults who were now abusing themselves and their spouses and their children. We all knew, and had discussed it openly, that people who had been abusers (oppressors) were in the workshop, and that more would be in the audience. They were deeply oppressed oppressors, but oppressors nonetheless. It was, once again, as had been the case with *Out of the Silence* in 1992, and to a degree in *¿Sanctuary?* in 1989, extremely difficult and problematic to separate the oppressors from the oppressed.

Play 2 The second and present-day play starts in a bar. Penelope[104] is passed out. Bert enters with two beers, muttering that he hasn't been able to get into her pants yet and she's already asleep. He wakes her up. She says she wants to go home. He suggests they go to his room in the hotel. She says no and asks him to take her to her own home – she wants to sleep. He says she can sleep in his room, she can trust him and after she rests a bit they can party some more. She agrees. They stagger out of the bar and into his room. Bert hugs her. Penelope puts her head on his shoulder and ever so slowly brings her hand up his back, into an embrace. It is obvious from this theatrical moment that they are going to have sex.

---

[104] Once again, these are character names, not the names of the real people.

Six months later they meet on the street. Penelope is pregnant. She does not really want to see Bert, but is caught. She tells him she is pregnant with his baby. He denies any possible responsibility, saying he knows she sleeps around a lot. She says, "Well, fuck you, then." He says, "Well, fuck you, too," and they part company.

It is five years later. A five-year-old girl, Francine runs onto the stage playing with a Game Boy. Carol, her eight-year-old sister, runs after her, trying to get her toy back. They fight. Penelope yells at them, saying if they don't shut up she is going to "Kick them to Kingdom Come!"[105] She yells at them to go to bed. Francine protests that it's too early. Penelope threatens her, saying she'd better behave because Chuck, Carol's father, is coming over. Francine shuts up. The sisters go off to bed.

Chuck enters, bringing alcohol and asking what all the yelling is about, he can hear it down the block. Penelope complains about her "two brats." Chuck wonders what the problem is. He buys his daughter all the toys she wants. Is that other little brat, Bert's daughter, trying to steal them from Carol? He says he has to go to the toilet.

Penelope lies on the sofa, drinking. Chuck goes to the girls' room. Carol looks up at him. He tells her to "shhh." He sits on the bed and strokes Francine's back. Francine remains motionless. Carol rises onto her elbow and glares at her father. He tells her to turn around and go to sleep. She shakes her head "no." He tells her to do as she's told. She does.

Chuck takes the blanket off Francine and folds it over onto Carol. He crawls onto the bed and rapes Francine. He leaves. Carol puts the cover back onto her sister.

In the morning, Penelope comes into the room, yelling that the girls have slept in and are late for school. She starts to take the cover off them and realizes that Francine has soiled the bed (again). She screams at her about using the toilet. Francine

---

[105] This is an echo of a line that the nun says in the previous historical play.

apologizes. Penelope wraps the soiled blanket around her daughter's head, calling her a "dirty Indian!"[106] and yelling at her to "smell that!" while making her put the blanket into the washing machine. Francine goes to the washing machine. Penelope tells Carol to get the strap. Carol glares at her. Penelope yells at her not to look at her that way. Carol gets the strap and hands it to her mom. Francine is returning and Penelope grabs her. Francine starts to beg her mother not to hit her. Penelope yells that it is for her own good and raises the strap to her daughter. This is the end of the play.

After creating and rehearsing the plays, we returned to the mainland (the town of Tofino) to perform in the school gym. We were told by the people who had remained to do the organizing for the event, which was also going to feature traditional singing, speeches and food, that the nuns from the local church had been going around taking the posters down! Their efforts to silence the community were in vain. Approximately 250 people, mostly Nuu-Chah-Nulth, packed the school gym. The audience ranged in age from infants, to small children and teenagers, to adults and Elders.

The interventions in the Forum started quickly and went on for over two hours. Some interventions in the early part of the Forum included:

- Penelope having a friend with her at the bar
- Penelope yelling "Fire! Fire!" in the bar when Bert wouldn't leave her alone, which scared him away
- Bert struggling with his image of women
- Penelope refusing to have sex with Bert unless he uses a condom
- the girls doing battle against Chuck in various ways

---

[106] A repetition from the historical play. Something the nuns used to say.

it's clear what you *don't* want. what *do* you want?

Once we got into the section of the play with Chuck, the Forum got into a repeating loop of people yelling "Stop!" and replacing the oppressed character – either one of the girls or Penelope – and 'doing battle' on their own, with Chuck. It was at this point that something became clear for me.

The audience members were coming on stage to try to *get rid of what they didn't want.* We were asking them to come onto the stage, replace an oppressed character, and try an idea to break the oppression. They didn't want to get abused, so they were doing that – trying not to get abused. That's what they *didn't want.* I asked if this was indeed what was happening. If so, what *did* they want? Did some of them have ideas to try to get what they *did want*?

Instantly the interventions changed. Instead of entering the playing area and doing battle alone against Chuck, interveners started talking with their sister, with their mother, trying to reach out of their isolation and create safety, not alone, but with other members of their family. Sometimes these interventions included treatment for Chuck. Changing the invitation created a subtle but profound change in the investigation in the room.

This was another step for me in redefining the central question of the *Theatre of the Oppressed* as I understood it, and had been practicing it. What kind of language would make it possible to encourage an investigation of healthy family, without potentially polarizing the community and without being prescriptive – that is, while still leaving space for the community to do this themselves?

Some later interventions included:

- Frances telling her mom why she was afraid of Chuck
- many women, men, boys and girls yelling for Mom, or finding different ways to say no to Chuck along with the sister or alone
- an intervention near the end of the play from an eight-year-old boy

This led to a conversation in the auditorium about how kids deal with abusive adults. The clear message from some of the Nuu-Chah-Nulth leaders (men and women) was that they must find a way for their children to be able to say no, and to feel that there are people that they can go to for help, even if that is the beginning of a painful journey.

Then something terrible and amazing and wonderful happened: a middle-aged, Caucasian man stood up and started yelling that the event was abusive and we had to stop it. "Children should not be told they could have said no – they found a way to survive and the pain has to be dealt with later," he said. He told us that the children were not responsible for being abused, and that we had to stop making them feel guilty for not saying no. This man was a senior counsellor in the community. Doing what he was accusing us of was certainly not our intention. I was preparing to respond somehow, feeling like I needed to, as the co-director of the event. But, thankfully, before I could, one of the participants, who was a Nuu-Chah-Nulth Chief, came onto the stage. He was so angry, he was shaking. He pointed at the man, who held a senior government ministry position in the community, and said:

> "Can I say something? Sit down. Sit down. Sit down, please. What we are talking about is our pain. The pain we went through for years. We're not asking anybody to change. What we're saying is, 'Hear us.' Please hear us. Let us talk. Let us be able to say, 'This is ours.' Maybe you never gave it to us. Somebody gave it to us. But it's time that, that man, and that man who was up here [pointing to two people who had done interventions] are able to work with the people who know what they're talking about. This man and woman [two of the workshop participants who had been key in organizing the project], who have gone through what we have gone through. Please honour us on that. Thank you."[107]

The room burst into applause and cheers and whistles.

---

[107] Transcribed from the video of the event, shot by the Nuu-Chah-Nulth Tribal Council.

This led to a number of speeches from other Nuu-Chah-Nulth audience members about how the cycles of violence had gone on for too long. Then we continued with the Forum.

Many, many people spoke formally after the Forum. Simon Lucas, another Nuu-Chah-Nulth Chief and Elder spoke very forcefully about his own journey in life and in the workshop as a participant, and how the experience had been so powerful for him that he would support any attempts to deepen the theatre work in the community. The evening finished with a feast and drumming and dancing, which went on late into the night.

legacy

It was because of the positive impacts of this first workshop that the Nuu-Chah-Nulth Tribal Council decided to sponsor *Reclaiming Our Spirits* workshops in up to nine other First Nations communities throughout British Columbia, two of them inside their own ancestral territory. Explanations of the process and what was possible went out from Headlines and the Tribal Council, and invitations came from seven other First Nations. In each community we started from 'zero'; that is, came in with a process for making the Residential School plays, but no pre-determined product. All of the plays were terrifyingly similar. These same kinds of stories were told over and over again, by very different communities.

The Nuu-Chah-Nulth took a leadership role in this, partly because they were at the forefront of a legal process that was taking the churches to court over the abuses meted out to children in the Residential Schools. They knew the theatre would be healing for the communities, and would also prepare people who had been abused for testifying in court. The impetus was both spiritual and practical.

"The [Gitxsan] *Reclaiming Our Spirits* training and performances were excellent! The awareness created on both a personal and community level has brought us one step closer to addressing the Residential School issue and its effects. The [theatre] training provided a wealth of information and new tools for caregivers and/or facilitators."

Sharon D. Russell, North West Coordinator,
Provincial Residential School Project, 1996

"The *Reclaiming Our Spirits* workshop [in Terrace, BC] has affected me deeply. I feel like a new person now, having let go of the past negative experiences that I had throughout my life. I've learned to control the cops in my head."

Men ga den wii hayastk – Helen Johnson,
Lax Kw'alaams Band, 1996

The *Reclaiming Our Spirits* project was a small part of a larger process of moving a consciousness forward, not only of individuals, but of the living organism of the community. Now it's time to discuss group consciousness.

AWAKENING THE GROUP

CONSCIOUSNESS

In my travels, I have worked with many different Aboriginal cultures across North America, in Namibia and in New Zealand. Even though the results of colonialism have been devastating, in most instances, the core belief systems of these cultures are still apparent, and, in many instances, are still being handed down from generation to generation. The belief systems vary, but they all seem to share one thing: a knowledge that the birds, the fish, the animals, the humans, the rocks and the trees are all 'brothers and sisters' somehow.

Here is a beautiful game to help participants experience the interconnections in a group.

blind magnets[108]

Joker Tip: I will most often place this game at the end of a sequence of blind games, on the first day of a six-day process. Clear all obstacles out of the room, or move them

---

[108] This game is in the *feel all that we touch* category. I first encountered a version of *Blind Magnets* in 1971 when I was a first-year acting student at the University of Alberta. A different version, *The magnet – positive and negative*, is in Boal's *Games for Actors and Non-Actors*, p. 109.

all to one side. Then, create an artificial 'wall' by gently taking participants by the shoulders and turning them if they reach the area with obstacles.

Find a space to stand in the room, arms either by your sides, in your pockets or across your fronts. Close your eyes and when you are ready, start to walk very slowly. Please do this in silence. Remember to keep your heads up. Lead from the heart. You are going to bump into each other. That's OK. When that happens, please try not to open your eyes or to talk, just make your way around the person. If you get panicky, don't forget to breathe. Try not to open your eyes. Walk for a while.

Now, as you walk, I want you to think of yourselves as magnets. Magnets do two things: they repel and they attract. For now, I want you to think of yourselves as magnets that repel. It's as if you have a very gentle force field around you that makes it impossible for you to touch anything or anybody. Try to feel this. Extend your senses out. You are magnets that repel. It's impossible to touch. (Wait for a while.)

Now, you are magnets that attract. If you touch someone, like shoulder to shoulder, for instance, you are stuck there. But you keep moving together. Keep your eyes closed and try not to talk. Feel yourself drawn to the energy in the room. You are magnets that attract. (Wait for a long while.)

Now, very gently, and without violence, you are magnets that repel. It's impossible to touch. (Wait for a long while.)

Now, one last time, you are magnets that attract. Feel yourself drawn to the energy in the room. (Give the group enough time to arrive at one or two bunched up groups.) Now, freeze. I am going to ask you to do something; please do not do it yet. I am going to ask you to open your eyes and, without talking, look around the room and think about some things: Where are you? Who are you near? Who are you not near? Take a moment to reflect on this in silence. Do that now, please.

Joker Tip: After completing this and all games in a workshop, I will sit with the group and ask them what they experienced and also if it connects up in any way to the issue we are investigating. Comments from participants after this game will inevitably include their fascination at being a magnet that repels. They discover their ability to sense other people around them. Is it body heat, I ask? No. Is it odour, then? No. So, what is it? Most often one or more participants will identify that they feel the person's energy. I will take the opportunity to ask how many also experienced what this person is talking about. Usually, at least half of the people in the room will raise their hands.

I ask the participants if they have ever heard of René Descartes. It is very rare that anyone has, although they recognize the famous phrase, "I think, therefore I am." After explaining who he was and a bit about his work,[109] I take the opportunity to talk briefly about the separation of mind and matter. I share discoveries coming from physics and other disciplines about the interconnectedness of all matter.

I make a point of saying that there are practical boundaries between me and the person sitting next to me that must be respected. On a subatomic level, though, if we could wander around in the particles of matter, we would experience no difference between me, the floor we are sitting on and the person next to me. We are all energy. This is not science fiction. It is fact. In our reductionist culture we are not taught to pay attention to things like this, but that doesn't mean such realities don't exist.

All the blind games open up the possibility of experiencing each other and the connections in the room this way. *Blind Magnets* is the clearest example. Whatever the focus of the workshop, and regardless of the cultural origins of the participants, it is now possible to ask the

---

[109] See *Prologue.*

参与者 participants what it means to our subject matter if we *really are all connected to each other*. Does it change our relationship to the issues? It then becomes possible to have conversations about how the subject matter of the workshop affects not only the individuals in the room, but also the living community.

Emergence

A group of people will most often enter a *Theatre for Living* workshop knowing some people in the group, but not all, and having a sense of what we are going to do, but not really knowing, because it must be experienced. Each participant also enters the workshop at the present tip of their own life journey, and this is sometimes from a disempowered place in terms of their own experiences of speaking and being heard. Often people talk about feeling isolated.

The creation of art is not a linear process. It can be quite chaotic. When working with a group, various elements come together, but not necessarily in the same order each time. Some members of the group start to understand how to work with frozen images (a tableau of a participant's particular life experience), while others are more comfortable with spoken dialogue, and others understand the essence of movement with no words. Some characters get defined early on as recognizable flesh-and-blood characters, while others emerge from large symbols.

It is in the process of having to work together, of entering a state of disequilibrium and trying to achieve equilibrium, that the group transforms from a collection of isolated individuals into something larger than the sum of its parts – an organized body. As the organized body works, story emerges.

Nobel Prize winner Ilya Prigogine[110] described a "dissipative structure" as "an open system that maintains itself far from equilibrium, yet is

---

[110] Prigogine (1917-2003) was a leader in the field of nonlinear chemistry, whose research helped create a greater understanding of the role of time in biology and the physical sciences. In particular, he contributed significantly to scientists' ability to analyze dynamic processes in complex systems. See the Ilya Prigogine Centre for Studies in Statistical Mechanics and Complex Systems at www.order.ph.utexas.edu

nevertheless stable: the same overall structure is maintained in spite of an ongoing flow and change of components."[111]

A living cell is a dissipative structure, existing in a state of constant disequilibrium. It is always decaying and, if this continued, it would die. What keeps a cell alive is that the decay process is balanced by a constant intake of nutrients that are used to repair the cell's parts at least as fast as they decay and are excreted as waste.

Prigogine discovered that dissipative structures reach bifurcation points – let's call them 'forks in the road' – that are created at points of extreme instability. In these points, the living system can emerge into new structure and/or new forms of order.

> "This spontaneous emergence of order at critical points of instability is one of the most important concepts of the new understanding of life. It is technically known as self-organization and is often referred to simply as 'emergence'. It has been recognized as the dynamic origin of generation of new forms – is a key property of all living systems. And since emergence is an integral part of the dynamics of open systems, we reach the important conclusion that open systems develop and evolve. Life constantly reaches out into novelty."[112]

Capra explains emergence this way:

> "Emergence results in the creation of novelty, and this novelty is often qualitatively different from the phenomenon out of which it emerged. This can readily be illustrated with a well-known example from chemistry: the structure and properties of sugar.
>
> When carbon (C), oxygen (O) and hydrogen (H) atoms bond in a certain way to form sugar, the resulting compound has a sweet taste. The sweetness resides in neither the C, nor the O, nor the H; it resides in the pattern that emerges from their interaction. It is an emergent property. Moreover, strictly speaking, the sweetness is not a property of the chemical bonds. It is a sensory experience that arises when the sugar molecules interact with

---

[111] Capra, *The Hidden Connections*, p. 13.
[112] Capra, *The Hidden Connections*, p. 14.

> the chemistry of our taste buds, which in turn causes a set of neurons to fire in a certain way. The experience of sweetness emerges from that neural activity."[113]

The whole is greater than the sum of its parts.

Emergence is critical to a discussion of creating art. An artist, or a group of artists, bring elements (like the atoms) together to create art. These elements may be actual, complete items as in visual art that is comprised of found objects, or they may be colour and brushstrokes, or spoken words and image, or a series of strikes of a chisel, etc. When, though, do these individual elements become something we can call art? Recall that C, O and H become the experience of sweetness through their interaction with our taste buds and neurological activity in our brains. Dialogue, image, light and sound become theatre when they interact with our eyes and our ears, stimulating complex neural activity and creating a transformative moment – the experience of art.

Entrainment

Entrainment is a step along the path to emergence. Humans entrain to rhythms all the time. Sometimes we do it consciously and sometimes we do it subconsciously. When we are walking along the street, and there is music, and we start to walk in rhythm to the music, that is subconscious entrainment. When we take on the jangled rhythm of a traffic jam, that is also subconscious entrainment. When a person comes home and puts on soothing music, this is a conscious act of entraining into a different, calmer rhythm. The following game helps groups experience entrainment in a conscious way.

clap exchange[114]

This game is a conscious way to bring a group together into the same rhythm. It is a tremendous aid in group building, in developing those intangible links that are necessary in a working group. It also develops an essential skill: listening.

---

[113] Capra, *The Hidden Connections*, p. 41.

[114] This game is in the *listen to all that we hear* category. There is a very different version of a clapping game called *The clapping series* in Boal's *Games for Actors and Non-Actors*, p. 92.

step 1   Let's sit in a tight circle, knees almost touching. I am going to send a clap around the circle. It will travel like this: Turn your body, twisting at the waist, to face the person on your left and that person turns to face you. Each person claps their own hands together in unison. One sound. The person on the left twists to face the person on her left. They clap in unison, and so on around the circle. Listen to the rhythm. All around the circle. Now again, faster – and faster – and again, faster – numerous times around the circle, until we are throwing the clap around the circle as fast as we can! One sound. Listen to the rhythm.

step 2   Instead of a single clap, try a more complex rhythm. The way this clap moves is that the person on your right and you clap your hands against each other's hands (like a high-five) then you clap your own hands together in some rhythm. Then you twist to your left for a high-five with the person on your left, who then claps his hands together in the same rhythm you made and then twists for a high-five with the person to his left...and around the circle the rhythm goes a couple of times. Listen!

Now start to send many, as many as possible, of this same rhythm around the circle. Keep them together – listen to the rhythm. We should hear one sound, not applause.

step 3   The same as step 2, but with a more complex rhythm.

> **Joker Tip:** This is a listening game, not a looking game. Participants will often think that if they watch the clap go around, when it comes to them they will do the rhythm well. But watching can keep them outside the rhythm. It is a listening game. Also – remind participants that each of them has the power to bring the clap back into rhythm if it comes to them out of rhythm.

The Joker is disturbing

> "A machine can be controlled; a living system, according to the systemic understanding of life, can only be disturbed."[115]

> "The goal of the *Theatre of the Oppressed* is not to create calm, equilibrium, but rather to create disequilibrium which prepares the way for action."[116]

We see through the work of Prigogine and Capra how disequilibrium, being off balance, is necessary in nature and in organizations; it is in reaction to disequilibrium that novelty occurs. It is how life has evolved. Interestingly, I have also heard Boal, in discussion, refer to a Joker as being a 'difficultator', not a 'facilitator'.

It is the role of the Joker to create working space that is a safe place for the participants to be able to enter disequilibrium. *They must want to do this.* It is in the risk-taking that the people find themselves off balance, or in Capra's terminology, 'disturbed'. It is in this collective disturbance that creativity exists.

Depending on who the participants in a creative process are, some may be very familiar and comfortable in this place of disturbance, and others might experience discomfort. They might complain that they don't know what to do; some might rebel against it because it is a state in which there appears to be little control.

Image Theatre and Forum Theatre disturb the living organism that is in the room. The theatre presents and explores crisis with no resolution. This throws the participants and/or audience into disequilibrium. Because of this, just as a single cell must adapt because of a disturbance, the living community must adapt, to try, once again, to find equilibrium. Early in a workshop process, it does this by taking part in Image Theatre activations. In a Forum Theatre event, it does this by making interventions.

This is a key to the group transformative process. The disturbance that the image or the play creates in the community in turn creates the

---

[115] Capra, *The Hidden Connections*, p. 112.
[116] Boal, *The Rainbow of Desire*, p. 72.

potential for a journey from disequilibrium to equilibrium, in which both learning and transformation can occur. When this happens, it is as if the group enters a new level of consciousness. There are interesting parallels here with the exploration of how consciousness manifests.

Epoché

Francisco J. Varela, PhD, (1946-2001) was, among other accomplishments, a director of research at CNRS (National Institute for Scientific Research) at the laboratory of Cognitive Neurosciences and Brain Imaging (LENA) located at the Salpêtrière University Hospital in Paris. He was the head of the Neurodynamics Group there. He was also senior faculty at CREA, École Polytechnique.

Varela's work indicates that consciousness occurs at a moment when different regions of the brain connect together in such a way that their neurons fire at the same time. Temporary and transient "cell assemblies" are formed. This state can be triggered by sensory perception, memory, emotion, movement, etc. I see this happen on a larger level in workshop groups. The group itself becomes conscious as various members of the group – inspired by a game, an image, a discussion, an emotional connection – gain new understandings and perspectives about an issue.

How, actually, does this occur? Again, Varela's work provides insights that match my own observations. In *The Gesture of Awareness – An Account of Its Structural Dynamics*,[117] Varela and colleagues describe the act of an individual becoming aware as:

> "...an initial phase of *suspension of habitual thought and judgment*, followed by a phase of *conversion of attention* from 'the exterior' to 'the interior', ending with a phase of *letting go* or of *receptivity* towards the experience."

---

[117] Co-authored by Varela, Natalie Depraz and Pierre Vermersch, published in *Investigating Phenomenal Consciousness*, Benjamins Publishers, Amsterdam 1999. Note 1 in this paper states: "This text is adapted from a forthcoming book: *On Becoming Aware: The pragmatics of experiencing*." It was published by John Benjamins Publishers, Amsterdam 2003.

Varela and his colleagues call these three organically linked phases "epoché".[118] A workshop group goes on a journey together in a *Theatre for Living* process that mirrors epoché in remarkable ways.

Individual and group *suspension of habitual thought and judgment* is triggered by games and exercises that challenge how we normally *see*, *listen* and *feel*, and by asking the individuals and the group to accept all other participants' perceptions of individual and group images. Suspension of habitual judgment is also encouraged by the use of traditional talking circles, where each participant is given space to speak and be heard, without being judged.

Individual and group *conversion of attention* from the exterior to the interior is encouraged by theatre-making exercises that ask the individuals and the group to focus inside the experiences of *this group* – not absent friends, relatives or Hollywood movies.

Throughout the process, individuals and the working group are challenged to *let go* of preconceptions and individual agendas – to not to make theatre that already has the answers, or theatre about one person's experiences. They are asked to invent group images and then collectively create plays that ask the hardest and truest questions possible about the issues at hand. In order to do so, the individuals and group must often *let go* of long-held assumptions about the story, and about characters in the story, in order to represent the characters with the complexity of real life. In order to accomplish *this*, the individuals and group must also be *receptive* to each other's perceptions and to new ideas. Each participant/actor must be in *this moment*, so that he can find the truth of a character's motivation. This *letting go* and *receptivity* is encouraged on each day of the workshop through all the theatre games and, in particular, the trust games. These progress from simply leaning over and giving one's weight to other members of the group in *The Glass Bottle*,[119] to falling off a table backwards, eyes closed, into people's arms in *The Fall*.[120]

---

[118] *Encyclopædia Britannica 2003* states epoché originates in Greek philosophy and means 'suspension of judgment'.
[119] See the *Trust games* section in the *Appendix*.
[120] See the *Trust games* section in the *Appendix*.

The workshop process continues with everyone seeing participants' images, accepting various interpretations of the images and then, in rehearsal, challenging both individual performers and the group to discover and embrace the meaningful motivations of characters – even those who are doing things with which we might all disagree.

Finally, in the Forum Theatre performance, the workshop group must also *let go* of being the focus of the workshop itself. The exploration is no longer about the microcosm that is the workshop group; it now belongs to the macrocosm that is the larger living community, which passes through the boundary of the workshop space or theatre to participate in the interactive plays.

Epoché, an awakening of the group consciousness, does not generally happen on the first or second day. I see it manifest in groups on the third, fourth or sometimes fifth day of an intense six-day, eight-hour-a-day process.

Is it also possible that the process contributes to an awakening for the even larger living community that may *not* have attended the event?

While I see the proof of epoché in workshop processes and at Forum Theatre events, I don't have a concrete answer for this larger question. However, epoché on a larger community level, outside of the actual event, may be linked to the existence of what are called "morphogenetic fields".[121] These are energy fields that are thought to contain behavioural patterns. As a microcosm of the living community (i.e., the workshop group) experiences epoché, the 'new consciousness' may indeed spread to the rest of the living community.

In her paper, *Embracing the Earth Charter: Community Transformation through Inter-Being*,[122] Dr. Mukti Khanna, a clinical psychologist and expressive arts specialist, writes:

---

[121] See Rupert Sheldrake, *A New Science of Life* (Tarcher, 1981) and *The Presence of the Past* (Times Books, 1988). The concept of morphogenetic fields is controversial. A good portal for more information is
http://en.wikipedia.org/wiki/Morphogenetic_field
[122] Presented at the International Conference on Conflict Resolution, St. Petersburg, Russia, in May 2003.

"In witnessing David Diamond's *Theatre for Living* work with communities in conflict,[123] I have seen how working intensively with images, interactive theatre and dialogue with key members on both sides of a conflict can create a morphogenetic field of resonance and healing. I have been most interested in how this has decreased incidences of violence in the larger community. Other parts of the community may have been unaware of the intensive conflict transformation work that was occurring in both high school environments infused with racial violence and Reservation communities experiencing multiple homicides. However, after a core group of key participants on both sides of a conflict in a community have worked intensively on community issues through expressive arts and image theatre modalities, the energy field of the larger community has appeared to shift towards greater communication and harmony. Violence had significantly decreased."

Praxis

Praxis, the creation of intentional feedback loops, is an essential part of group process.

Antonio Gramsci (1891-1937), an Italian socialist, political theorist and activist, wrote about a cycle of planning, action and reflection that is necessary in any developmental process.[124] Praxis implies the necessity of all three stages in building any movement. Take any one stage out of the process and the possibility of effective development or growth is diminished:

- if a group only plans and reflects, there is no action
- if there is never analysis (reflection) of action taken, adaptation because of new insights is not possible

---

[123] Dr. Khanna organized two *Theatre for Living* workshops in Ignacio and Durango, Colorado, in 1998: one with the Ute Nation on issues of respect/ disrespect, and another in the Durango High School on issues of school violence.
[124] See *Letters from Prison* by Gramsci, published by Harper and Row, New York 1973.

- if action and reflection occur, but no planning, actions are always improvised in the moment and therefore not benefiting from analysis

Planning in a *Theatre for Living* workshop happens in various ways. The consultation between the Joker and the organizers and then the Joker and the group about what their needs and desires are in the work; check-ins at the start of every day that help define the day's activities; ongoing feedback from the group that does the same; and also the clarity with which games and exercises are explained – all of these are forms of planning and preparation for action within the workshop.

Actions are the games and exercises, the various activations that are done on images, the rehearsals, etc. Within these actions, the participants have a lot of freedom, making decisions inside the actions.

Reflection happens in group discussion, directly after every action. This also happens in the closing circles at the end of every day, and in private ways over meals, and outside the hours of the working sessions. Reflection in the form of assessment also takes place with participants, sponsors and organizers after a project has ended.

group reflection

After every game and every exercise in a *Theatre for Living* workshop, I suggest we have a relaxed and short conversation, in which I ask one question – which is really two questions: "What is inside this game/exercise for you?" All the games are experiential and symbolic, and they will all have different meanings for different participants. The question invites the group to reflect on what each of them has experienced on a personal level doing the activity, and whether or not the symbolism of the activity relates to the subject matter we are investigating. There are no right or wrong answers to this question. It is important only that the participants express themselves and that they are heard. As a result of the conversation, connections are being made. Individual's ideas and perceptions are both validated and challenged when someone has the same or different perceptions of the image as they do, or when someone has seen something that is an insight for them. Sometimes, simply the act of articulating a feeling or an idea can be a great risk for a person. Being heard in this moment is very important.

The Joker must create space for the individuals to express their thoughts in an environment where their opinions are being validated. Then, through the repeating cycles of praxis, epoché can occur, not only for the individuals, but for the larger consciousness that is in the room.

In some way, every decision in a workshop is aimed at this awakening of the consciousness of the group, of finding ways to facilitate praxis that leads to epoché. In order for this to happen, it must be safe for people to disagree. In fact, disagreement should be encouraged. This is where the seeds of meaningful dialogue with others and oneself reside.

Encouraging complexity

Each and every one of us has an ongoing internal dialogue that argues about the pros and cons of certain decisions, and mulls over various perspectives on events in our lives. It's normal. It's human. If we embrace the idea that a community is a larger living organism, it becomes simple to see that a workshop group will function in the same way. It is part of the Joker's role to create enough safety for these disagreements to exist without having to be resolved. Disagreement must be allowed and encouraged, because in the creation of the frozen images and plays, we are not looking for solutions. (Solutions will be offered in the Image Theatre or Forum Theatre that is a response to the images and plays.) In the creation process, we are looking for complexity, and richness. True images, like life, are full of contradiction.

The articulation of different perspectives in the group is part of the thought process of the larger organism. It must not be feared, or 'dealt with', unless it becomes disrespectful, in which case, in order for everyone to feel safe and able to continue, rules may need to be established. Different groups of people function differently, and rules, if they do need to exist, should emerge as the need arises, not be imposed upon the group from the very beginning. The Joker, however, needs to be vigilant, so that rules are not established out of crisis, but out of evolving need.

Boal has a wonderful expression that I have heard him say in workshops many times: "Whatever is not expressly forbidden, is allowed."

the knowledge in the room

There are times in a workshop when it is important that the person offering the moment (the protagonist or storyteller) gets to direct whatever image or improvisation is being developed. The *Groups of 4*[125] exercise, which can be a first instance of image creation early in a workshop, is a good example of this. *Groups of 4* is a first articulation from the individual. These first images give the individuals in the room an opportunity to see all the other individual's images – windows into their particular life experiences. This validates individual's experiences and builds connections between the participants. When person 'A' sees that person 'B' has made an image that could be from their own life, or that they relate to very strongly, this builds a sense of trust and common purpose, which makes it possible to do deeper work.

But the challenge of *Theatre for Living* is to move beyond the individual and to work with the living community. Exercises most often begin with an individual's moment, which acts as a core, or an inspiration, that the rest of the participants respond to and add to, creating an image that *belongs to the room* and not the individual. But, the protagonist must give up ownership of the moment at some point in the exercise. After initially setting up the image or improvisation, he is not allowed to say to another actor, "You must play the scene this way," or "Hold your arms like this."

We are not creating a therapeutic moment for the individual. We are making theatre that is an expression of the larger community by working with a microcosmic representation of the whole – the participants in the workshop.

We must trust the knowledge in the room, and trust that it is connected to, or is an implicit part of, the knowledge the larger community

---

[125] See the section *Making images* in the chapter *In the Workshop Room.*

has, outside the physical boundaries of our workspace. Sometimes this knowledge is hard to access, because members of the living community are not used to being listened to as a group, asked questions or recognized as collective authorities on anything. In our mechanized, reductionist culture, where everything is disconnected from everything else, it is the *individual* who is supposed to be the authority, not the *group*. Ironically, within our hierarchical structures, many individuals also are trained to believe that they are stupid and that their thoughts are not worth expressing. This makes the challenge of accessing the knowledge of the living community doubly difficult.

In the same way that individual consciousness is created when seemingly disconnected neurons in our brains fire in relation to the same stimulus, the group consciousness is awakened through this process of seemingly disconnected individuals' minds activating in response to an image, an improvisation or a discussion. What must happen, in order for the group consciousness to awaken, however, is individual expression.

getting over the fear of silence

Years ago, I read a study about teachers. I think of myself as a theatre director and a Joker, but not a teacher in the traditional sense. The study has relevance, nonetheless.

In the study, it was discovered that the average teacher will ask a class a question and wait 2.5 seconds for the answer. One, one thousand, two, two thousand, three. If the answer does not come in this extremely short period of time, the teacher, it was discovered, would give the answer. Perhaps the teacher feels pressed for time. Perhaps the teacher interprets the short silence as an indication that the students do not know the answer. Being human and needing positive reinforcement, he panics – perhaps the silence means he is a bad teacher. Whatever the reason, the average teacher will give a class the answer after an average time of 2.5 seconds to reflect on the question. How disrespectful.

This, of course, creates a cycle of silence in the room. Is the teacher really interested in the answers the class might have to the question? It would appear not. Why bother answering? He either isn't interested, or he thinks we are all stupid.

In a *Theatre for Living* workshop, individuals in the group are being asked important questions, deep questions about their lives, their place in the community, their struggles. They are being asked to think in a new way and to express the connections they are discovering between other people's images and their own experiences. They are being asked to physically and emotionally offer moments of their own lives for group investigation. On a deeper level, the group consciousness – which is sometimes like Rasputin, in a deep sleep – is being asked to awaken.

Sometimes it can take 15, 30 or (gasp) even 60 seconds for someone to respond. An eternity of silence in a room full of people! Years in the theatre!! And yet, it is only 30 seconds or one minute. Hardly any time at all.

The room has the answers. Always. The answers given might be different than what the Joker, sponsors or organizers had assumed or sometimes even hoped they would be. But the answers the living community gives are their true answers and will guide the workshop to its next phase.

The result of creating space where praxis that leads to epoché can occur, will be theatre that has *emerged* from the living community; theatre that speaks the truth, but is not about any one person in the group, because it is about everyone. It is not a documentary truth, which captures real people in a real situation. It is a fictional truth, in which real people create and enact a symbolic representation of what they agree is their reality, and that we (the Joker included) trust the living community will see and recognize as the truth.

The case study *Dancers of the Mist*, in the *Appendix*, is an example of a group reaching across generations to speak the language of dance, and through the dance, to tell a story about truth in the present. But first, let's investigate internalized voices.

The Rainbow of Desire

Rainbow of Desire and Cops in the Head[126] (Cops is described in the next chapter) are currently the most directly therapeutic techniques in Boal's body of work. They were conceived in France.

In 1971 Boal was the director of the Arena Theatre in Brazil, and working in opposition to the military regime. He was jailed and tortured. He moved to Argentina until 1976 and then to France.

While in France Boal started a centre for the *Theatre of the Oppressed* in Paris to continue his work. France and Brazil are very different culturally. He started to find that the working methods he had developed in Brazil did not work the same way in Paris. Boal tells a story about how the people who were in his Paris workshops sometimes had difficulty naming their oppressions and their oppressors. It wasn't that they didn't have any. They were having a hard time manifesting them in images.

Boal came to realize that in France, which has a generally more affluent culture than Brazil, the people he was working with had a different experience of oppression. They had internalized their oppressors. He started to develop techniques that dealt with this kind of oppression. This exploration gave birth to Rainbow of Desire and Cops in the Head.[127]

In my own work, Cops and Rainbow have become valuable tools in the investigation of the complexity of the feedback loops in which we all exist. We all have our own internalized struggles that manifest as behaviour that is detrimental to both ourselves and people around us.

---

[126] These two exercises, which I have also adapted, are discussed in detail in Boal's *The Rainbow of Desire*, published by Routledge, 1995.
[127] For a wonderful account of this process see Adrian Jackson's introduction to Boal's *The Rainbow of Desire*. Adrian is the translator of many of Boal's books and is artistic director of Cardboard Citizens in the UK.
See http://www.cardboardcitizens.org.uk/

choosing between Rainbow of Desire and Cops in the Head

Generally, if a moment is about two people who approach each other with good will, but through the complexities of their fears and desires, or through their ignorance, the exchange goes badly and they walk away from the moment confused, hurt, disempowered, etc., I will do Rainbow. My choice in this exercise is always to animate the Rainbows of both the *Protagonist* and the *Antagonist*.[128] This exercise is a beautiful way to explore assumptions and misunderstandings between two people, to look at two sides of an issue. Because we are making theatre, the exercise is highly symbolic and easily translates from the individual to the group. A full explanation of the mechanics of the exercise follows this discussion.

I will choose to do Cops if the Protagonist finds that he gets paralyzed somehow in the moment, or always makes the 'unhealthy choice' if the story is of a repetitive nature. Often, when developing stories for Cops, I find that the Protagonist is either alone or the Antagonist is secondary to the internalized life of the moment. I have, for this reason, to date, chosen to do explorations of the Protagonist's Cops only.

The nature of 'cops in our heads' is that they can be triggered by almost anything. (I once Joked a wonderful Cops exercise about a woman, alone in a supermarket, trying to choose between ugly organic and beautiful genetically modified tomatoes.) The focus of the exercise is not the relationship between two people, but a person and her inner voices. As with Rainbow, this is a theatrical and highly symbolic exercise, that translates quickly from individual exploration to the group.

---

128 *Protagonist* is the person at the centre of the story – the storyteller. She supports the concept of the action. It is easy to assume this person is the oppressed, although, upon deeper investigation, this might not always be the case. *Antagonist* is the person in the story who opposes the concept put forth by the protagonist. The opposition. Likewise, it is easy to assume this person is an oppressor. This, also, might not always be the case.

Rainbow of Desire

I have used Rainbow in week-long workshops, as a half-day workshop, as a technique for character development in a rehearsal process for a mainstage play, and as a two-hour, stand alone event in a theatre or conference in which all the stories and Rainbow fragments come from a paying audience[129] or conference delegates.

This exercise of manifesting conflicting internal voices is most useful in exploring complex relationships: children and parents, lovers, employer/employee, for example. In order to do Rainbow of Desire, the workshop participant (the Protagonist/storyteller) must offer the group a situation that is filled with internal conflict for both himself and his Antagonist. He chooses an instance where the relationship in question becomes confusing, contradictory, filled with complexity. It must be real, not imagined, although identities can be protected. It is enough, for instance, to say "my employer" or "my doctor" without naming the employer or the doctor.

setting up the exercise

All of the games and exercises are always evolving. I believe it is valuable, though, in the context of this book, to detail the steps of the exercise. What follows for Rainbow, and later for Cops, is one clear instance of doing the exercise.

If the exercise is not part of a multi-day process in which the group has already been working with images, I suggest doing *Complete the Image*[130] first. It is a wonderful tool to help the group understand images and internal monologues.

To begin the Rainbow exercise, solicit three stories from the group. This involves inviting volunteers to come into the working space without yet telling their stories. Once three people have offered to participate, then let them tell their stories. The reason for this has to do with not naming images. If the first person tells their story right

---

[129] One such event was *Safe Sex*, produced by Headlines Theatre at the Havana Theatre in Vancouver in 1996. See http://www.headlinestheatre.com/pastwork.htm
[130] See *Making images* in the chapter *In the Workshop Room*.

away, this leads to immediate internal comparisons and stops others from offering. The group needs to be able to choose one story from a few options.

The group picks one of the stories to work on. The reason to choose one story over another is that it resonates most deeply with the majority of the people in the room. Ask as many participants as would be willing and able to play the Antagonist to volunteer themselves. It is not their goal to create a cartoon or a caricature of this character, but to honour what she thinks and feels, portraying the Antagonist with integrity. Those offering to play the Antagonist should understand something about the character. The Protagonist then picks someone from the volunteers to play the Antagonist; that person comes and sits onstage.

Everyone gets to ask questions of the Protagonist for a few minutes to get as clear a picture of the relationship and the event as possible. Even though we are not trying to recreate exactly the Protagonist's life, we want to start from the same 'here' as much as possible. It is particularly important for the Antagonist to ask questions. The character she creates is not going to be the same as the real Antagonist, because it will be a blend of herself and the information she has received. She does, however, need a solid reality base from which to improvise.

Here are some guidelines for the initial improvisation. The Protagonist tells the group, including the Antagonist:

- where the incident took place
- how he was feeling
- what happened
- what he wanted
- what he imagines the Antagonist wanted

The Protagonist sets the stage, with the Joker's help, using whatever is available in the room. The Protagonist and Antagonist improvise a short scene. They should be as true to each moment as possible and keep improvising until asked to stop. The Joker looks for a moment of emotional engagement and true complexity, where the conflicting fears and desires of both parties are the most evident. When this moment becomes apparent, the Joker 'freezes' the improvisation there for the rest of the exercise.

Joker Tip: It is important to note that once the group has chosen a story and has started to turn it into a symbolic representation, it is no longer the Protagonist's story. Also, the participant playing the Antagonist is not the true Antagonist, but understands something about the Antagonist. She is creating a character that is a hybrid of the Protagonist's information and her own life. In other words, the 'room' is starting to own the story.

creating the Protagonist's Rainbow

In this frozen moment, the Protagonist has desires towards the Antagonist. The Protagonist shows one, without speaking, making the shape of the desire, using as much of his body as possible. A person from the audience or workshop group offers to play this Rainbow fragment by taking on the shape. Why would someone do this? Not because they know what is inside the Protagonist, but because they think and/or feel that they understand the desire being shown. It is also their own desire. And so, the viewer becomes a character that is frozen in space physically, but that can hear and speak. This character is *not the Protagonist in his entirety*. It is a very focused character that wants a very specific thing, which is embodied by the shape.

Now request that the Protagonist show another desire to be portrayed by a new person.

Now, a fear. It is also the case that fears set up actions inside us that can be physicalized by making a shape. Someone from the group becomes a fear. Then another fear is portrayed by another person.

Is there a fear or desire that the group believes is in the Protagonist that has not been offered yet? Yes? Show us. Is this fear or desire in the Protagonist? If he says yes, it can stay. No? It must return to the audience, until one (or more) acceptable Rainbow fragments are found.

The Fears and Desires (which are now characters) are placed in their shapes and proximity to the Antagonist by the Protagonist. All together and at the same time, they do an internal monologue. After about a minute, ask each of them to say a sentence. I like this sentence to begin with "I want." This simple restriction will force them to come up with something that will also create clear action based on the shape their body is in.

activating the Protagonist's Rainbow

Now we have the Protagonist's Rainbow of Fear and Desire. It is his *team*. The Protagonist and his Rainbow go to one side of the stage. One by one, in an order determined by the Protagonist, the Fears and Desires enter the playing area to improvise with the Antagonist. Their job is to get what they want from her. They take their place, frozen in shape. They can move around, but they must stay in the same body shape for the entire improvisation. The body shape acts as a filter through which everything they say, hear and do is interpreted by the Antagonist, themselves and the people watching the improvisation. The Antagonist can walk and talk and listen. The Antagonist must be the Antagonist character as honestly as she can, mixing her own desires and fears along with the information she got from the Protagonist, all the while trying to tell the character's truth in this symbolic moment. The challenge is to be as authentic as possible. Authenticity cannot be forced. It must be allowed to emerge out of silence. The actors need to be aware that telling the character's truth may also mean being flexible. If they are really listening and seeing, then things the other character says or does may change their tactics. Or not. The actor is the expert in this moment.

The improvisations can happen in one to two minutes, which can be a long time on the stage. One by one, we see all the Protagonist's Rainbow fragments improvise with the Antagonist. Although it is difficult to do, the Antagonist must try to erase each improvisation from her emotions and psyche after it is finished, so that she can receive the next fragment as a clean slate.

During this sequence, it is often very useful to freeze the action and use various Image Theatre techniques to explore the moment more fully. Our purpose here is to investigate how the characteristics of each fragment (e.g., the desire to strangle the Antagonist, or a fear of being alone that makes the Protagonist cling to the Antagonist) are affecting the exchange.

Some Image Theatre animation techniques:[131]

NAME	EXERCISE
Shape of Emotion:	Freeze. I am going to clap my hands. When I do, using as much of your body as you can, make a new shape that is the shape of the strongest emotion you are feeling *as the character* in this moment right now. Clap.
What You Want:	Freeze. I am going to clap my hands. When I do, using as much of your body as you can, take one step in the direction of getting what you want right now *as the character*. Take a further step each time I clap. Clap...clap...clap...
From Each Other:	(as above)...one step in the direction of getting what you want *from each other as the character* right now. Clap...clap...clap...
Secret Thought:	Freeze. I am going to touch you. When I do, speak your *secret thought* – the thing the character is really thinking deep inside but would never actually say out loud in this moment. Decide what it is in silence, and commit to it. Don't change it when you hear what the other person says.
What Do You See?	Ask the audience this question and have a brief discussion.

---

[131] All of these simple animations are usable at any working moment in a workshop, rehearsal or performance and with any character or group of characters.

creating the Antagonist's Rainbow

I *always* create the Antagonist's Rainbow. I do this because the living community is as full of complex contradiction as the individual members of the community. It is the dynamic between the two characters that is the puzzle, not just the fears and desires of the Protagonist. If we are trying to investigate issues that are relevant to the living community, then stopping the investigation having heard only one side of the equation is not appropriate. This is not dialogue, it is monologue. There are great insights to be made into ways to navigate the issue at hand to the benefit of all from investigating the Antagonist's rainbow, and doing so with the same integrity we afforded the Protagonist.

Repeat the same process as for the Protagonist. The Protagonist also now receives the Antagonist's Rainbow fragments in improvisations.

deeper into the group consciousness

After investigating the Antagonist's Rainbow, place the two teams, including the Protagonist and Antagonist, on either side of the playing area. The Antagonist sends one member of her team into the playing area where he takes up his place as if the Protagonist was there. The Protagonist looks at which character has been sent in and chooses one of his team that he thinks fits together with the Antagonist's choice. It is important that the Protagonist, who is the originator of the story, controls the choices. So, the Antagonist decides the order and the Protagonist chooses which Rainbow fragment of his fits best with the Antagonist's.

The Protagonist's chosen Rainbow fragment enters and places herself as if the Antagonist was there. The two characters are frozen in shape and *cannot unfreeze their bodies, although they can move through space.* They can listen and speak. This means that they may be in a physical orientation to each other where they cannot see each other. They must get what the characters want from each other, but they must also be as authentic as possible. There can be emotional, psychological and physical movement, if they are truly motivated as the character. Because of the frozen body shape restriction, these are highly metaphoric improvisations.

The group sees all the Rainbow fragments this way, teamed up, two by two, in improvisations. As previously, the Joker may stop the action and use any technique necessary to investigate more fully the relationship that is unfolding. The task here is not to find answers or solutions to the problem, but to peel the layers of complexity away from the symbols.

At any time in any of the improvisations, the Joker can turn to the whole group or, if it is a public event, the audience, and ask them what they are seeing. This question is about the generic relationship, not about the Protagonist (whose story it is) in a personal way, or about the acting ability of the participants.

After the group has seen all these improvisations, the Fears and Desires are thanked, asked if there is anything any of them would like to say, and released.

fluid-Forum

A fluid-Forum can be a very energizing and positive way to end the Rainbow of Desire exercise, although it is not absolutely necessary.

The group has used the theatre as a laboratory to take the original image (the story) apart, analyze it and put it back together again. By doing this, we have all gathered a lot of information about what we believe is happening inside the symbolic representation of the community. Do we now have ideas for ways to solve this dilemma, from the perspective of either character?

The initial improvisation is repeated, as close to the original as possible. The actors must try to be true to the original scene, and not incorporate insights they have gained during the exercise. Now, members of the audience can yell "Stop!" and replace either character if they identify with the struggle in which the character is engaged and have an idea of how to navigate the moment in a healthier way. In this fluid-Forum, it is not necessary to return to the original players. The cast can keep changing very quickly. It is as if the two characters become fluid, able to be played by anyone in the room, as long as that person is replacing them to engage in their struggle. However, it is the Joker's job to make sure that no one gets replaced before the person onstage has tried his or her idea.

winding up the exercise

The Antagonist and the Protagonist are individually thanked, asked if there is anything they would like to say, and then released. At this point it is important to acknowledge all the people who offered stories at the beginning of the exercise. Only one can be chosen, but it takes courage to offer a story for an exercise like this.

In group discussion after the exercise, I make a point of asking the participants to give the Protagonist a break and not pepper him with questions. He has been generous enough. It is not the purpose of this discussion to psychoanalyze the Protagonist's actions, or to ask him what he has learned from the exercise. If the Protagonist wants to offer this information, fine.

the benefit of humanizing the oppressor

The following is an example of Rainbow of Desire in practice.

March 21 is the International Day for the Elimination of Racism. In 2005 the Equity Ambassadors at the University of British Columbia (UBC) put together three days of anti-racism events. One of the events was a *Theatre for Living* workshop. The very nice request from the Ambassadors was to do something that would shake people up and challenge their perceptions about racism. I chose to use Rainbow of Desire.

The people in the room chose to work on this story offered by a member of the workshop group: A woman of Chinese ancestry is shopping in a drug store, in an affluent and not very diverse neighbourhood. She hasn't been to this store before. When she finishes finding what she wants, she goes to the cashier, who is Caucasian. The cashier looks her straight in the eye, so obviously knows she is there, and then turns around, fusses with a shelf for a moment, and leaves. The woman, who realizes that the cashier is pretending she isn't there, wants to say something but doesn't – and, having not said anything in that moment, doesn't when the cashier is leaving and gone. She places her full basket on the counter and leaves the store. Many of the participants mentioned that this kind of thing happens to them regularly.

I want to be clear that the exercise, while based on a real life story, is also symbolic – the woman playing the cashier is not the cashier. But we agreed that, even though this was just one example, we could recognize the cashier in ourselves in some ways, through her anger and fear at her own place in life. In one of the Rainbow fragments (a fear) that was presented, we discovered the probability that the cashier spends her day serving people who very often don't treat her like a human – she is 'just a cashier'. Now, her perception is that 'all these people' are coming from another country – people who she perceives have a lot more money than she has; people who she feels she is going to spend her life serving; people who, from her perspective, rob her of chances to advance. She is furious with them, without knowing them.

Again, the exploration was not a case of condoning the character's racism in any way. However, the participants, many of them anti-racism activists, found the insights from the exercise very profound. What we realized during the exploration is that we are already very familiar with the fears and desires of the customer who experiences the racism. While this is interesting to all of us, and there are important discoveries to make about how to combat racism through the exploration, to a large degree it verifies things we already know. It is the fears and desires of the racist that are most hidden and unexplored and, because of this, they are of real value in our desire to confront the causes, and not just the symptoms, of racism.

There was an animated and very positive group discussion after the exercise. All of us were confronted, I believe, by our symbolic connections to this character – even though we are all people who are engaged at some level in anti-racism work – and by the ways that we are ourselves racist, or classist or sexist, or exclusionary in some manner.

We were only able to investigate the issue at this level, because we risked creating the Rainbow of Fear and Desire of the racist cashier. We honoured her humanity, while not condoning her actions.

Cops in the Head

While the Rainbow of Desire is about internal voices of fear and desire – different aspects of the same person – Cops in the Head[132] deals with other people who have taken up residence inside our heads. These learned voices from parents, bosses, teachers, friends, lovers, etc., that tell us we are stupid, or are incapable of achieving something we want, are not voices that are inherently our own. They have come from somewhere else and are masquerading as our own voices. How do we identify these voices and exorcise them from our psyche? Or at least learn to recognize them and cope with them in healthy ways? I would also ask, do these voices exist in our collective psyche? If they do, is it possible to work on them at the community level in the same way it is possible to work on them at the individual level?

I use the same kinds of warm-up games and exercises for Cops as I do for Rainbow. The stories that are asked for are ones in which the Protagonist must make a choice about something, and in that moment of decision, gets paralyzed or taken down a path that is not in her best interests. This could be a story where the Protagonist, chosen by the same process as in Rainbow, is alone – in which case, the scene will be a monologue. Or there could be an Antagonist, also chosen by the same process as in Rainbow. (For the sake of this description we will assume the Protagonist is not alone and that there is an Antagonist.)

As in Rainbow of Desire, the group picks a story to work on that resonates with the majority in the room. The Protagonist picks someone who is volunteering from the group to play the Antagonist, and tells her story in greater detail. The Antagonist and the group listen and then ask questions; then the moment to be explored is improvised. The Joker looks for the moment in the improvisation where the Protagonist gets 'stuck', when it is apparent all the voices in

---

[132] Versions of *Cops in the Head* are also in Boal's *Rainbow of Desire*, p. 136, and *Games for Actors and Non-Actors*, p. 192.

her head are at full volume and we can see the confusion that they are creating in her. This is where the improvisation freezes. From this freeze on, we are investigating this one second (or millisecond) of the scene.

discovering the Cops

With the actors rooted emotionally in the frozen moment, the Joker asks the Protagonist to make a shape of what the loudest voice is saying to her. The Cops are very particular voices. They are not fears or desires as in Rainbow. They are the voices of *other people* who are now living inside the Protagonist's head, and giving her *bad advice*. The Protagonist self-sculpts the shape of the loudest Cop, using as much of her body as possible, and positions it as if the Cop was talking to her, where she is standing in the scene.

"Who understands this Cop?" Lots of hands will go up. "Who could come here and play this Cop, *with integrity*?" Many hands will go down, but someone will come.

> **Joker Tip:** There are a number of stipulations in this invitation. As in all of the *Theatre for Living* work, one of the challenges for the participants is to take on roles of characters that they understand and who might be doing things with which they disagree. It does not help us in our investigation to make fun of these characters or to demonize them. They are doing what they are doing for their own good reasons. We might disagree with them, but their actions are, from their perspective, valid.
>
> Why would someone come up to play a voice in the Protagonist's head? Not because he knows what is inside the Protagonist, but because he *recognizes* something about the Cops in his own head, in this Cop that the Protagonist is offering. Once again, we are starting from one person's story, but are moving to a pluralized moment. The 'room' is starting to own the story.

The audience member takes on the shape of the Cop. The Protagonist must approve of the interpretation. If the shape, the facial expression, etc., is not right, then she shows the audience member again until he is doing it to her satisfaction. He is placed, by the Protagonist, in relation to herself.

Another Cop, different from the first. Same process. And another, and another. Do the people in the audience believe there are Cops inside the Protagonist's head in this scenario that she has not offered, but that they could offer? Yes? Come. Show us the shape, without speaking. The Protagonist must agree that this Cop is in her head. If she does not, the audience member returns to his seat. It is important, though, that some Cops come from the audience. This deepens the pluralization of the story.

first activation of the Cops

The Cops are frozen in place around the Protagonist. All together they do an internal monologue, each articulating the thoughts and feelings of their very focused character. The body shape gives them clues, as does their own experience of this Cop. They must be clear that they are not playing the Protagonist. They are now a character who is in a scene with the Protagonist. They are no longer in her head, but present and visible on the stage.

Freeze! The Joker goes to each Cop and when they are touched, they speak a sentence that begins with "(name of Protagonist), I want you to..." This sentence is their desire for the Protagonist. For example: "I want you to protect yourself by staying silent." "I want you to run away." "I want you to remember that you are not worthy." "I want you to do what you are told." Etc. They are giving the Protagonist advice that is paralyzing her somehow, or sending her down an unhealthy path. They are very particular voices.

The Protagonist now gets to go to each Cop, in any order, and tell the Cop two things:

1. Who they are: "You are my brother (my mother, my teacher, etc.)..."
2. A key phrase that they are saying to the Protagonist.

The workshop participants playing the Cops now have these two specific instructions from the Protagonist, plus their own sentence and internal monologue discoveries. Each of them will incorporate all of these to create as full a character as possible.

Now, all the Cops start to 'go after' the Protagonist, all at the same time. Everyone can move, but the Cops must stay in their shapes as much as possible. They must do whatever they can (no actual violence – theatrical violence is allowed) to convince the Protagonist to do what they want. The Protagonist must do whatever she can (no actual violence – theatrical violence is allowed) to deal with the Cops. She may move them around, try to escape, argue, sing, dance, etc. This will, in all likelihood, demonstrate that the Protagonist needs our help, that the combination of the voices all together create too much pressure for her to be able to function in a healthy way.

activating the anti-bodies to deal with the Cops

All the Cops go to one side of the playing area. One by one, the order being up to the Protagonist, we have a chance to deal with the Cops. A Cop comes and places him/herself in the position and relationship to the Protagonist that has been set earlier in the exercise. The original improvisation is repeated between the Protagonist and Antagonist. At the moment where the action froze, it's as if the lights go down on the Antagonist and up on the Cop. The Antagonist goes silent and the Cop takes over the scene. He tries to convince the Protagonist to follow his advice. The Protagonist must be truthful to her struggle with the Cop.

When someone in the audience sees a way to deal with the Cop on behalf of the Protagonist, the audience member yells "Stop!" and takes the Protagonist's place (becomes an "anti-body" in Boal's terms), trying an idea, just like in Forum Theatre. Many different ideas can be tried for each Cop. Slowly, we make our way through all the Cops.

During this part of the exercise, it is possible to use various animation techniques in the same way as in the Rainbow exercise. It is not necessary to actually find real solutions to defeat the Cops, although this can and does occur. What is important is the investigation, because many insights for redefining one's relationship to the voices will arise for many people in the room and, by extension, for the living community.

analyzing the original placement of the Cops

Once the investigation with the Cops is complete – which could take two or more hours with breaks – all the Cops, the Protagonist and Antagonist come back into their original places. Now the Protagonist can put the Cops in different proximity to her, based on how she feels or thinks, having experienced and witnessed the exercise about their power over her. Has anything changed? Perhaps she has learned new things about the Cops, their weaknesses or strengths; maybe one or more are actually useful in ways she hadn't thought about; and so on. Each Cop could, at this point, say a few sentences from this new place. Now is a very good time to ask the audience what they are seeing and hearing.

winding up the exercise

The Cops are thanked, asked for comments and released. The Antagonist is thanked, asked for comments and released. The Protagonist is thanked, asked for comments and released. Again, as in *Rainbow*, I make a point of asking the participants to give the Protagonist a break and not pepper her with questions during the discussion that follows the exercise.

I have used Cops in the Head in many different circumstances. As discussed, during *Reclaiming Our Spirits* we used Cops to investigate issues arising from Residential School. I have also used the technique on issues of climate change to investigate: What stops us from taking action?

In 2000 Headlines produced a Forum Theatre production on globalization issues called *Corporate U*.[133] As part of the research on that project, I had the idea of using Cops to investigate how the voices of corporations had invaded our collective psyche, and whether or not we could use theatre to both better understand those voices and exorcize them.

---

[133] Created and performed by: Emme Lee, Valerie Laub, Kevin Millsip, Charlene Wee. Stage Manager: Kelly Creelman. Directed and Joked by: David Diamond. For a full report see http://www.headlinestheatre.com/pastwork.htm

We booked a small theatre space and, as we had done previously with productions like *Safe Sex*,[134] advertised a theatre event in which there would be no script, no play and no actors. We called it *Corporations in Our Heads* and had five interactive evenings.

the innovation of Corporations in Our Heads

Corporations communicate with us hundreds, perhaps thousands of times a day. Their messages come to us from television, radio, newspapers, magazines, billboards (both static and mobile), the labels on people's clothes and the branding on the luxuries and necessities that inhabit our lives. It is possible that corporate voices are more recognizable to us than some humans. These are not the voices of human beings, not the voices of CEOs, but perhaps they are the voices of living entities.

In *Culture Jam: The Uncooling of America*,[135] author and founder of *Adbusters*[136] Kalle Lasn details how corporations have acquired the legal rights of human beings. A turning point in this evolution was the Santa Clara Railway decision in 1898, in which a US Court declared the railway corporation had the rights of a "natural person". This case has been used as a precedent in corporate law ever since.

As troubling as this sounds, if one investigates corporations under a systems theory lens, they do appear to have the characteristics of living systems. Capra writes:

> "...metabolic networks in biological systems correspond to networks of communications in social systems; chemical processes producing material structures correspond to thought processes producing semantic structures; and flows of energy and matter correspond to flows of information and ideas."[137]

What follows are my notes of the first evening of *Corporations in Our Heads* as a sample of what happened.

---

[134] See http://www.headlinestheatre.com/pastwork.htm
[135] Published by Eagle Brook, New York 1999.
[136] The birthplace of Culture Jamming. See http://www.adbusters.org
[137] Capra, *The Hidden Connections*, p. 261.

September 21, 2000

I was nervous starting out this first night, because there were things I had no way to know would work without trying them. I am wanting to look at the voices of *Corporations* that have taken up residence in our heads, voices that try to get us to do things that may not be in our best interests, in the best interests of the planet, the ones we love, etc. Can we use the theatrical exercise to do this? Can/will people be able to manifest the voices onto the stage and play them as characters? Yes. The people in the room did this wonderfully tonight.

The story that was chosen: A woman who is an anti-globalization activist is walking down Robson Street (a very trendy street in the shopping district of Vancouver), having just come out of an international conference she is attending. She comes to The Gap. She explains to us, "It is the only place that sells jeans that fit me. I know that The Gap makes its jeans in sweatshops. I end up going in anyway."

The improvisation she creates is a monologue; there is just her, and the Gap store.[138] I ask her to play the scene once in silence, just to find the physical pattern. Then again, speaking all of her thoughts out loud. There is a moment where she looks around the street and wonders if anyone she knows will see her. She checks her watch. She decides it is safe and she will go in. I froze the scene when she is looking up the street, while she is concerned about someone seeing her, just before she decides to go into the store.

In the same way as happens in Cops in the Head, I ask her to create the voices in her head that she feels are giving her bad advice, by making a shape with her body of what the voice is telling her. I ask people from the audience to come and play those voices. Once they are all in place, the voices do an internal monologue and then say a sentence to the Protagonist. Then the Protagonist gives each voice both another sentence – and, in this experiment, a brand name.

---

[138] In retrospect, I am wondering what would have happened if we had turned the store itself into a character – the Antagonist. Something to play with someday.

The first and loudest corporate voice is The Gap itself – and it tells her that she knows she is fat and these jeans will make her look thinner. The second is Eddie Bauer, a different clothing label. This one is telling her that the garment industry really supports human rights and is changing its labour practices, so going in is nothing to be concerned about. The third is Revlon, the make-up manufacturer, telling her she deserves these jeans because she is beautiful and they will make her more beautiful. The fourth is Nike telling her she is a loser if she doesn't 'just do it' – go in and buy the jeans.

Naming the voices generates a lively discussion with the audience about how remarkably easy this is for her and the rest of us to do. It is like a revelation in the room. As she names the voices, there is lots of applause and laughter. We really do all have these voices of corporations inside us. The people in the theatre are experiencing a collective moment of recognition. (In retrospect, I suggest this is a moment of collective epoché.)

There were lots of interventions from audience members to try to exorcise the Corporate voices. Something happened over and over again: people needed to argue, sometimes vehemently, with the Corporate voices, and the Corporate voices really wanted us to engage with them on a deep level. It became apparent, though, that 'getting into it' with them, was not necessarily a solution. Often, this was exactly what the Corporate voices wanted. They wanted us to engage with them in any way, knowing we were susceptible to the power of their messages.

On the other hand, one intervener pointed out that, as he found out more and more about the character of an individual voice, as he understood the tactics of the voice more, he felt more empowered to disarm the voice's control over him. So, the manner in which we engage with the voices is important. Are we engaged critically?

Another moment highlighted how, inside the culture in which we live, it seems to be one of our responsibilities now, as good citizens, to shop. When we do manage to stop buying, the response from the Corporation is sometimes that we are robbing them of their right to do business and make a profit.

Generally speaking, the audience had an easier time dealing with voices they could personalize. The voices that remained distant were the hardest with which to cope. There are big clues here, I think, about tactic. We have to take the time to understand specific corporate messages' underlying meanings, before we can hope to exorcise the control they have over our lives and our collective psyche.

A suggestion that came out of this evening is having classes in elementary school and through high school about how to view commercials and other forms of advertising. This seems appropriate in the consumer-oriented world in which we live. We could be giving young people the tools to be conscious of the effects these voices have on our lives.

There is, in fact, a wonderful group in Vancouver attempting just that in secondary schools. They are called Check Your Head.[139]

Rainbow and Cops are examples of Boal's work evolving as his life journey took him from one context to another – from Brazil to France. Part of the power of his work is that it adapts to meet people where they are focused, whether it is externally or internally, or a mixture of both.

I began to notice in my own work how so many of the individuals and communities I was invited into were struggling with their emotional and psychological location. They were very uncomfortable with their 'here' and were eager to find some 'there'. This got me thinking about using the language of images that is in Image Theatre and Rainbow and Cops to create a community visioning exercise that could plot a symbolic course from 'here' to 'there'. The result, *Your Wildest Dream*, is explained in the next section.

---

[139] See http://www.checkyourhead.org/

Getting there from here

Paulo Freire, in *Pedagogy of Hope*, writes: "...you never get *there* by starting from *there*, you get *there* by starting from some *here*."[140] In order not to take this sentence out of context, let me explain that Freire is writing about how an "...educator needs to know that his or her 'here' and 'now' are nearly always the educands' 'there' and 'then'." He is explaining that when one enters a community as an educator from the outside, one must begin where the educands[141] are, not where the educator wishes they were.

It is not the role of a theatre director or Joker working with a community to teach participants in a workshop about their lives. If the Joker is a 'teacher' in any way, it is about the techniques of the theatre. The participants are the experts when it comes to their lives. Their own exploration in the workshop process is bound to give them insights into their lives and the life of their community. The collective process of theatre creation and community analysis itself provides an educational process, of which the Joker is a facilitator.

When a group of people come together to create theatre through an improvisational process, it is imperative that enough time be taken to try to find the 'here' of the group. This serves both the group and the Joker. Never, in my experience, has a group, even an already coherent working group, had clarity or been in consensus about their 'here' in relation to an issue. The 'here' I am talking about is not an individual 'here'. It is a collective 'here'.

I have witnessed, on numerous occasions, the resistance in a group to investigating 'here'. This resistance, however, makes sense. 'Here' may not be a very comfortable place. (If it were comfortable, it is unlikely we would be making theatre about it for the purpose of stimulating dialogue in the community.) The tendency of groups is to want to get

---

[140] Freire, *Pedagogy of Hope*, p. 58, originally published by Sheed and Ward, Lanham MD 1972; subsequently published by the Continuum Publishing Company, New York 1994.

[141] The relationship between teacher and student is similar to the relationship between educator and educand. However, in the former, traditionally the educator is an expert, filling the student with knowledge. In the latter, the educator is a guide, taking the educand, who already has knowledge, on a journey of discovery.

'there' very quickly. There are no shortcuts – only assurances that after doing the work to understand 'here' in all its complexity, the resulting dialogue-creating theatre event will investigate how the community as a whole can journey to some 'there'.

I have also witnessed communities who have extreme difficulty imagining 'there'. They have, perhaps, been so entrenched in 'here' that it seems impossible to look up and see any horizon. As with individual people, a community's health is attached to its capacity to imagine. Following is a community visioning exercise developed to help the living community to imagine, to dream, together.

Your Wildest Dream

In 1997, after encountering the Freire quote above for the first time, I started developing a technique that incorporates Image Theatre and Polaroid photography, to help communities envision a path from 'here' to 'there'. I have used Your Wildest Dream with the Nuxalk Nation in BC, and with a group from the Passamaquoddy Nation in Maine, US, and New Brunswick, Canada.[142] After five *Theatre for Living* work-shops in three years, the latter formed a theatre troupe called The Passamaquoddy Players, using theatre to focus on issues of language and culture. People who have attended our *Theatre for Living* training workshops have also taken the exercise into the Regina School District in Saskatchewan, for instance.[143, 144]

The focus of Your Wildest Dream is not an external issue that may concern the community; the focus is *the community itself*. How can a community work effectively on issues of concern if it is, itself, dysfunc-tional?

Wildest Dream is best done over two or three days and works best in a community of people who know each other and live/work together; a

---

[142] The Passamaquoddy ancestral territory spans the boundary that separates Canada and the United States.

[143] Just before going to print with this book, I got word from Adam Perry, a 2006 *Theatre for Living* training participant who was working with an organization called InterChange. Adam was preparing to conduct Your Wildest Dream workshops with members of the Rwandan Diaspora community in Toronto, Canada.

[144] *Your Wildest Dream* evolved in a workshop in Calgary, Canada and was subsequently updated on July 30, 2007 creating version 1.1 of this book.

community that has geography in common somehow, even if that geography is place of work. Participant numbers have ranged from 15 to 40. This exercise is more difficult, but still possible when the only thing that creates community is that the participants share a common focus; perhaps they are all social justice activists or all teachers. In either case, they will have travelled into the workshop to create the wildest dream of the social justice community, or of the teaching community.

Day 1

I would begin a Wildest Dream process with some of the following games and exercises; they would vary depending on what is happening in the room:[145]

Balancing
Hypnosis
Lead the Blind
Blind Cars
Complete the Image
Sculpting Partners
Glass Bottle
Groups of 4

Wildest Dream: Stage 1

Ask the group if anyone can create *an image of the dysfunction* of the community. What does the dysfunctional community look like? The image can be realistic or symbolic and can contain from two to all of the participants. Someone starts by making an image. Everyone looks at it, walking around it if desired, seeing it from various perspectives. Another, different image is made. See that. No discussion at this point, just seeing, feeling, absorbing. Another. Another. Spend time throwing images of the dysfunction of the community into the space. After six or eight or maybe 10 images have been created, ask if anyone has an image that is really different than the ones that have been seen. Maybe there will be some. Look at them and then move to the next stage.

---

[145] Games not already explained are in the *Appendix*.

Wildest Dream: Stage 2

Having seen these images of dysfunction of the living community, try to synthesize them and create *the* image – the *one* that encompasses them all. It can be realistic or symbolic, and can include as many people as there are in the room, or as few as two. In this case, the image of dysfunction must contain at least one protagonist and one antagonist.

So now the task is not to create *an* image of the dysfunction, but *the* image of the dysfunction – that is, a representation of *the* core dysfunction of the community.

Someone creates *the* image. The group votes. If a majority of participants do not think this could be *the* image, ask for another image. When a majority of people in the room agrees that this could be *the* image, keep the image, and now only add to, subtract from or slightly alter this image. This process continues until everyone in the room is satisfied, or as close to that as is possible. This can take time. It's important that everyone remembers to breathe.

Take a Polaroid (or if you have the printing equipment, a digital photo) of the image of *the* dysfunction of the living community, and put it on the wall. This can be the end of an emotionally hard day's work. A formal circle in which each individual has the chance to speak and be heard (if they want to) is recommended.

Day 2

I would start this second day with games that were more challenging than the selection on day one. Depending on what was happening I might choose these:

Point and Turn
Fill the Empty Space
Blind Busses
Clap Exchange
The Intestine

Wildest Dream: Stages 3 and 4

After the group-building work with the games, repeat Stage 1 – but this time, imagine that the dysfunction of the living community does not exist. Dream! First seek *an* image of the dream, to get the collective juices flowing, and then the image of *the wildest dream of the community*. Not *an* image, but *the* image. In the group's wildest dream, what does the healthy, functional community look like?

It is important to differentiate between this 'wildest dream' concept and Boal's "Image of Transition", or "Ideal Image".[146] We are not seeking an image that is a reaction to an image of oppression, or even the image of dysfunction from the previous day. This is one of the reasons I like to separate the work from one day to the next. In Wildest Dream, we are imagining that the dysfunction, struggles, oppression do not exist. In this wild fantasy, what does the community look and feel like?

When everyone in the room is satisfied, or as close to that as is possible, take a photo of the Wildest Dream and place it on the wall, six to 10 feet from the image of dysfunction. Again, this can be the end of an emotional hard day's work. A formal circle is recommended.

Day 3

Again, I would start this third day with games that were more challenging than the selection on previous days. Depending on what was happening, I might choose these:

Fear/Protector
Clap Exchange (different rhythm than previous day)
Effective Hand
The Fall

---

[146] Boal, *Games for Actors and Non-Actors*, p. 173.

Wildest Dream: Stage 5

After some group-building and trust work, ask the group to start offering images that exist anywhere between the image of dysfunction and the dream. Someone makes an image. It can be realistic or symbolic, and can contain from one person to everyone in the room. The image can now have only one person, because it does not have to have the tension of antagonist/protagonist in order to physically identify the dysfunction. The group is now seeking images that exist somewhere on the path from the dysfunction to the dream. They can be realistic or symbolic. All images are accepted without question or explanation.

Take a photo of each image as it is created. Ask the group to determine where, in between the two extreme images, the new image should be placed. When there is disagreement in the room, a point in between the two suggested extreme points is found. Images are not frozen in place; they can be moved later if necessary. Slowly, images go up on the wall.

> **Joker Tip:** The voting to place the images is not the same as the voting in the image activation work. Decisions are not based on a majority vote, neither is consensus being sought. The Joker is gauging the consciousness in the room regarding each particular image and where in the continuum of images it is placed. Compromise is the word for the day.

The first half dozen or so image placements are usually relatively easy. After this, more discussion is required to place each image. Maybe two images that the group thought were side by side have to have space opened up between them to accommodate a new image. Maybe the group decides that a new image exists outside the boundary of the extreme images – in other words, this new image has redefined the extremity of the dysfunction (the community's ability to define it's 'here') or the dream (the community's ability to imagine a collective 'there').

> **Joker Tip:** During this process, the images must be placed in a linear way, horizontally, across the wall.

Think of the photos as a symbolic map, like a bus route put on paper. We know busses don't necessarily travel in one straight line. However, in order for passengers to be able to read the map clearly and see which stops follow the other, the transit authority creates the route in a straight line. Holding to this rule creates a structure in which the group must analyze which steps follow which.

As many images go on the wall as possible. I have not seen a group create more than 40 or less than 10 images.

Wildest Dream: Stage 6

Ask that everyone sit and look at the Wildest Dream images. Can any individual in the group volunteer to trace either their own life journey, or their impression of the living community's journey, through the symbolic steps in the map?

It is astounding the varied and complex stories that are told from the same photographs. Individuals come to the map and are able to trace their own journeys, referring to particular events in their lives, getting to a point and moving backwards and going through steps again, most often ending somewhere in the map. "I am here now – I hope someday to move further, to there." The same happens with individual's impressions of the community.

Once the exercise is complete, number the images in sequence. This will facilitate them coming down and going back up in the same order at a later date, if that is useful.

In every instance of doing this exercise in a community setting, I have left the photos with the community. In Nuxalk Territory in central British Columbia, the map remained on the wall for months, with people coming back to refer to it again and again.

In another instance, with the Passamaquoddy, the group realized we had to take a second photo of the dream, because they needed to place the duplicate dream image *before* the image of dysfunction. The community was working back to a state of equilibrium that existed before Europeans invaded their land.

CASE STUDIES

The best way to illustrate how the concepts in this book actually work in a community setting, is to share some in-depth case studies from actual projects.

As I mentioned in the *Prologue*, every time I work in community, I write after the workshop or rehearsal session each day. The writing helps me get some perspective on what has happened during the day, which helps me plan the next day. If I am going to make a document about a *Theatre for Living* workshop public, I will always run the report past the organizers and/or participants first, and, *if the project is not a mainstage project*, will also make the document anonymous, changing names of participants. What follows is a series of case studies, from my journals, on a diversity of projects.

Dancers of the Mist

This project was a wonderful experiment in 1998, and is a powerful example of how we can use theatre to access collective consciousness.

During the years of early contact with Europeans and the Residential Schools, the Canadian government made the dances and feast system of the Gitxsan and other First Nations illegal. People were severely punished for practicing their culture, so it went underground. The old, traditional Gitxsan dances remained, but it had been about 100 years since any new dance was made. This project was an opportunity to do that and to have the dances grow directly out of relevant issues in the dancers' lives. Once again, we were using dance to tell the living community's stories.

The invitation to do this project in Gitxsan Territory had history attached. Eleven years earlier, in 1987, Headlines had embarked on a four-year project with the Gitxsan and Wet'suwet'en Hereditary Chiefs, whose combined ancestral territory is approximately 22,000 square kilometres in the North West of British Columbia.[147] The project was called *NO`XYA` (Our Footprints)*.[148] This agit-prop play was an articulation, from the Gitxsan and Wet'suwet'en perspective, of their relationship to ancestral land. It was created and performed for diverse audiences across BC and Canada, with discussion sessions after every performance,[149] during the build-up to the now famous *Delgamuuk'w vs. The Queen* land claim case.[150]

Integral to *NO`XYA`* was Hal Blackwater,[151] a core group member, choreographer and cast member. *NO`XYA`* performed in Vancouver and toured BC in 1987, toured coast-to-coast in Canada in 1988, and toured into Maori communities in New Zealand, as an exchange between the Gitxsan and Wet'suwet'en and the Maori, in 1990. On August 19, 1987, in Kispiox, BC, Hal's father, Chief Baasxya laxha (Bill Blackwater Sr.), threw a feast at which the non-Native members of the

---

[147] The combined territories encompass both the towns of Smithers and the Hazeltons on a map of BC.
[148] Written by: David Diamond with Hal B. Blackwater, Marie Wilson and Lois Shannon. Cast: Sylvia-Anne George, Hal B. Blackwater, Sherri-Lee Guilbert and Ed Astley. Director: David Diamond. Co-producer: Maasgaak (Don Ryan). Administrators: Doug Cleverley, Honey Maser. Technical Directors/Stage Managers: Paul Williams, Marian Brandt. Consultants: Gitxsan Chief Baasxya laxha (Bill Blackwater Sr.) and Wet'suwet'en Chief Gisdaywa (Alfred Joseph). Designers: (poster graphic) Maas Likinisxw (Ken N. Mowatt); (sound) Skanu'u (Ardythe Wilson), Ray Cournoyer; (set) Vernon Stephens; (regalia and masks) Gitxsan Chief Wii Muk'wilsxw (Art Wilson), Gitxsan Chief Wii' Elaast (Jim Angus), Gitxsan Chief Sekwan (Silena Jack), Gitxsan Chief Iswoox (Lorraine Morgan), 'Alluksa'xw (Cheryl Stevens), Gitxsan Chief Niiyees Haluubist (Rita Williams); (cartoons) Don Monet.
[149] Representing the Chiefs in the discussion sessions were Marie Wilson in 1987, Chief Gisdaywa (Alfred Joseph) in 1988 and Skanu'u (Ardythe Wilson) in 1990.
[150] *Delgamuuk'w vs. The Queen* was a landmark land claim first in the Supreme Court of BC and then Canada that sought recognition of the jurisdiction of the Gitxsan and Wet'suwete'en in their ancestral lands. See http://www.gitxsan.com/ and http://www.wetsuweten.com/ and http://www.delgamuukw.org/
[151] Many thanks to Hal Blackwater for feedback on this section of the book.

touring company, myself included, were given Gitxsan names. My relationship with Hal, his family and the Gitxsan has remained very strong over the years.

In 1998, when the Supreme Court of Canada overturned an initial negative ruling by the BC Court and found in favour of the Gitxsan and Wet'suwet'en, I called Kispiox to speak with Hal and his family to share in the good news. In the course of that conversation, Hal mentioned that he thought it was time for another theatre project.

Both Hal and Bill Sr. had been members of the K'san Dancers and had toured extensively showcasing traditional Gitxsan dance. Hal had also been working for a few years to develop a youth dance group in Kispiox. The group was learning the traditional dances. This led us to an innovative idea.

We would do a *Theatre for Living* workshop with the dance group and others from the community, but instead of working the images created into a theatre piece, we would work with the group to create new dance about issues in their lives. These dances would then be performed in Gitxsan Territory.

It is in this spirit that I drove the 1,200 kilometres from Vancouver to Kispiox, where we began a six-day workshop process. The journal entries, written in present tense and edited for this book, follow.

> Day 1   There are 24 participants and four support people (counsellors). The organizing work by Hal and by Doreen Angus has been very good. A wide age range, from an eight-year-old boy to a woman in her 70s.
>
> One of the images made today was of a funeral. It was very recent and caused a lot of tears in the room. This is not a bad thing in and of itself, but it was one of the first images offered and, I think, it scared the participants. Some of them literally ran away – for a little while. Those who stayed and worked the image showed a lot of courage.
>
> We all know that there are a lot of issues of violence in this community and that participants are bound to be dealing with issues of breaking long-held silences and the ramifications of

that. This is just one of the legacies of Residential School and colonization. It will be important to allow them some distance on the characters, so they can not only make images, but can have the confidence to activate them into dance for the public.

I was very impressed with the eight-year-old boy today, who seems to have wisdom beyond his years. A number of times, he was a very calming influence in the group, grounding them in nervous moments.

Day 2   This was a dense and intense day. I decided to repeat some of the activity of yesterday. I felt that the group didn't really finish the day with a grasp of what the Image Theatre work is, and we need this in order to proceed. This was a good decision. They needed to feel comfortable with the theatre language we are speaking in order to be able to explore.

The game *Knots*[152] was very difficult and there are interesting reasons for that, I think. The first time we did the game, the group made three intertwined circles. There was very little they could do to undo the knot. More importantly, few tried. They just stood there while a small number of the group tried to solve the problem. We stopped and remade the knot. Again, they made three intertwined circles. The odds against this are huge, as they are randomly reaching across the group with their eyes closed! Again, it was a small core that were trying to solve the problem. I acknowledged this out loud, and then, once they all started to move, the game progressed. In discussion later they mentioned that this was a realistic mirror of the community, as it contains the Hereditary Clan system, which can sometimes create very small circles in the community. There are also, they said, a small core of 'doers', who do a lot of the problem solving; many members of the community, though, just want things fixed, but are not willing to do anything so that will happen. Interesting how this manifests in the game.

---

[152] See *knots* in the *Several senses* section of the *Appendix*.

The game *Animals*[153] was wonderful. I don't find the opportunity to do this game very often, but in this workshop it seemed appropriate. Gitxsan dances are often based on animals. Hal provided a list of 12 animals (male and female = 24 participants) that are indigenous to the area. Each participant picked the name of an animal out of a hat. They started as the animal asleep and then, without speaking any language, had to find their mate and court each other. When they were all partnered, pair by pair, I asked them to show us their mating rituals. Many of the group shone at this, and there was great focus and laughter.

We made more images of the community's struggles with violence, and some were very strong. In the midst of making these images the counsellors got very busy. For some of the participants, simply the acknowledgement that these issues are in their lives was a major step.

During activation of the images, I discovered a new technique that I called *Orchestra of Emotion*.[154]

Once the image was made, I asked each character to make the sound of the emotion they felt. Then, with them standing in a line, I conducted them like an orchestra. The connections of one sound to another, the dissonance, how the sounds of the image are like music, was wonderful, and will be of value to the dance group. We made notes about the sounds. We also took Polaroid photos of all the images we worked and will go back to them later in the workshop, seeking motion, characters, etc.

Near the end of the day, the young people asked if they could make an image. It was of many of them standing around a dead grandmother, who they never got to know well. They put her into a chair, 'dead'. She looked passed out. Images of alcohol were present (we discussed this later), but not raised in the moment. They spoke of how the grandmother represents the culture and of the youths' struggle and regret at the severance of

153 See *animals* in the *See all that we look at* section of the *Appendix*.
154 See *orchestra of emotion* in the *Image Theatre animation techniques* section of the *Appendix*.

their connection to her. They have knowledge of her and so they understand – but the time is late – what do they do? How much do they have to reinvent?

In the final circle today, it was obvious that the 'lights are going on' as to what the possibility is in this week. Also, many more spoke today than yesterday.

In retrospect, years later, I understand that epoché was occurring in the larger living organism, although it was difficult to know at the time. As you will see, the next day it felt as if we had taken a step backward, but this was, also in retrospect, a natural part of the journey.

Day 3   This was a complex, wonderful and frustrating day. Some moments were painfully honest. Still, some of the teenage participants, who keep coming back every day, were so disruptive, out of nervousness perhaps, that they started blocking other people's ability to work.

This is so complicated. I really believe and can see that these young people want to be here. They are deeply hurt, and also sense that something important is unfolding. I know this from sparks of understanding that seem to fly sometimes, or from their level of engagement in certain moments. But they will not stop talking, giggling and running around the room, even when other people are working very hard to express something and really need the focused support of everyone else. Hal and I have tried to talk with them many times, asking if there is something we can do, something they want, if something is bothering them. We've given them lots of breaks, and the support people have met with them as a group and individually. Nothing. "Nothing is wrong," they say – but the behaviour stays the same and is getting on other people's nerves (not just Hal's and mine) and is stopping some of the group from participating.

One young girl left this afternoon, after talking with a support person. He was questioning her behaviour and she mentioned to him that it was her friends in the workshop who were bugging her and she had to do what they wanted – they were her friends. Rather than say no to them, she said no to herself by removing herself. While it is very sad that she has left, it may also be the right thing for her in this moment. Maybe she needs some reflection time. One of the support people is going to check in with her tonight. If leaving and staying away is the thing she really wants to do, then that needs to be honoured.

The game *The Intestine*[155] was a big leap of trust for many of them, but they did it and expressed how wonderful it was to be able to trust people in the group.

Magnetic Image yielded three strong and very different images. The first was of a mother about to hit her young son for not cleaning his room. One daughter is standing there, not knowing what to do, and another daughter is grabbing the mother's arm to try to stop her. In activation, something became clear that wove itself through many of the images and, really, is in a lot of this workshop. We were doing a mini-Forum on this image and someone replaced one of the daughters. She and the mother got into an argument about how the mother is always lashing out at the kids. While this was going on, the son cleaned up the whole room in silence. No one in the scene noticed. Even though he was doing what he was told, the fighting continued.

The second image had three young people in the foreground fighting. Behind them were three adults, each isolated. When we activated the image, none of the characters seemed to be able to do anything. No matter what we did, each adult character remained in her own world, wishing things were different but not doing anything, while the young people continued to beat the crap out of each other. When I asked the group what they were seeing, no one mentioned this. They saw each isolation, but not the larger picture. I pointed this out to them – that the larger image of the isolation and people not noticing seemed to me to be repeating itself in images in the workshop. Is it possible that this is what the larger community is facing? Having asked this, I let the image sit onstage. After a long reflective silence, someone wanted to re-sculpt part of the image. This involved taking the kids and having them pull the

---

[155] See *the intestine* in the *Trust games* section of the *Appendix*.

mother in different directions. Not a happy picture – the mother going from the frying pan into the fire, as it were, but at least she was no longer isolated and, perhaps, as someone in the group pointed out, now not on the path to suicide.

The third image was a fragmented symbol of a journey from pain to healing. Hal commented that the image had an energy flow. This inspired me to ask the people in it to reposition themselves in a straight line. Then I asked the group to start filling in the steps between the shapes that were already presented. This started slowly, but as the pieces started to fit together, more and more people jumped in. In the end, we had created a very beautiful image of steps that showed the creation of self-doubt and hatred, how that turns into abusive behaviour, how that turns into despair and then self-questioning, then perhaps more despair, reaching out, sharing and then strength again. Writing this, it sounds kind of corny, but doing it was not. The people in the workshop talked about how just taking this image around in the community would have a very strong and positive effect on people. (The experiment with this image was one of the first impulses that led to the technique developed years later called Your Wildest Dream.[156])

A number of the participants spoke about the power of the *Magnetic Image* exercise. They said that even though they see each other every day, they never imagined that they shared emotions, concerns and experiences the way they do; that the links made in the exercise will remain and will change the patterns of relationships in this community. Patterns create structure.

The work today was very moving. In the final circle, I felt that I needed to thank them. Regardless of my connections here, which are strong, I am an outsider – a White outsider – and always will be. The trust and co-operation that happened today touched me deeply.

---

[156] See the section *Getting there from here* in the chapter *Awakening the Group Consciousness*.

Day 4   We went into uncharted territory today, in four hours instead of eight. We have started short days, because school is back in now.

The girl who left came back today and brought me a beautiful hand-done drawing and a note. It was eloquent and self-aware and spoke of the work opening her heart and how that was frightening for her. In the note she asked if she could return. I told her how much her gift meant to me and that, of course, it would be wonderful if she came back. This also pleased many in the group.

As would be expected, *The Fall* (falling off a table backwards into participants' arms) was very challenging. Many did it, though, and there was much celebrating and discussion of the distance we have travelled together.

We found titles for the photographs of all the images we have taken. This took some time, but was very worthwhile. By asking the group to come to consensus on an evocative title for each image, we have had to analyze each one, share our insights and agree on some things about them.

Having done the titling, we moved into the grand experiment of this workshop. Hal and I were nervous, because neither of us have ever done anything like this before. Although we have done a lot of talking about how we might proceed in theory, in reality we are now making it up on the spot. How could it be otherwise?

We asked one of the groups to re-create their image from the photos we had taken earlier in the workshop. Then we asked this group to close their eyes and, frozen in position, to do a silent, internal monologue, allowing that to turn into a sound – no language – and then on a signal, all at the same time, to let that sound come out. After letting them play with this for a while, we asked them to allow the sound to take on a rhythm. Once the rhythm was established, we asked them to allow that rhythm to reach into their whole bodies, while staying rooted in their shapes. This took time. They needed to focus and really reach deep within themselves.

Then we stopped and asked each character to decide, just inside themselves, without saying anything out loud, what 'essence' they were in this image. A human? An insect? An animal? A bird or fish? An element of the weather? A plant? A smell? They would know. Then, keeping this 'essence' in mind, we asked them to go back to the image, to the sound (silent, though, just in their heads) and to let the sound drive the rhythm, which would then move their bodies, eyes closed, through space and into dance.

One of the images was called *Abusive Love*. The dance results were raw, but spectacular. Chilling. People spoke of goose bumps, of deeply communicated emotion and a very clear story. The movements were intertwined between characters and echoed each other. This all happened in silence and with their eyes closed. When they stopped, we asked each person in the dance image to say who or what they were and what they were doing:

- a mother caribou yearning for her lost child – she is searching through the forest, which is on fire
- a child, lost and hiding
- fire
- a flower that has been stepped on

They did this without speaking to each other, and without planning it. We all just stood there, looking at each other, not knowing what to do. Someone said the hairs on the back of his neck were standing up. Hal turned to me and said, "There's something you don't know: In Gitxsan, the word for child is 'flower'."

It feels like we have plugged into something much larger than ourselves – many spoke of this – we were stunned by the results. Really, like sticking our fingers into an electrical outlet.

I believe that what happened here was the accessing of a consciousness that was larger than any individual in the room. Later, Hal described this moment as "something that would have happened hundreds of years ago. Now, with technology all around us, we don't do it. It would have come from someone going onto the land and going through a time of intense soul-searching, reaching into the culture at a subconscious level. Instead, the collective came together and did an ancient thing in a unique way, and we did it in a building, not out on the land."[157]

The consciousness of the living community is connected across generations. It was as if we had accessed the quantum field together, a place where all knowledge exists. It reached across a multi-generational gap in the community – a gap created by the policies of the Canadian government and by the Residential School experience that was an attempt to negate Aboriginal knowledge. These young people tapped into a language that their great-great-grandparents spoke as an everyday part of their lives. A metaphoric language of dance. We all saw it, felt it.

> Day 5   The energy in the room today was really ragged when we started and to some degree we didn't manage to smooth it out. Part of the difference, I think, is that the participants all came from a full day of school and work today. It didn't seem to matter what we did, focus was always a problem. This also may have had to do with the power of what happened yesterday. A strong experience like that will often temporarily throw a group off balance.
>
> We worked three images today. They seemed to happen with chaos around them and also a lot of emotion. Lots of processing. I am going to document one.
>
> The image was extremely violent. A woman standing with her fists on a young girl's chest and face, with two very young kids holding each other in fear on the floor. Same process as yesterday, except when we got to the movement part, we asked the participants to open their eyes and play the scene, having found a rhythmic pattern of movement. It was brutal. The woman was a "mad dog" (she said later) and the beating she was giving her daughter, pounding her fist into her face, was relentless. She said that in the middle of it she wanted to stop but couldn't. It was really ugly and mesmerizing all at the

---

[157] Hal Blackwater, in a telephone conversation, September 21, 2003.

same time. It was mechanized, somehow, and as she pounded, the girl seemed to go deeper and deeper into the floor.

These images have been made by the participants. They have a strong desire to perform them. To tell these stories. In the final circle, the girl who was at the centre of the image talked about how it was a good thing to show that image, even though it was so intense. Many spoke about the power of the day. As young as some of the participants are (one is eight years old), they know what they are doing. They are living these issues. As frightening as some of this is, truly respecting them means creating the space for them to make the theatre/dance that they want. This is one of the reasons there are counsellors from the community in the workshop.

Day 6   We started this day with a focus game and a final trust game. Then I formally handed the workshop over to Hal, explaining that for the first three days, it had been me facilitating everything, in consultation with Hal. Then, as I was sure they had noticed, two days ago we started to facilitate activities together. Now, Hal would take over and work in consultation with me. Hal explained about the difference between my work and his.

Hal started with the first image, *Abusive Love* – the one we had activated into dance two days earlier. He asked the performers to go back into the image and for people from the audience to come and stand with the character they felt the closest to. Then he asked the performers to let go of the emotional content for now, and to focus on externals: What were they? How did they move? What sounds did they make? They worked and deepened the movements with their eyes closed, going through a stage of just standing and waving their arms in the air, to really using their whole bodies to be what they represented with authenticity – tall grass in a storm, a volcano, fire, smoke, etc. This took some time, but after an hour of stopping and starting, it was obvious that new characters were emerging who would be able to interact in dance forms that are traditionally recognizable to the Gitxsan.

Hal explained that this was just a taste of the work they were going to do. His own realization during the hour was that he needs to work one-on-one with people.

A reporter from the local paper was in this morning, with the permission of the group. She watched the games and this session with Hal and then, when we took a break, sat down with four of the group: the eight-year-old participant, a teenager, an Elder and a counsellor. They talked for about 20 minutes. This will form the basis of an article featuring the dance group in the local paper. The exposure will be exciting and valuable for them.

After the break we gathered back together and Hal and I let them split up into groups any way they pleased. They were given the task of making a short 'anything' to express themselves at the end of the workshop. We told them it was OK, if they wanted, to use any of the skills they had learned, in any way, to say anything, including making fun of me, Hal or the counsellors. Great laughter about this. They had 15 minutes. Hal and I left to give them privacy.

There were two groups. The first did a ritual of letting go of energy. A tight circle with energy spouting out its centre like a fountain. Then a warm greeting to me and Hal.

The second did a long song in Gitxsan that kept sliding into rock and roll, to great hilarity in the group. At the end, the Elder in the room, who had been singing with the rest, danced up to me, took my hand and danced me around the room – also to much laughter. It was very good to do these skits after all the heaviness of the last few days. Then we played their favourite game, *Fox in the Hole*, for an exhausting 15 minutes!

In the final circle, more spoke than ever before, but still not all. During this time, the girl who left and came back spoke at length for the first time in the week, saying yesterday had been hard, but she woke up this morning feeling different than she had been feeling for so long. The heaviness was gone from her, she said, and she felt happy for the first time in a long time.

We entered party mode with lots of food. We had made certificates of achievement for all the participants and thank-you certificates for the counsellors. Hal did a wonderful job of introducing each participant and speaking briefly, in positive ways, of the journey he observed in them during the week. Each one got a certificate and a small honorarium. I made the introductions for the counsellors. The energy in the room was wonderful – people appreciating all the hard work that had been done. Many of the kids spoke short, heartfelt speeches, some doing this for the very first time. In a culture that is based in oral traditions – traditions that were forced underground for many years – the speeches from kids who are always silent had great meaning, both for the rest of the group and for the handful of respected adults who had come to witness our ceremony.

After the workshop, the parents of one participant came to me expressing the changes they were seeing in their son. They wanted me to tell them what he had done in the workshop. I explained to them that I thought it was best if they were patient and learned this from him through his actions and the things he chose to share with them. I explained that it wasn't that I was being secretive, but I knew the things I interpreted about him would not be the same as what actually happened to him. And so if I explained these things, it would set up expectations of their son that would be false. Wouldn't it be better to eliminate me and allow time for this conversation to happen naturally, through word and deed, with their son? They thoughtfully agreed.

legacy

August 23, 1998

I got a triumphant call from Hal last night. The Anspayaxw Community School opened officially and, to mark the opening, Dancers of the Mist (the name of the dance group) performed new Gitxsan dances for the first time in over 100 years. This is a truly historic event. I am in the middle of a *Theatre for Living* training session in Vancouver and couldn't be there, but Hal explained one of the dances to me:

It starts from the *Abusive Love* image in the workshop and also the funeral image, and links the violence in the participants' lives to the violence on the land – the rape of Gitxsan Territory and the sense of mourning in the community. The dancers are a caribou, flowers, the wind, a grouse and salmon.

Hal mentioned that the dance was received with great enthusiasm and emotion from the community – and with awe that the young people who were performing the dances were expressing themselves in such creative, clear and courageous ways.

Here and Now (ਏਥੇ ਤੇ ਹੁਣ)

In late 2004, a series of articles on Indo-Canadian gang violence appeared in the *Vancouver Sun*. Many people, including us at Headlines, considered the articles to be sensationalist. The articles stimulated a conversation in our office, which was eventually reflected in the lobby display audience members saw coming into the theatre at performances of *Here and Now (ਏਥੇ ਤੇ ਹੁਣ)*.[158, 159]

Canada is a multicultural country. Isn't it interesting, we thought, that, 15 or so years ago, these kinds of articles were being written about the Chinese and Vietnamese communities. Then, seven or so years ago, the focus shifted to Latino communities. In 2004, it's the Indo-Canadian community. In five or six years, in all likelihood, the focus will be on some other recent immigrant community.

The truth of the matter is, the issues of violence and gang violence are woven through all of our communities. Why is it, we wondered, that the Hell's Angels just get to be called the Hell's Angels and are not

[158] *Here and Now (ਏਥੇ ਤੇ ਹੁਣ)* was created and performed in 2005 by: Shawn Cheema, Balinder Johal,* Jas Grewal, Natasha Ali Wilson,* Raminder Thind, Seth Ranaweera* and Jagdeep Singh Mangat. Directed and Joked by: David Diamond. Technical Director: Craig Hall. Stage Manager: Kitty Hoffman. Movement Coach: Sudnya Naik. Set, Props and Costume Design: Julie Martens. Lighting Design: Caitlin Pencarrick. Sound Design: Amos Hertzman. Project Support: Sarjeet Purewal. Community Scribe: Kashmir Besla.
*Appeared with permission of the Canadian Actors' Equity Association.
[159] To view the lobby display created by Dafne Blanco go to http://www.headlinestheatre.com/Hereandnow/display1.html

identified as a 'Caucasian gang' or an ethnically defined gang, and yet it is Honduran gangs, Indo-Canadian gangs, etc.?

Out of this conversation the idea for the *Here and Now* (ਏਥੇ ਤੇ ਹੁਣ) project bubbled up. Because the current focus of the media was the Indo-Canadian community, we approached people in that community who knew Headlines' work. We got a very positive response.

And so, almost a year later, after a great deal of networking and fundraising, 22 people from the Indo-Canadian community who were living the issues of gang violence gathered together in a week-long *Theatre for Living* workshop. The cast were part of that group. When I say "living the issues" I mean that some of them were ex-gang members, and some of them were from inside families who were touched by the issues. The age range in the group was 19 to mid-70s.

After the week-long workshop, the cast, production team and I had almost three weeks to make the play. The play did not tell any one person's story. No one portrayed themselves or any one workshop participant. Our job was to make the best theatre possible, to tell the truth of the living community.

Headlines' staff and our many partner organizations worked very hard to invite the general public to the production. Our hope was, because theatre is symbolic, that diverse audiences would come to the production and be able to recognize that the symbol on the stage – a gift to all of us from the Indo-Canadian community – belongs to us all. That the family on the stage could be any family. That the gang members could be any gang members. And that if we could agree that we all share the problem, we could use Forum Theatre to work on the issue together – to seek grassroots solutions to the issues that we share.

As well as the public interactive Forum events each night, there was another layer to this project. Kashmir Besla was the project's *community scribe*. She attended every performance and, in the same way as would happen in a *Legislative Theatre*[160] project, she notated, analyzed

---

[160] In *Legislative Theatre*, interventions from audience members are notated, analyzed, collated and then transformed into legal language as suggestions for law and/or government policy. For full explanations of this process see *Legislative Theatre: Using Performance to Make Politics* by Augusto Boal, published by Routledge, London and New York 1998. See Headlines' report on *Practicing Democracy* at http://www.headlinestheatre.com/pd/index.html

and collated the interventions into a Community Action Report.[161] Instead of this report being aimed at government, it was meant for social service agencies that deal with community issues of violence and family.

pre-production

We will be doing the community workshop at the Moberly Arts Centre in Vancouver. The creation/rehearsal process and the first two weeks of performance will be at the Ross Street Temple, in the Activity Room, adjacent to the actual Temple. The decision to perform the project at the Temple is a challenging one. The room itself poses difficulties – it is relatively small and a very strange shape, but we feel confident that we can get our 14-platform portable stage, lights, etc. in – and seat 100 people – although it will be tight. The reason to be at the Temple is to really reach into the community.

Suki Grewal, who was on the project Advisory Board, did the initial negotiations with the Temple Executive. A signed contract came from the Temple with ease. We met with Kashmir Dhaliwal, who became our Temple contact, and with some of the Executive, and had a productive and straightforward meeting in which we discussed the parameters of the project, including but not limited to:

- There would be no meat consumption or smoking at any time on the premises.
- The play and Forum would be an expression from the community and would need to be portrayed with a sense of reality. This would likely mean violence on the stage and also rough language. The Temple Executive were concerned about nudity, but we assured them that we did not see the potential need for nudity in the project.
- We would have exclusive use of the space.
- We would provide 10 free tickets for each performance, 100 tickets in total, to be distributed by the Temple, so its members, who are used to attending free events, would have access.

---

161 Ms. Besla's full report is available as a PDF document at
http://www.headlinestheatre.com/Hereandnow/finalreports.html

We knew before we started that we would be putting a family on the stage. All of our discussions with community members have been about how gang violence is, in one form or another, a family issue. The participant interviews were intense. We saw 32 people and have space for 25. There were a good number of strong young men and women, all of them with direct experience in the issues. Some grandparent possibilities and mother possibilities, who have experienced the issues from that angle. We have no one right now who could play a father. I have considered simply accepting this and making the mother character a single mother, but feel strongly that this signals a very bad message: broken family = gang violence, which is simply not the case. It feels imperative that we find a father.

We have gone to the people we know to try to network the search for a father, but without success. Many men of this age range are either working at jobs that make it impossible for them to commit the time; others are simply not be interested. Today we started looking through the talent agencies. This may mean that the person in the role will not have the kind of direct experience I feel is necessary, but, I will keep my fingers crossed.

The talent agencies netted zero. I finally did find a father by, interestingly, re-calling someone I had already interviewed. This was a big lesson for me. I had eliminated him initially, because we had so much trouble communicating. He has a difficult time communicating in English, and I have no Punjabi. When I opened myself to the realization that this might in fact be a strength that he brings to the process – part of the complexity of the issue here in Canada – I was able to recognize that he was actually a very strong candidate. I didn't have to speak Punjabi. Other cast members who do could translate when necessary.

And so we have a confirmed cast: Balinder Johal (Grandmother), Raminder Thind (Father), Jas Grewal (Mother), Natasha Ali Wilson (Daughter), and Shawn Cheema and Jagdeep Singh Mangat who, at the moment, may or may not be members of the onstage family.

the community workshop

Day 1 It feels like a sudden start, but as Dafne Blanco, Headlines' outreach coordinator, mentioned in the introductory circle, it has taken us over a year to get to this day.

We have 22 participants. It's a strong, very diverse group and the work today was great. They took to analyzing the imagery in the games pretty much right away. Some of the things that rose up early on were: how some people follow blindly; how, in the community, one is either a leader or a follower; and how there is a sense among some that it's better to be a follower, so people follow. Also discussed were the many reasons people have for not getting involved in trying to deal with the issues: respect for others, not wanting to expose them, fear of others, fear of what others will think, and fear of shame to the family – each of these, in their own way, being silencers.

We have already had images of extreme violence – of parents beating their children – and discussions of how that violence leads kids to seek out others with whom they feel they can belong and feel protected. These violent images are similar to family violence images I encounter in any group wanting to look at that issue. We also had an image of a · funeral and a family in mourning and shock, wondering how the death of their loved one could have happened though such violence.

In one of the images, a grown son is on the floor, curled up, while a woman is slapping him, very firmly. Has he done something terrible? Does the violent reaction from his family drive him further away?

The final circle took almost an hour – a surprise on the first day. People had lots to say about how amazing it is to have a space to really discuss the issues, and about the diversity of experience in the room. One concern I have is that some of the cast members are being quite quiet right now. I am wondering if this comes from me suggesting, when we all met for the first time, that they should "be sponges during the workshop." Do they think I don't want them to participate fully? I will sort this out with them tomorrow.

Day 2 I spoke with the cast first thing in the morning and told them that I thought some of them were sitting back a lot yesterday, and that when I talked with them I didn't mean that they should not participate fully in the workshop. They seemed to understand why I was saying this and acknowledged that they knew they needed to be more activated.

The final *Groups of 4* image was very strong[162] – a mother begging her son to stay – he is on his way into violence. In the background is a father, reading a newspaper, not paying any attention – and a daughter on a cell phone, deeply inside some other world. On animation, this image led to a long discussion about various aspects of the issue.

Many mothers came onto the stage to 'stand with the mother', and when they spoke, none of them knew what they wanted for themselves. Always it was: "I want him to stay, to stop his behaviour, to be a good son," etc. That's what you want HIM to do, I kept saying – what do YOU want? They couldn't answer – and so this was obviously the answer – and also, we realized, part of the problem. The mother, being focused so completely on the son, wanting the best for him, also pushes him away. The group talked about how he leaves because he has no space – he goes to find 'family' in which he can feel safe, because he does not feel safe in the claustrophobic environment in which he is living. The mother gets exactly what she fears, by allowing her fear to govern her behaviour.

At the same time, the father keeps saying (in the image animation), "I want to be back in India." He leaves the problem to his wife – he has 'already left'.

Throughout this, the daughter is walking out the door – to do what? No one knows. No one asks. Why? In discussion, we hear from many participants that the daughter does not matter. She does not belong to the mother or the father – she will belong to some other family and so is not a concern to them. This caused quite an uproar in the room, but when I asked the group if anyone felt it was true – they didn't have to think it was good, or right, or agree, but was it true? – about 70 percent said yes, it's true.

All of this from one image.

---

[162] For an explanation of this exercise see the *Making images* section of the chapter *In the Workshop Room*.

We have created five groups with *Magnetic Image*[163] and have animated one of them. We are at a funeral of a young woman. The scene is complex. Young men are there, very upset, guilty, blaming each other. Young women are there, some of them saying, "She got what she deserved" and "I am so glad this happened to her and not me." Some of the characters are also, as they mourn in a traditional manner, admitting secretly that for them the traditions have no meaning. They are following the traditions because they want people to think well of them. A lot of the image is about how things look on the surface.

On animation, the young men at the funeral get into a physical fight about who is to blame for the death.

In the final circle, many spoke about how amazing it is what has happened in two days; how they had no idea how deep the work would be, many saying the whole community should do this. One of the women talked about how the games draw so deeply on traditional Indian culture.

What is happening in this workshop is what so often happens. The work itself is extremely flexible: it gets inside individual people and the living community on primal levels. If they are still attached to traditional ways in their culture, the work seems to fit those traditional ways. I have witnessed this in Namibia, in New Zealand and in First Nations communities across North America.

Day 3   We got the news this morning that it is possible that on Friday the workshop hall we are in, a civic building, may be behind a picket line. Dylan Mazur, Headlines' administrator, has made arrangements for us to go to the Temple that day if necessary.

The games went well in the morning, and most of the group did *The Intestine*, in which an individual gets moved through a tube of the other participants' arms. This was a big deal for many of them (trust is an issue) and, as I hoped it would, the experience seems to have deepened the connections between people in the room.

---

[163] For an explanation of this exercise see the *Creating plays* section of the chapter *In the Workshop Room*.

There was a really strong image of three men – one is on the ground, knocked out. Another has a gun and is trying to get his friend to shoot the man who has passed out. The scenario is that they beat him up and then realized he is from a more powerful gang than theirs. If he lives, he and his gang will come and kill them. But they don't kill him. The improvisation about needing to kill him, but one of them not wanting to, was very powerful. Most powerful was a moment when one of the men put the gun to his friend's head and threatened to kill him if he didn't shoot the other man. But then he backed off. The decision to NOT pull the trigger was huge.

This improvisation affected the room very deeply. Many of the participants recognized the truth of it, which made me wonder about something: I asked how many of them had held a gun that was not for sport. About 65 to 70 percent of them raised their hands. These are people who are in the room because of their struggles with gang violence, but the numbers still surprised me and the participants themselves.

Day 4   A lot of the activities this morning were chosen to bring the group 'into the moment' in preparation for Rainbow of Desire this afternoon and making plays tomorrow.

The Journey[164] helped them understand, experientially, that reality is perception based. In one of the pairings, the leader created a scene where her partner was getting ready to go to work at a construction site – putting on boots, a hard hat, etc. The partner's experience was of taking off his shoes, preparing for prayer. Which one is the true experience? Both, of course. And it's easy to see how this translates into different perceptions inside a family. This doesn't mean that everyone is right – the abusive father isn't correct in what he is doing, but can we understand that he has a perspective on the events that lead him to believe he is correct? We must do this if we are going to portray a character with integrity – especially a character with whom we disagree.

---

[164] See *the journey* in the *Several senses* section of the *Appendix*.

I spent a lot of time on *Speed Gestures*[165] – an exercise I have developed to stimulate improvisation skills. By the end of an hour of moving from simple sound and gestures into exchanging gestures and sentences, and accepting realities that were being created, participants were making complex, focused improvisations.

The group chose the story of a young woman for the Rainbow of Desire. It's about her and her father. She is sitting watching TV. The mail is on the table. He enters the living room and picks up the mail, a bank statement in her name, and goes to open it. She tells him not to – it's her mail. The ensuing argument is all about power, about her being under his control, about his desire and perceived right to open her mail and look at her money if he wants to.

A young man offered to play Dad. The young woman's Rainbow fragments included: wanting to punch him in the face; wanting respect from him; wanting the letter; and a fear that he would hit her. His Rainbow fragments included: a fear that she would never understand him; a desire to leave the room and have peace; and a desire to put her in her place by slapping her.

The work was very deep. Her fear seemed to empower the father; it gave him exactly what he wanted and, in the end, he had no respect for her. In another improvisation the levels of anger rose so high, the two characters were screaming at each other. Many of us thought the scene was certainly going to escalate to violence. Then there was a moment, when he was talking about how he wanted her respect, and she replied very calmly, "Well, if you do, then you must see that the mail belongs to me." Somehow he heard this. He tried to ignore it, but he couldn't. We all saw the understanding of what the daughter had said go into him and discussed it later. It was like emotional judo – and it was done so calmly.

In another moment, when the father's desire to slap her was onstage, he was saying, "What's wrong? Don't I take care of you and your mother? Why are you afraid?" All the while he had his hand raised above his head, ready to slap. She said, "Well then, why is your hand raised?" It was amazing. The father had forgotten it was there – a 'true

---

[165] See *speed gestures* in *The power of gesture* section of the chapter *In the Workshop Room*.

moment'. He is so accustomed to this, it is normal now. How can he stop being aggressive if he has forgotten his raised hand is even there?

The insights in the exercise today are not about finding actual solutions to that story – the story is a symbol. We are all reflecting the moments back into our own lives and investigating what we do and how we perceive the actions and behaviour of others – deepening our understandings of character for the play.

The final circle took just over an hour today – the longest yet. For the first time everyone spoke – and there were some long stories and lots of tears from some of the very young people, who told stories about their fathers and mothers and home life, stories about friends who died. We make plays tomorrow.

We will be working at the Ross Street Temple tomorrow.

I have been considering that we may not be able to tell the story we may need to tell with one young woman and two young men, and one grandmother, one mother, one father. We may need another youth. I checked the budgets today and we do have funds in the year to hire another actor. I am talking with Seth Ranaweera, one of the workshop participants.

Day 5 At lunch break I asked the cast to join me for a quick chat and explained my sense of needing another youth. They responded immediately that they had been talking among themselves about exactly that, and for the same reasons: they feel the work right now is weighted too far into the domestic and not enough into the gangs. I agree. With a fourth youth in the cast, the weight will shift in creation. They asked me who I was considering and I told them Seth. They were very, very happy with the choice. He is a strong performer and also brings experience into the group. Then I talked with Seth, and he agreed.

The reason to make these plays in the workshop is not that they will necessarily provide material for the larger project. The plays are a continuation of a research process – they are not product. I feel it is important for the workshop participants to have some closure by the end of the workshop. Making the plays and doing Forum helps this a great deal.

Play 1 (Secrets at Home) Grandmother, Mother, Father and Older Daughter (22) are at home. Grandmother is making tea. Mother is wandering around the room, while Father and Older Daughter are watching TV. Father wants his tea and Grandmother tells Mother to take it to him. In the process, the sour relationships between Grandmother and her daughter-in-law, and between the husband and wife, are revealed. Because she is upset, Mother sends Older Daughter into the kitchen to help Grandmother.

Son comes home – the favourite (and only) son. He is in a rush. He wants the car. And he wants $500 for hockey tickets. Mother and Father work out between them how to give him the money. Older Daughter is outraged and says, "Do you want to know what he is doing with the money?" He quickly silences her. Grandmother pulls him aside and wants to know what he is doing with the money. He knows she knows it's for drugs, and she knows he knows she knows. He gets his way by loving her. She tells him to promise to be good. He kisses her and leaves.

Younger Daughter enters (14). She is getting into fights at school and has had detention. Her parents want to know where she has been, but she won't say. She goes to the kitchen. She loves her grandma and compliments her on her cookies. She eats one. Grandmother takes the opening and brings over a book with pictures in it – of a man in India, a man she wants the Younger Daughter to agree to marry. Younger Daughter is repulsed – she is 14. An argument starts between her and Grandmother in which the Younger Daughter is disrespectful. This infuriates Grandmother, who grabs her by the hair.

Younger Daughter starts yelling. Mother gets involved and backs Grandmother up. She starts to slap Younger Daughter. Older Daughter, who has tried in vain to stop it, calls the police.

The police come and there is nothing visible happening. They question Younger Daughter, who stands up for her family. The police leave. The family think Younger Daughter called the police. When they find out it was Older Daughter, they gang up on her and beat her.

Day 6 The three other plays are:

Play 2 (The Perfect Daughter) A mother and father are in their home. Mother is up late and worried about both older kids who are not home yet. It's 3:00 AM. Father enters and, in a caring way, wonders what is going on. Realizing she is waiting for the kids, he says he will wait up with her. She doesn't want this, knowing if he is there when they arrive, there will be trouble. He insists.

The two youth are in the car. Son and Daughter. Daughter is very drunk and Son is taking care of her, getting her home. On the way there, they discuss how he is always getting into trouble and how she gets away with everything. She promises that he won't take 'the heat' over this.

They arrive home and the father immediately launches into his son. Son says he was just driving his sister home from a party. In an attempt to save her brother, Daughter says it was she who drove home and she is the reason they were late. Now they are caught in a lie and it escalates. Father assumes Son has been driving drunk.

Little Sister enters and tells on them, saying that Daughter has a boyfriend – something the parents do not believe, because they think their daughter is perfect. Little Sister tells them that Son is hanging out with a drug dealer. Father confronts the son – it gets physical and violent.

Play 3 (Reluctant Killer) This is a very complex little play. Sister and Young Man are in love. They are in Young Man's car, sharing life stories.

Brother (Sister's brother) is on the phone in their home, talking to a member of his gang. Brother and Sister have been robbed by Sam (who we never meet), a member of another gang, in a drug deal gone bad. Sam is Young Man's cousin. On the phone, Brother gets the news that Young Man and Sister are seeing each other. He sees them in the driveway when he looks out the window.

Brother calls Sister's cell phone. She sees it is him on call display and is immediately worried. She silences Young Man and answers. Brother interrogates her about who she is in the car with and orders her into the house. He hangs up on her. She knows she must go and tries to explain to Young Man. He insists on taking her to the door, saying he isn't afraid of Brother.

Brother meets them at the door. He is civil, in a very cold way, and gets Sister inside, stopping Young Man from entering. Young Man tries to make a connection, but cannot. He is sent away. He returns to his car.

Inside, Brother and Sister argue about how much control he exerts over her life. He explains about Young Man being Sam's cousin, and Sister yells that Young Man is not Sam. Brother does not operate at this level.

He notices Young Man hasn't left yet. Sister knows that it means the car won't start. She runs out with Brother and tries to give Young Man her keys, just to get him out of there. Young Man sees it as an opportunity for him and Brother to bond, over car talk, and sends her away. Brother starts Young Man's car and then suggests they go for a drive to get to know each other. Young Man agrees.

Sister watches through the window and is panicking. She calls Young Man's cell phone. Brother tells him not to answer it – it's likely Sister and she drives him crazy with her interfering. They stop at a beer store. Brother says he has forgotten his cell phone and asks to borrow Young Man's – who agrees. Brother enters the store and throws Young Man's phone away. He buys a case of beer and gets back in the car.

They drive up the mountain. Brother plies Young Man with beer, keeping his own consumption down. At the top of the mountain, they exit the car and look out over the city. They have a talk about Sister – Young Man loves her. Brother talks about Sam. Young Man says he isn't close to Sam and he knows he's into heavy things, but he isn't Sam – and whatever has happened between Brother and Sam has nothing to do with him. The conversation feels friendly. Understanding.

Brother laments that Young Man is a good guy – too bad the circumstances are not different. Brother walks behind Young Man and shoots him in the head.

Brother goes home, where Sister is waiting. She is frantic. She has been calling Young Man. Young Man wasn't answering his phone. What did Brother do to Young Man? Brother, in a loving way, tells her it's all OK – he took care of Young Man. Sister knows what this means and screams at him – crying. He tells her she will get over it and, exiting, tells her he's going to bed and not to bother him.

Sister goes to her drawer and, in a moment of revenge on her brother, takes a great many sleeping pills.

Play 4 (The Meddling Brother) Grandmother is making tea for Older Brother. Older Brother is waiting for his Younger Brother. Younger Brother enters and Older Brother confronts him with what he found when he was going through his drawers. (A bag of drugs) Younger Brother is very angry that his brother has gone through his drawer, and they argue about privacy and who's house it is and who has control in the house.

Grandmother intervenes and says the house is home to all of them. The argument escalates, and Mother enters. She tries to separate her sons, but the yelling is escalating. Father arrives home and is immediately drawn into the fight. Older Brother tells Father what he has found and Father is furious. Younger Brother yells at his dad, "Why would you be concerned now – you never have been before!" He pushes Father. Older Brother attacks Younger Brother physically for this, punching him in the face.

We did Forum on all the plays. There were a lot of powerful moments, but two were particularly powerful.

In the 'Reluctant Killer' play, a male participant replaced Brother when the two guys were up the mountain. He recognized Brother's struggle in having to shoot Younger Man. It sounds strange, but it is very important, I think, to recognize that from the character's perspective, in order to retain his place in the community, in order to remain 'safe' in the world in which he now lives, he must retain a reputation for brutality. A part of him does not want to kill this kid who loves his sister, and who she loves. He is convinced, though, that he must.

The heart of this, and something I think that is important to the play we will make, is the human side of the Brother character. He cannot be a monster. He must be a recognizable human trapped in a seemingly impossible situation, even if it is one of his own making.

The other moment was in the 'Secrets at Home' play. The interventions were all about the youth – none of them dealt with the terrible situation in the home with the mother or grandmother. I asked the room if they saw the struggles of these women. "Yes," many said. "Then why no interventions?" I asked. This brought us into the same conversation we had a couple of days ago: Elders, particularly women, participants said, can be beaten, emotionally abused, etc., as is too often the case, and no one notices. No one wants to know.

A female participant replaced Mother in this play and refused to give Brother any money. Brother was on the verge of agreeing to stay home, when the grandmother decided to give him the money herself. This was a great shock to everyone. Off went Brother to the drug deal. "Why did you do this?" I asked the grandmother. "Harm reduction," she answered. "Well, what I observed," I said, and asked her to correct me if I was mistaken, "was that you gave him the money because his mother wasn't going to – it had very little to do with Brother – it had to do with the battle between you and your daughter-in-law." She thought for a moment and admitted that this was likely the case – on a subconscious level. Many in the room agreed. The two women are at war, and the battleground is the young people in the home.

In the final circle, the group was very happy, very moved by the Forum. Many of them have expressed interest in helping with publicity or other tasks necessary to make sure the larger play is a success. I have reminded them all that they are very welcome to drop into rehearsals.

On Tuesday, the cast of seven, Kitty Hoffman (stage manager), Sudnya Naik (movement coach) and I meet at the Temple and start the process of figuring out the journey of the play.

creation and rehearsal

October 25, 2005
We got a lot done today – all 'background work', but it will pay off shortly. We started to understand the characters' relationships in the family. The more solid these are, the more coherently we can do Forum Theatre. We accomplished this through a lot of talking, but I also had the actors make images about how they feel their characters might fit into the family relationships as they evolved.

It took the actors weeks to find their character names. For the purposes of this report, I am going to start calling them by their character names now:

Balinder Johal is Grandmother	Daadi
Raminder Thind is Father	Jeewan
Jas Grewal is Mother	Rupa
Natasha Ali Wilson is Daughter	Sonya
Shawn Cheema is Son	Jay
Jagdeep Singh Mangat is a gangster	Kam
Seth Ranaweera is a gangster	Sunny

Daadi and her late husband came to Canada with two of their children when she was 40 years old. Jeewan (her eldest son) was 22 at the time and he stayed in India. She had him at 18. After eight years her husband died. She didn't want to return to India, so Jeewan, the dutiful son, came to Canada when he was 30. He left behind a young woman whom he loved. He came on a visitor visa. In India, he had been overseeing their family land. They are an agricultural family. He was a landlord.

One year after arriving, his mother arranged for him to marry Rupa so he could stay in Canada. It is a loveless marriage. Shortly after marrying, they had Sonya, who is now 20. This makes Jeewan 51. Daadi is in her early 70s and Rupa is in her late 40s. We don't know right now if Jay is their child or not, but we think he is. We know he is 16.

Jeewan is driving taxi. He was a powerful man in India. Rupa is working, we think, in an office. It's clear they are both working. Jeewan feels that everyone – his mother, his wife, his kids – blames him for the trouble in the family. They do not communicate internally. No one in the family feels respected. We acknowledged today that the respect issue is important. It isn't that the kids and parents don't respect each other; it's that the respect doesn't manifest the way they want it to. The parents aren't respected the way they want to be. The kids aren't respected the way they want to be. And so, no one feels respected.

Jay is smoking marijuana pretty much every day and may, we think, be sometimes selling cocaine. He finds somewhere to belong and it is with Kam, who provides him with 'materials' and a phone with which to do business. Jay believes he is going to be rich – going to have everything he wants – which includes being nothing like his 'loser' father.

We don't know a lot at the moment about Sunny or Sonya.

The young cast members also agreed that the idea of having a 'park' as part of the set was very important, as this is where their business tends to be done.

Today Sudnya (movement coach) gave some of the cast individualized and interesting exercises to do at home and throughout the day. She is starting a physical process: we are trying to build an awareness of their bodies and their movements, because there is a plan to experiment in this play with frozen, suspended image and shadow.

October 26, 2005
In the morning we looked at each character, by asking the character to create an image of themselves in the play. I have never done this before – it's a nice discovery. The images led to deep and complex discussions about each character and the other characters' relationships to them. I took Polaroid photographs of each image.

Then we started putting together a list of 'things that need to happen in the play'. Here they are, in the order they came to us in discussion:

- Jay gets recruited into a gang or 'crew'. We believe this happens to Jay, although at this point it's still open.

- A family member is assaulted (inside the family). There is some kind of abuse, physical and/or emotional aimed at either the grandmother or the mother. It is a secret inside the home.

- There is a cultural disconnect between generations. There was a long discussion about how the generation (sometimes agrarian) coming from India has great difficulty communicating with the younger generation (in the city and now urban) in Canada. They have different values, experiences, expectations. Words, which are always symbols, have very different meanings for each 'side'.

- Someone gets shot. Someone in this play either gets shot, or is threatened with getting shot. We don't know if it is Jay, Sonya, the father, the mother, Kam or Sunny. It doesn't appear to be the grandmother.

- We see the family in a good light. If we need to see the dysfunction of the family, we cannot understand it without contextualizing it from within the caring aspects of the family.

- Convenient denial empowers Jay. Jay starts getting money. Someone in the family (Father, Mother or Grandmother) knows exactly what is happening and where the money is coming from and could stop it if they tried. Instead, they are either as allured by the power of the money as Jay is, or they are frightened by the possibility of exposure and 'decide' to not know.

- There is a power struggle in the gang (of two). Kam and Sunny have known each other since early childhood. Kam is about 27; Sunny is about 30 or 32. As children, Kam looked up to Sunny, but in adulthood, it has become Kam who holds the authority. This, and other factors we do not yet know, creates tension. There is a power struggle inside the relationship, which represents a larger gang.

- Sonya tries to assert herself. Sonya cannot fit into her family. She cannot be the compliant girl that her grandmother and father, in particular, want her to be. She has tried. Somehow, we need to see her try to assert her individuality as a young woman and to see how the reaction to that alienates her even further from her family.

- A youth struggles to get out. Sonya and/or Jay get embroiled in the gang, and then have to face their desire to 'get out' of gang life and how difficult this is. The discussion centred around the addictive nature of entering that world and how the struggle is not with others, but with one's self. I believe this scene could be highly symbolic and be, somehow, about internal voices.

- A youth seeks safety/'home'. Sonya and/or Jay are both in a home that they do not feel is either 'safe' or 'home'. It is the reason they go looking for somewhere else to belong. They find safety in a much more unsafe place.

- Reaching the point of no return. There has been a lot of discussion about reaching the point of no return – of having to kill someone, having to do the drug deal, having to commit to the violence. We need to see this happen onstage, but are not certain at the moment how this will happen.

There are holes in all of this, of course – some of it will be in the play and some of it will not. There will be other scene ideas that come, which we have no idea about right now. It is remarkable how much of what we talked about today came from images, discussions and the plays that got made in the community workshop. That consciousness is at the table. Tomorrow we will start the process of finding an order in what we have and turning the ideas into physical improvisations.

October 27, 2005
We have been in talking mode this last couple of days. Part of my task today was to move us into working on our feet.

The better part of the morning was taken with discussion, which started with BC Attorney General (AG) Wally Oppal's statement yesterday, in response to recent gang shootings, that "sometimes there are people who we just need to give up on." The feeling of the group seems to mesh with my own, and that is that as government policy, this is an extremely dangerous and highly inappropriate thing for the AG to say. If we embrace this concept, where is the boundary? Is it not the case that Jagdeep, who is an articulate, concerned and active part of the solutions in his and other communities – and who was a deeply involved gangster years ago – would have been beyond caring about?

We also explored, in the morning, how the family functions: sitting watching TV, reading, just being together. It was like getting our toes wet. I had meant to do the same with Kam and Sunny, but the exploration with the two friends evolved into a far more meaningful exercise.

I asked them to be the small children they were when they met, when Sunny was 10 and Kam seven. The actors rolled their eyes and I knew it would be hard for them. I am very pleased that they trusted me. And so, Farina (workshop participant), who had come to visit, played Sunny's mother and introduced the boys. Kam's parents had come for dinner. The adults were upstairs drinking and the boys had 30 minutes downstairs alone until dinner. Sunny wants this potential new friend to like him and so he starts 'playing host' – getting Cokes from the downstairs fridge (knowing he shouldn't) and chips from the cupboard, and the boys bond eating food they shouldn't eat before dinner. We realize later that this first moment sets the relationship and is the reason there is tension between them now. For so many years, Sunny has been 'getting sugar' for Kam – it's just the definition of sugar that has changed. We skipped forward 10 years. Sunny has his first car and is taking his friend Kam for a ride. They stop at a drive-in for burgers. We can see how close they are – even when Kam spills ketchup and mayonnaise on the seat of Sunny's prized car. Sunny brings his friend into a crime world that he himself has entered.

Now they are 27 and 30. Both adults – not kids anymore. And it's Kam who is the more ambitious of the two. Sunny moves too slowly, is too conservative. The leadership role is switching and this is making these best friends tense with each other.

(Like a lightening bolt – I think I know who gets shot at the end of the play! It's Sunny. Kam forces Jay to shoot Sunny. Is this too much? I will run it by the cast tomorrow.)[166]

---

[166] This realization came in the evening while I was writing the journal entry for the day.

After lunch we went into 'mush land' and it was scary. I think it happened because I chose the wrong moment to focus into — trying to find perhaps the most difficult thing we need — the bridge, the connecting scene that brings Jay to Kam and Sunny.

And so I decided to look at the family dynamic again and had a lovely surprise. I think we may have found the opening of the play. I asked that we investigate the 'rituals' of the family's morning. We worked this a lot. It's 'normal land'. It's mostly movement, with some phrases thrown in. And it's all about physical timing.

> It's morning. Jay is asleep on the sofa (so — now we have a sofa as part of the set — a big decision). Daadi enters with tea for him, stands and admires him, puts her finger in his ear — toying with her grandson. He moves. She touches his neck, and having fun, tickles him. He wakes up, startled, but knows he is home and safe. She gives him tea.

> Before he can drink, Sonya runs in from her bedroom, takes his cup, sips, gives it back to him, goes to the kitchen to get her own tea.

> As Sonya is crossing, Mother enters (up the stage right stairs) from her night work; she is exhausted. She sees Daadi and Jay, but says nothing and heads for the kitchen. She meets Sonya and they say good morning. Sonya crosses, asking where her shoes are, and exits stage right to her bedroom, while Jay goes after Mother, looking for food. She tells him to ask Daadi. Mother turns back and crosses stage right, while Father comes (up the stage left stairs) from Temple. They circle each other and exchange hellos. Mother says she is going to bed and exits stage right. Father watches his wife go and says "OK" to himself and is left at the sofa with his mother, for whom he has brought a morning ceremonial sweet. She pulls up her shawl; eats the sweet. A prayer moment.

> While this has been happening, Jay has crossed stage right and entered the bathroom and is brushing his teeth (this works in mime — does not need a material location). Sonya knocks on the door (good naturedly, as happens every morning) and tells him to hurry up. He exits and goes to the sofa

> where Daadi and Father are, while Sonya enters the bath-
> room. Jay asks Father for money – Father signals he should
> go to Mother. Daadi says, "Give him the money." Jay gets his
> daily $20 from Father, kisses Daadi (not thanking Father) and
> runs out the door – down the downstage stairs. Father says to
> Daadi, in Punjabi, "You are spoiling that boy." Sonya exits the
> bathroom, yells goodbye and runs down the same stairs as
> Jay. Daadi says, in English, "I am not spoiling him."

This works in a choreographed way – a morning ritual, and through it
we are introduced to the family. The next thing that will happen will be
meeting Sunny and Kam, in mid-argument about something that went
wrong on the street last night.

October 28, 2005
In our morning check-in I mentioned the idea that had burst in my
head about it being Sunny who gets shot at the end of the play by Jay.
Daadi gasped and then there was a very long silence at the table. Kam
and Sunny and Jay were looking at each other and nodding, nodding
and staring into each others' eyes. "Of course. It has to be that," said
Sunny. Kam agreed that with what we know about them now and how
Kam is climbing the power ladder, and the power he has over Jay, that
it made sense. Jay just kept nodding his head, absorbing, I think, what
this might mean.

Perhaps partly because of this new knowledge, the Sunny/Kam
relationship is becoming beautifully clear in rehearsal now. The two
guys play very well together. Their first scene will be in the park in
daytime. In it, we meet the two young men, who are childhood friends,
in mid-argument. We understand they are gangsters and see that Kam
is far more ambitious than Sunny. Even in this first scene we can see
that the power relationship between the two is shifting.

Then we fast-forward to dinnertime.

> Daadi is making chapatis in the kitchen. Mother is watching
> TV from her chair beside the sofa. Father is watching TV from
> the sofa.

Jay comes home and claims the sofa and the television. Father gives up on TV and moves behind the sofa, on his way to the kitchen.

Sonya enters, talking on her cell phone (to Sunny, but we don't know that yet). She is laughing, making plans to meet later. She moves through the living room on her way to her bedroom when Father calls to her. "Sonya." And again. She stops. "Who are you talking to?" (in Punjabi) "No one...a friend." "Who are you talking to?" "A friend." "You don't say just a friend." Father takes her by the arm and drags her away from the bedroom, into the living room. An argument starts between Sonya and Father. Mother intervenes and gently tells Sonya to go, that it's OK. Sonya kisses her mom and leaves.

Father feels that Mother has undermined him. He says that Sonya needs to behave, and Mother says that he has to try to understand her better. Father says he would never have been allowed to talk with his father that way, and Mother responds that he isn't in India anymore.

Daadi has by now come from the kitchen and stands with her son against her daughter-in-law. It gets more and more heated until the two women are yelling at each other about who is the head of the family. Because Mother is disrespecting his mother by talking back to Daadi, Father slaps his wife across the face. Jay has been trying quietly to stop this as it has escalated, but when Father slaps Mother, Jay leaps at his father who, in a rage, turns and pushes him onto the floor. Jay, shocked, yells "Fuck you!" at his father and runs out of the house.

Sonya, who has come back into the living room as the fight has escalated, goes out after her brother.

Lunchtime was filled with a production meeting. The design team are, rightly so, impatient, wanting to know what the play is that they are designing. Of course, we don't really know yet.

After lunch: What follows is a lovely little scene between the brother and sister – on the stairs.

They sit in silence for a bit. Sonya breaks the tension by joking with Jay about his muscles and being a tough guy, but this quickly turns into her embracing him. He has stood up to his father for the first time. Silence. She tells him that she is meeting some friends for dinner. He suggests that they should probably get into the house for dinner there, but it is she who says, "No way." She asks if he wants to come with her. "Really?" She has never suggested he hang out with her friends before. "Sure." And they leave together.

Kam and Sunny are at the restaurant. They are once again in the conversation from the first scene, but it is interrupted by Sonya and Jay arriving. They like Sonya and are happy to see her and are surprised about her bringing her little brother. We get a lovely scene here, full of friendly chat and banter. They joke with Jay, because they know he is dealing a little marijuana, being a 'kid gangster'. At the same time, they are congratulating him – building him up – because they hear good things about him. The scene is full of warmth and laughter and it is obvious that this 'dangerous place' is a much nicer place to be than at home. Eventually, the banter ends, and they sit in silence. Sunny and Kam have things they need to discuss and can't do it in front of Sonya and Jay.

But, in the silence, Kam has an idea. He sees Jay in a new way and, without consulting Sunny, which would be normal, he starts to sound Jay out about working with them. Jay is eager for this. It makes Sunny very uncomfortable. He is insulted that Kam is doing this on his own and tries to shut it down, but can't. Sunny makes an excuse to leave – angry.

Kam gets straightforward with Jay. There is work for him if he wants – he could make a lot of money. Sonya hadn't intended bringing Jay so he could join Kam, who she knows is into very heavy gang activity, and she tries to get herself and Jay out of the situation. But Jay wants to work with Kam, and the two guys tell her to relax. Kam tells her to leave; he wants to talk with Jay alone. She doesn't want to go, but Kam insists in such a way that she knows she has no choice. Jay allows this. Once alone, they agree to proceed – Jay will work for Kam, and not tell Sunny anything.

I think we are about halfway through the play. Before we went home, we ran what we have and it held together pretty well. But there is also a lot of work still to do.

I had to confront a design dilemma today: as we understand more and more of the play, it increasingly takes place in very strange, undefined space. I have to allow the play itself to define the space, not the other way around. So I have decided to throw design concerns aside and just let the drama become what it needs to be. I know this will put us into a time crunch later, but it feels like the best way to proceed.

I am also thinking seriously about letting go of the shadows idea.[167] I talked it over with the cast, as Sudnya isn't around right now, and we agreed that the shadows will only work if the people making them are not identifiable. It would be easier if all the actors were playing multiple roles in the play, but they are not; each cast member will be identifiable, even in shadow. The shadows seemed like a good theoretical idea before work started, but they may not fit into this play.

At the end of today a couple of the cast expressed how intense they are finding the process of all this discovery through improvisation – and, as a result, the deep questions they are asking themselves about their past experiences. I had a long and good talk with one of them after rehearsal. I have also reminded them that Sarjeet, the support person, who was part of the community workshop, is also still available if they want to access her.

October 29, 2005
We reworked the restaurant scene so that Sunny leaves, but secretly waits outside. At some point in the scene, Sonya's phone rings. She checks it, notices it is her home number (Daadi) calling, and doesn't answer. Eventually Kam sends Sonya away – she tries to stay but he and Jay insist she leave and wait for Jay in her car. Kam and Jay strike a deal for Jay to do work for Kam. Jay leaves.

Kam leaves and is confronted by Sunny in the parking lot. Kam is so surprised that he pulls his gun, not knowing for a moment that it is Sunny. They have an intense conversation

---

[167] I had a directorial idea very early on about using the actors' bodies to project shadows on screens as a way to underline or counterpoint scenes.

about the inappropriateness of Kam recruiting Jay without first talking with Sunny. The gulf between them is widening.

We go to black. In the darkness, we hear Sonya's voice-mail greeting and her grandmother's voice leaving a message: "Sonya, dinner is waiting. Where are you? Is Jay with you?"

Lights come up slightly onstage. Daadi is waiting. It is 10:30 or 11:00 PM. Rupa has gone to work. Jeewan is asleep (or trying to sleep). Daadi is waiting up. The kids come home. Sonya is trying to get her brother to tell her about the conversation between him and Kam. He won't and orders her into the house, the way Kam ordered her out of the restaurant. She stands her ground (which I think, at the moment, is the wrong choice for the scene), so he goes in.

I think Sonya needs to enter first, because we then have the potential for her to tell her grandmother about what has just happened. She won't tell, but the potential creates a space for the audience before Jay enters.

Daadi is very relieved to see them, and the kids try to calm her down. When Daadi feels safe, she gently confronts Sonya. Daadi says that Sonya should understand that she is her father's "honour". Sonya has heard this lecture before and tries to escape, but Daadi won't let her – she is doing the best she can for her granddaughter.

Jeewan has heard the voices and enters. He is also very relieved they are home. He approaches his daughter, but she doesn't want to be near him. He asks her if a father doesn't have the right to ask his daughter questions. She answers he has the right, but the daughter has the right to not answer. He says that he needs to know sometimes what she is doing, where she is going. She replies that, in Canada, girls talk to boys. He says to her in Punjabi that she doesn't understand, but when she has children of her own, she will understand. She replies in English that she doesn't have to have children to understand this – and tells him to speak English.

Sonya confronts him about the violence to her mother. Daadi comes across and behind Sonya in support of Jeewan. Sonya is trying to stand up to them, but is outnumbered. Her brother, who could help, and who no one has asked about anything in this exchange, announces he is going to bed. He exits.

It took hours to get this scene today. The cast members, while saying that they wanted to get under the surface of the scene, kept finding ways in the improvisations to avoid doing just that. This happens sometimes in any rehearsal process. But if finding some hidden truth is something we all agree we want to do, then the director (in this case me) has to find ways to help it happen.

In one moment, just when we were getting somewhere in what had been quite a superficial improvisation, Sonya exited to her bedroom. Jeewan stopped the scene. I suggested he go after her. He just looked at me. Go, follow her to the bedroom, continue the conversation, I suggested. I decided, as a director, to push things, to trap the Sonya character. Jeewan said, "But she has left the stage." I reminded him, as we have discussed so many times, that there is no offstage. He went to the daughter's bedroom, and the characters agreed to 'talk about it in the morning'. "OK, it's morning," I said. It took two or three more exchanges to get the father and daughter sitting together, actually having the conversation that the daughter and father needed to have.

What we are experiencing in rehearsal is the difficulty of confronting the issues in real life. This is why we rehearse. It is theatre about real life, but it is not real life – it is the theatre. There is no point just putting real life on the stage; we can see that at home. If the theatre is going to be an opportunity to get deeper into the hidden issues, then we have to find ways to put those hidden issues on the stage in theatrical form.

At the end of the day, we ran everything we had. I am trying to remember that I have been in these self-questioning moments before with both *Practicing Democracy* (2004) and *Don't Say a Word* (2003) and perhaps every other mainstage project. In the middle of creation, running what we have got so far, I suddenly found that what seemed like strong material yesterday, or three days ago, now seemed so thin. Well, all of us were exhausted by the end of the week. The work has been extremely intense, and the cast don't really know what the scenes are beyond the skeletal structures. Although I know all this, I was, nevertheless, in a panic for a while after the run.

I have to remind myself that material like this – material that is not script based – relies on emotional engagement, not on words. It's very difficult at this stage for the actors to feel their way through the emotional engagement – they are too busy trying to remember what happens next. We all have to be patient.

We have a photo shoot for publicity Tuesday morning and then have Tuesday and Wednesday to finish finding the skeletal story. Then we have to get into the scenes in detail and start putting flesh on them. We have a lot to do.

November 1, 2005
We did a terrific photo shoot with theatre and dance photographer David Cooper[168] this morning; it was time very well spent, because of the quality of the work.

Before lunch I went over various suggestions with the cast that I had considered on the weekend:

- Mother can't work nights, which will mean reworking the opening. Working nights eliminates her from the night scenes, and therefore from the rest of the play.

- Kam and Sunny need to work out the minute details of their current situation. The two actors did this over the course of the afternoon, and it's great. They have charted out who their own and the other local 'crews' are – names and numbers. And they know the size of an upcoming drug deal (with amounts in kilos) and the reasons, both financial and territorial, that Kam wants to take it over and eliminate the man who would be their superior, and why Sunny feels it's all getting out of control. Doing this led them to understand that they were not, in fact, working in the 'same world' last week. So, this was a great step forward for them and they had a good time doing it. They also agree that the Sunny character wants to get out of the gang life. This becomes the reason he finds

---

[168] http://www.davidcooperphotography.com

himself at the end of a gun at the end of the play, in the same way that people today are being shot for wanting out.

- Jay can't be a gangster off the top of the play – the character has nowhere to travel.

- Sonya needs to stay in the house after Mother gets slapped, and not run directly out to Jay. This will extend that family scene and let us explore the Sonya character's dynamic in the family more.

- When the kids return from the restaurant, Sonya must enter first and decide not to tell Grandmother what happened at the restaurant.

- Kam and Jay need a scene in which Kam gives Jay a gun.

- We need to find our way to the end of the play.

After lunch, Sudnya did her first movement work with the group. This was also very good – reawakening their body awareness after the workshop, and also, at a very basic level, waking them up. We will try to do this 20-minute routine every morning from now on. The cast seemed to like it, too.

We did detailed work today on the first family scene and then the scene where Mother gets hit. Because the scene escalates into an argument in which the characters are overlapping each other vocally and then into violence, it needs to be very detailed. The actors need to be completely confident and safe inside the chaos of the scene.

The scene, which is two or three minutes long, took over three hours to work. When we ran it at the end of the day, the structure was there, but all the lovely builds, the ebbs and flows that had been in it, were gone. We will come back to it.

Tomorrow we must redo the scene where the kids come home from the restaurant, to bring the mother into that scene.

November 2, 2005
We did what at one point today I thought was highly unlikely – we made it to the end of the play. We may have a very strong story.

We reworked the scene where the kids come home – now that Mother is no longer working nights. Daadi is pacing. Mother enters from her bedroom, and we see them try to speak about the earlier violence but not be able to. Jay enters the porch area, followed quickly by Sonya. She is trying to get information out of him regarding his exchange with Kam. He tells her it is none of her business and orders her into the house. Furious and frustrated, she goes. Jay remains on the stairs.

> Sonya is hoping everyone is asleep, but there are Daadi and Rupa (Mother). "Shit," says Sonya, under her breath. Daadi asks Sonya where she was. "Out for dinner." "Was your brother with you?" "Yes." "Where is he?" "Just outside." Daadi goes to the door and Sonya calls to her, wanting to tell her about Kam, but she chickens out. Daadi calls Jay into the house while Sonya goes and checks on her mother.
>
> Daadi calls the two kids together and, in a loving way, admonishes them. Jay tells her not to worry – they are safe. Calming down, Daadi turns her attention to Sonya. She is her father's pride...etc. Sonya doesn't need to hear this right now and tries to get away. Daadi insists. Mother tries to get her mother-in-law to stop, but Daadi has to get it out. It's not angry – it is full of caring. If only Daadi can get her granddaughter to understand...
>
> Jeewan enters and listens to his mother tell his daughter that she is his pride. Jeewan thanks his mother – both meaning this and also telling her he will take over. Sonya does not want to deal with her dad at all and heads for her room, her refuge. Daadi and Jeewan stop her – she is going to listen.
>
> Jeewan tries to reach out across a great cultural divide to his daughter. But she laughs at his Punjabi and his insistence that he has rights over her. "Yes," she says, "you have the right to ask questions, and I have the right to not answer."

Jay, having been left alone, abandons his sister and announces he is going to bed – he has no need to listen to any of this. Sonya is furious that they just let him go. He's the boy and they are interrogating her – especially considering what she knows happened tonight. She yells at her father, "You have no idea – no idea what is going on in this family!" Her yelling infuriates him – he tells her he wishes she had never been born. She responds by asking him if he thinks she wants to be in this family. We escalate into a frozen tableau and, frozen in this terrible place, we cross-fade into a lively scene between Kam and Jay.

It is six to eight weeks later. Jay is excited about his new and expensive car and is like a puppy at Kam's feet as they walk along the sidewalk. (The tableau dissolves upstage and the actors exit.) We learn that Jay is managing to keep the car a secret from his family, because he is parking it two blocks from home. The family have no idea. (A true story from the workshop.) They enter the restaurant. Kam has something serious to discuss with Jay.

Kam compliments Jay on what he is hearing about him from the friend Jay is now working for. Kam lays out the trouble with Sunny and talks about loyalty. He starts to explain how serious the competition from other gangs is – and Jay, in a moment of bravado, suggests they just "blow them away." Kam, though, is a serious mentor. He tells Jay to relax – there is too much hot-headedness right now, too many headlines. Things have to happen quietly.

He explains to Jay that he is taking him to the "next level." When they are finished talking, they are going to walk out to the parking lot, and Kam will give Jay a gun. Is he ready? Jay wants to say no – he hasn't expected this. He is absolutely not ready. But he now owes Kam many things and both wants to please him and is afraid of him.

"Are you ready?" Kam asks again. "Yes – yes, I am," responds Jay.

They exit the restaurant, and, in the parking lot, the gun is given. Jay is very confused and internally conflicted. Kam walks around behind him, looking at him. They catch each other's eyes. Jay has this one last chance to say he doesn't want the gun, but he can't say it. Kam turns his back and walks away. Jay, literally, now has Kam's back.

Jay stands in the parking lot. He puts the gun in his pants – the only place he can hide it – and goes home. He sits alone on the sofa. He goes to sleep there.

In the morning, we start a repetition of the first family ritual scene. Daadi comes from the bedroom to the kitchen, gets tea, goes to the sofa and tickles Jay, like she did in the first scene. This time he jolts awake, frightened. He never sleeps deeply anymore.

Daadi, like all our grandmothers, knows many things. She says to her grandson, "Jay – who are you?"

"Your grandson," he says.

"Then why can't I tickle you anymore?" Jay won't have this conversation.

She continues. She wants to know where he got the expensive earring he is wearing, the coat, where is the money coming from? He is working, he says, "at his friend Kam's carpet company."

"You are making so much money?" she asks.

"I'm saving my money – I saved up for the earring."

"And the thousand dollars I found in your room? And the bag of ganja?" Daadi knows.

"You have no business going into my room!" he tells her – getting angry now. She is treading a fine line. "Look, my grandson," she tells him, "use the brain in your head. Don't get into something you will regret." But she will tell no one, and Jay knows it. He tells her he has to go – to school (adult classes he was going to in order to make up his grade 12, which he has secretly dropped).

During this scene, Sunny has wandered into the park (down-stage right). He is waiting. It is raining. Jay leaves his home and (lighting change) enters the park. Sunny takes the opportunity to tell Jay that if he keeps doing what Kam is telling him to do, he is going to get himself killed. Jay says he can take care of himself. Kam enters, asks why Jay didn't meet him at the car like he was supposed to. Jay says he came here instead. Kam puts him in his place, tells him to leave him and Sunny alone and to wait in the parking lot. Jay moves off.

We just found the skeleton of this next scene at the very end of the day today. We had time for one attempt.

Sunny tells Kam that he wants out of the gang. Kam's plan is too big, it's too dangerous. He is getting out. Kam has suspected this was coming and seems to understand. He tells his oldest and best friend that he is sorry to hear this, but knows it is inevitable. They embrace. He walks away and, behind Sunny's back, signals Jay to kill Sunny. Jay quickly moves behind Sunny and, pulling out his gun, puts it to Sunny's head. There is a scene here in which Sunny does not plead for his life, but tries to get Jay to understand that if he pulls the trigger there is no going back. Jay is at the precipice, at the point of no return that was discussed in the workshop. He is shaking like a leaf as the lights go slowly out.

We have the rough story and now, on schedule. The physical space will start to take shape. Next phase: rehearsal – making each moment work.

November 3, 2005
A good day. We all agree it feels like we have entered a new phase. The morning started slowly – a lengthy conversation about the CBC radio interview Kam and Sunny did yesterday evening.

I talked about how it is becoming apparent that this project poses a puzzle for the media and how we have to find a way to clarify what we are doing. On the one hand, we are saying the issue is everyone's, not just the Indo-Canadian community's, and on the other hand, we are making a play by and about the Indo-Canadian community. Why?

It has been the intention of the project from the very beginning to respond to the sensational newspaper headlines by using the current focus as an opportunity to tell a clear and specific story that will grab people's attention. We hope this brings the general public to the play. Once we have them in the theatre, we can use the play to ask many questions. One question is: Isn't it true that, regardless of our cultural origin, we all find connections to this particular story through our own lives and communities?

Sudnya did about an hour of movement with the cast this morning. They are enjoying their time with her, although some of them are getting sore – we must be careful. Even though we are letting go of the shadows idea, I am still hoping movement will be able to translate into the play. We need to start thinking about the specific spots where this could happen, as we have blocked out the story.

We got to some work on the play just as a reporter from CBC Radio arrived for her second interview installment. That was fine; we worked with her microphone in our faces – and the cast were great. We found the emotional content of the final scene, in which Jay holds a gun to Sunny's head.

After lunch we ran the opening, which works well – it just needed some fine tuning – and then we ran the first gangster scene. Kam and Sunny had done great planning work and I got them just walking circles around the room. The physicality and the precise detail of the conversation – how much drugs, how much money, how many people – really brought the scene to life. It will have to be played in front of the stage, though, in more stillness. The key, also, is that Sunny thinks Kam's plan is funny – it's so bad, so dangerous, it's laughable. He can't take it seriously.

Now, into the scene where Mother gets hit. We needed to get into detailed work again. The cast was really focused. And, something great happened. It got real. Mother (Rupa) has been so reluctant to 'go there'. This is completely understandable, but she is realizing, I think, that 'going there' is what the scene is about. Having been a part of creating it, she seems ready to make it work. I think also she is feeling safer. She is seeing the risks others are taking. I also freed it up in rehearsal and got all three (Mother, Father, Daadi) to do their lines in Punjabi. Miraculous! It flowed and the emotional content was there. This surprised them, as two of them are fluent in English. So we have agreed to work this way (in Punjabi, with translation for me) and to slowly transfer as much to English as necessary for the general public to understand.

I think the cast experienced, for the first time today, the depth of what we are doing – what really being 'in the moment' feels like and how exhilarating, and at the same time how draining, it is. It is the space we need to occupy.

November 4, 2005
The opening went well and they did the family fight really well the first time. I inserted a movement 'suspension' in the fight scene, which will work beautifully, we all think. Then, without making any actual changes to the scene, it started to change. We tried again and it changed more. We are having a retention problem. Some of the cast start to wander and I can't get them to repeat the scene the same way each time. The dynamic then is that they start to tell each other what to do, and it gets more and more confused and complex. It took so much of everyone's energy to sort this out. I wish I could find a way to get some of them to focus just on their own characters and to stop directing each other.

The woman playing Rupa, as I mentioned earlier, is also facing the truth of the scene and how it hits home for her. We had a lengthy talk about ways she can allow her character to surrender to the emotion that is necessary and not have it be her real self each time. We have agreed to start a costume ritual, so that the actor puts 'Rupa' on each day for rehearsal and takes her off at the end of the day. I have also made sure that Sarjeet, the workshop support person, is available for her.

We moved into the restaurant scene and found some more detail. Kam is drawing Sunny a diagram now – hoping he will understand the takeover plan. One of my concerns is that we don't get to know the two guys (Kam and Sunny) much at all. They need to be more than 'the gangsters'. And so, we have built a connection between Sunny and Sonya – she helped

with his sister's wedding a couple of weeks ago, and she comments on his appearance in a fun and affectionate way. They
have history. Then we have a lovely scene about making fun of
their the parents; there is a lot of genuine laughter.

Sonya does not stop, though. She continues the joking into the
moment when they are ordering beer, embarrassing her
brother, who is trying to impress the guys – and the scene
shifts. Kam sees this kid (Jay) in a certain way and questions
him about his reputation of being a 'one-puncher', of knocking
people to the ground with one punch. Jay responds with,
"Well, you gotta do what you gotta do." Sunny suggests that
Jay reminds him of Kam when Kam was a kid, and Kam turns
it around on Sunny: "It's true – you have to do what you have
to do." The subtext here, Kam to Sunny, is that Sunny has 'lost
his edge'.

Kam then starts to work on Jay. It's obvious what he is doing
– recruiting Jay. Sunny and Sonya both call him on it, but he
tells them it's just 'talk' and they should relax. We can see it's
not just 'talk'. This leads to a short exchange between Kam
and Sunny and Sunny leaves, very angry. The air is thick. We
see Jay transforming. Sonya takes the opportunity to try to get
her and her brother out, but neither Kam or Jay will let her.
Sonya is forced to go wait at the car while the guys talk. Kam
and Jay strike a bargain and there is a handshake – Jay paus-
ing, and then deciding.

Jay leaves the restaurant. Kam, pleased with himself, leaves also,
and Sunny confronts him in the parking lot. Kam is so taken by
surprise, he pulls his gun. We worked this in minute detail,
breaking the moments down into portions of seconds, and the
guys play it well. Sunny almost gets himself killed. There is a
short scene about trust. Sunny insists that he trusts Kam with his
life and that Kam MUST run the plan by Sanjay, their boss. Kam
refuses, and they part, further apart than before.

Jay and Sonya go home.

We ran into quicksand here – back in the family. This scene has become a repetition of the previous family scene. Also, the two women have been starting it in too heightened a state of distress.

The solution turned out to be simple. The women need to start from a very different place. The family fight was hours ago – they have let go of it. It's normal in the house. They are not terrified for the kids. They *don't know* about the restaurant (aha!). They are, in fact, mad at the kids now.

The technical/design side is coming together. After much searching, Kitty Hoffman (stage manager) and Craig Hall (technical director) and the electrician figured out where to put a 220V stove plug in for power. We have also made decisions in the last couple of days about stage size, restaurant size, photos hanging, how areas are defined.

We have six working days with actors until we perform for an 'invitation-only' Forum audience. Seven days to cue to cue,[169] when a lot of the work on the scenes stops and is taken over by runs and technical rehearsals. Nine days until preview. It sounds scary, but we are not in bad shape, as long as we can figure out the ending of the final family scene tomorrow morning.

I have found only one place so far for the movement suspension idea. We need at least three or four places to suspend the action if we are going to do this in the play. The shadow idea is gone. Is this the right piece in which to experiment with that kind of physical language? I am not certain.

November 5, 2005
We found the end of the final family scene this morning.

> Jeewan enters. Jay leaves and the family lets him, unques-
> tioned. Sonya can't believe it and complains. Father says the
> issue is about her and not Jay. She responds, "Oh, of course,
> he comes in every day, he watches TV, he does nothing. You
> have no idea what is going on in your own family." "Yes, it's
> true," says Father. "I work 18 hours a day." Daadi intervenes

---

[169] *Cue to cue* is a term for an early stage of technical rehearsal in which sound and lighting cues and levels are set.

again, accusing Sonya of lying about where they went, which
brings Mother in, and the whole argument starts all over
again. Father sits as the women argue and puts his head in his
hands. The lights fade out as the arguing continues.

Live sound cross-fading – we hear Kam and Jay's voices
emerging. Lights cross-fade – and now we are on the street. It
is three months later and Jay is bragging about his hot new
car. They head to the restaurant and we have the scene in
which Kam tells Jay about loyalty and takes him to the next
level – giving him a gun. The young man playing Jay is understanding Jay's dramatic journey and is starting to play with
the balance between his fear and his exhilaration.

Kam and Jay move to the street, and Jay is given the gun. He
goes home, falls asleep on the sofa, and Daadi awakens him in
the same way as in the opening scene.

We have what could be a lovely scene here, of Daadi interrogating Jay – he is changing, what happened to her grandson?
Jay would never hurt his Daadi, but he cannot tell her what is
happening. He escapes by saying he is late for school, which
he has dropped out of.

Sunny is now waiting at the park in the rain. Kam is supposed
to be meeting him. Instead, Jay shows up. They have a conversation in which Sunny tries to get Jay to see that Kam is out of
control, that Kam is going to get Jay killed. This is also Jay's
fear, but again, he can't admit it – Kam gets him everything he
wants.

After Kam arrives and sends Jay to the parking lot, Sunny tells
Kam he is getting out. Another friend was found dead in a
ditch, and Sunny knows that Kam's plan is going to get them
killed. He's too tired of it all. Kam is silent through most of the
scene. He asks Sunny if he has really thought this through. "I
have," says Sunny. They embrace and Kam walks away. He
touches Jay, who moves into the park, and, as Sunny is walking away, Jay puts the gun to the back of Sunny's neck.

The scene ends with Jay yelling over and over again, first to Sunny, but finally to himself: "You gotta do what you gotta do!" – trying to convince himself to pull the trigger. This terrified 19-year-old kid's mantra is repeated as the lights go down.

In the afternoon, we did a 'stumble through' of the play. I did this because Caitlin Pencarrick (lighting designer) and Amos Hertzmann (sound designer) and Julie Martens (set, props, costume designer) were coming. I wanted them to be able to see a run. I expected it to be a mess at this stage, but it was incredible, really, how much the cast held it together. There were many rough spots; some scenes disintegrated, but they kept going. There were some key moments missed, but all in all the cast did a terrific job.

Feedback from the three designers: there was some confusion about how the gangsters connect to the family (Sonya and Jay); also about the mother's relationship to her family. I think it's true that it is kind of invisible right now. We will work on these areas.

Design-side, things have come together very quickly in the last couple of days: a sofa is coming, the hanging photos are here, the kitchen unit is starting to get dressed, a restaurant booth is coming, the drapery for upstage that defines the home has arrived.

Things I am wondering about:

- Is it OK that we leave Sonya's story near the end of the play and focus only on Jay?
- Where are the other movement suspension points in the play?
- How do we make Mother more visible?

At the end of the day, in the circle, one of the cast members mentioned how amazing it is that they met three weeks ago – strangers. We did the community workshop. We met at the Temple and looked at each other and said, "What's the play?" And two weeks later, we have a play – seemingly out of nothing. The cast were very pleased and energized at the end of today.

November 12, 2005
Saturday morning
At about 7:00 PM last night the phone rang. Jagdeep (Kam in the play) was in Emergency at St. Paul's Hospital, having been beaten up badly as he was walking downtown.[170] Kitty and I both raced off to the hospital. The guys who beat him were quite young and called him by his old gang name. He has no real understanding of why this happened, other than them reacting to his reputation on the street, and their perception of their ability to boost their reputations.

We had our first invited Forum this afternoon, which I suggested we cancel. Jagdeep refused and insisted on coming in for the show.

We had to spend some time processing the events of the previous night with the cast and crew. During this time, we decided not to do any work on any of the Kam scenes, in order to conserve Jagdeep's energy. We focused on the family scenes. We cleaned up some areas and refocused part of the final family scene, where Mother brings Sonya back to her father. Mother has given up in a way. She decides not to get hit anymore by making sure her daughter listens to her husband. This brought a complexity to Mother that we hadn't had yet seen.

The cast really needed an audience. They had a great run, perhaps the best so far. Kam, with his stitches, swollen eye and bandaged ribs, was amazing. The Forum was very focused.

This was our first chance at Forum and my first chance to experiment with what to say, how to introduce it, how to Joke it. All in all it went very well, although it took three hours. It seems to me, though, that the first *Practicing Democracy* Forum was also that long.

some discoveries

This is the first time I have realized how very powerful the play is. People were stunned. Truly shell-shocked. I am going to have to find a way to transition out of the play and into the Forum.

---

[170] This story is included with Jagdeep's permission.

We should start the Forum at the third scene, after we have introduced all the characters. Doing so is perfectly appropriate for this play.

The audience members, even the community workshop participants, were very intimidated about intervening in the gang scenes.[171] We must expect this. I can deal with it, though, by talking about the need to experiment with how to get out of gang life once one has gotten in.

I need to keep it moving. This will be a challenge. We have a lot of material to get through and an audience's attention span is, generally, two hours.

The cast were great. It took them a couple of interventions to start to figure out the balance of how to respond to things – not try to be instructional and teach the audience anything; just be authentic. Once they did figure it out, and they all seemed to do that at the same time, the Forum really took off. This is why we did the invited Forum: to break through the barrier from straight performance to audience interactive event.

Tomorrow is cue to cue, where all the light and sound cues come together.

public performances

November 17, 2005
We had a very good preview last night and also a great media call in the afternoon – with eight television crews. Media call was like a scrum. This level of response from the media is so unusual in the theatre.

Then, as we were getting ready to leave the Temple sometime after 11:00 PM, a water main burst and raw sewage started pouring out. It took the City of Vancouver Engineering crew over an hour to arrive, after numerous calls. Finally, someone arrived who knew how to turn off the main underground pipes.

---

171 This was an invited rehearsal. In performance, I ask workshop participants, who have inside knowledge of the play and the process, not to make interventions, as it turns the Forum into a kind of demonstration.

It flooded the secondary Temple building with about three feet of sewage. We quickly removed everything from the basement of the building we are in, for fear of the flood reaching our building. We moved the Temple Education Program computers, turned off all the power and rescued everything from our dressing rooms. We did what we could to create a barrier to protect the building with rocks, sand-bags and other construction material that was in the courtyard. In the end, the bottom floor of our building got about an inch of sewage.

Kashmir (our Temple contact on the Executive) organized crews who came in quickly late last night and have done a great job of cleaning. But there is still a lot of work to do. We have power back, but will not have access to any water, so will be bringing that in ourselves. The basement of our building is sealed off for now. Access for both the company and the public to washrooms in the main Temple building next door, which was not directly affected, has been arranged. We were all very moved at how Kashmir and others at the Temple, working in a dire emergency, made certain that we could open the project with as little upheaval as possible.

November 19, 2005
We had our fourth performance last night and the Forums have each been so different.

Response to the play itself has been mostly fantastic. I have heard over and over again, from general public audience members, from people from the Temple, from workshop participants, and also from media people, that the play is so much more powerful than they expected it to be. This is very gratifying for us all.

I have also heard from a couple of people that they have had a hard time following the play. There are time shifts in it, for instance. When we did the invited Forum and the preview, I purposefully asked people who had not previously seen the play (also the designers when they came for the first run) about comprehension. Literally all of them said that the chronology of the story was clear – they understood the passage of time. And yet, there are some people who are expressing confusion. It is hard to know why it's working for most, but not for some.

For me, it feels like the most exciting Forum so far was the preview. It was the most engaged audience so far, I think. Navigating Forum is always challenging. We must be able to meet the audience where it is *each night* – not demand that it come to us, or be disappointed that this audience isn't at a level of understanding the issues that we wish it was. As the performances progress, it is very difficult not to compare one audience to another. Each performance, though, has to exist on its own.

At the preview, there was a really mixed crowd – people who were there because they were drawn to the issue. There was a level of knowledge in the room that made the investigation quite deep. We had interventions from various races and ages, from ex-gang members (known to cast members), from very tough young men, and also from the 'innocent but very concerned'.

One intervention, I remember, involved a young man replacing Jay near the end of the play. He gave Daadi the gun. This initiated a string of events that led to him going into hiding and a discussion (one that is coming up every night) about what mechanisms exist for people involved in gangs to get out. There are none, really. Going to the police is not an option, as they are going to want the person to name names, etc., which is going to put them and their family in extreme danger.

This was our first real (not invited) audience, and, while the Forum went well, I also felt that after the authenticity of the Forum rehearsal, now there was a great deal of 'blocking' going on in the family scenes during improvisations. Not from everyone, but from Mother and Father in particular. The actor's job is not to defeat everyone who comes on the stage, nor is it to be so agreeable that they will do anything – but to know their own character and tell the truth – even if the truth is inconvenient. I talked with the cast about this, in the hope that the 'family' would 'relax' a little on the stage and start to really be present in interventions. All those listening exercises from the workshop and rehearsals need to come into effect.

The first opening (we spanned opening invitations across the Thursday and Friday nights) was also a good night, with a deep investigation. This night a lot of the community-based supporters of the project came. Again the house was full.

An intervention that jumps out for me: A woman replaced Jay in the restaurant when Kam is giving him the gun, recognizing that he is surprised and uncomfortable with the news that he is expected to take it, but is unable to refuse. She did refuse. This led to understanding Jay's situation more clearly. He has said 'yes' to many things at this point – he has been dealing drugs for the crew, has made a lot of money and has a flashy car that is a secret from his parents. There are expectations of him. His refusal has ramifications. He is likely going to get beaten, although, after the beating, he may be allowed to back out. Again, calling the police is flagged as a dangerous option for him in this circumstance. It's what some of the public want him to do, but the cast and some audience members, who really are experts in this matter, are firm that this desire is naïve. The police can't protect him, even if they want to – and they have a history of just wanting information from him and then leaving him exposed to harm.

The second opening was harder. For some reason, this audience was mostly people representing funders, heads of agencies (instead of workers inside agencies), and old friends of Headlines. It was a far less directly engaged audience than usual; these people tended to observe the project.

We are getting interventions in the family scenes every night. Many people have come to me from various backgrounds (Indian, Iranian, First Nations, Chinese, Caucasian – to name some) and have commented on how the dynamics in the family are also the dynamics in their families, either now or as children. The family could also, in some ways, be my own family when I was a child. It's important for all of us in the project that this recognition – that it's not 'only' an Indian family issue – be operating with audiences. The issues we are dealing with in the play are social issues that span all boundaries – even though the case study we are using (because of the current headlines) is Indo-Canadian.

There are seemingly simple actions in these scenes that can lead to profound solutions. These may involve at least one of the family members (it could be, and has been at this point, any one of them) taking a leadership role and breaking the patterns that escalate the tension in the home. If this can happen, very often Mother doesn't get slapped around, the kids don't end up on the porch, they don't go off to meet Kam and Sunny in the restaurant, Jay doesn't get recruited, etc. But it's not as simple as it sounds. And we're not suggesting that the only factor is the home. However, it was very clear in the workshop that the participants were certain the young people were going into gang life partly as a reaction to their home life. We cannot separate the two influences.

A woman replaced Jeewan in the scene where he has good news and Sonya is talking on her phone. The intervener worked so hard trying to get the family to honour Jeewan's needs – and it was lovely, her understanding of his struggle, as an immigrant who is trying his best to provide for his family, in a culture that is contrary to his own. I was very grateful to her, because it's easy to overlook that he is not a bad father – he is trying to be the best he can be and, in the midst of that, is making some very hurtful choices.

People from the Temple are starting to come. In the last couple of days, I have noticed people from the Temple kitchen coming to the shows.

November 20, 2005
There was a lovely and controversial intervention from a young man who replaced Sonya in the scene where Mother gets hit. He started by saying to Father, "You're right, Dad. Mother deserved to get hit. I agree with you!" The audience let out a loud groan.

Then the intervener went on to try to get the father to also slap him (Sonya). "Hit me – I need to learn a lesson, too," he demanded. And he wouldn't stop. "Hit me!" The father and mother stared in silence. It was Daadi (Grandmother) who finally started to speak, in a very emotional way. "Are you listening to your daughter? Do you under-stand what she is trying to tell you?" Father was visibly shaken. In discussion about this, we talked about how stuck the family is in the pattern and how something dramatic needs to happen to shock them out of it. The father suggested that he had actually heard the subtext of this challenge from his daughter and that it would change his behaviour.

As is the case every night so far, there was also discussion about how the 'Sunnys and Kams of the world' get out of gang life. I asked the audience at one point how many of them have Sunnys (people who have entered gang life and want out) directly in their lives, and about 20 percent of the audience raised their hands.

November 23, 2005
The actor playing Jay came in all banged up today. He was at a club on Monday night and got 'jumped'. He has a broken wrist and a very sore ankle. He says it had nothing to do with the play – it's attached to previous events. He is in a fair bit of pain. Kam is almost fully recovered. So now, instead of making an announcement at the top of the evening about Kam's injuries, I am making an announcement about Jay. I am very impressed with his commitment to continue. We had to re-block some scenes to accommodate the injured actor. We cannot have Father throw Jay onto the floor now – we have changed it to a violent-looking push onto the upholstered sofa.

The run of the play went very well. The audience was completely stunned when it was over – there was stone cold silence. Some of the cast members have talked about how much they love this moment, when, instead of applause, sometimes, there is just silence. The lights come up and the cast are in a family photo configuration for the curtain call, and they can see the tears in people's eyes and they know that what they are doing has reached into the community.

There were some very considered interventions tonight, in particular regarding getting Jay and Sunny out of gang life. Kashmir, our contact on the Executive of the Temple came tonight and brought his wife, two kids and his mother. They loved it. His daughter made an intervention.

November 27, 2005
Every night I ask the audience members to remain standing if the issues in the play touch their lives or the lives of people dear to them, and every night at least 90 percent of the house remains standing. Most nights, it's higher than 90 percent. Yet on Friday, the interventions had a kind of naiveté to them. Saturday night they were spectacularly well considered. I don't think I have ever done a show where the depth of the Forum swings like this one does from one performance to the next.

It's so important to always meet the audiences where they are each night, and not to try to educate them, indoctrinate them or otherwise patronize them. Forum Theatre really keeps a cast and Joker on their toes.

People have started to bring their families, including very young children. We talk with them upon entry, to make certain they know what they are coming to see in terms of the coarse language and the violence.

On Saturday night, a young woman replaced Sonya and really asserted herself inside the family in a wonderful way. She embraced Sonya's passion for her cell phone and her need to connect with friends, and at the same time balanced that with the father's need to share his news with the family. It seemed so simple, but we all agreed that the way it was done empowered Sonya and at the same time respected the father. This woman, of Kenyan descent, came to me later and commented that the family felt like her own family. Jeewan, in particular, she said, "made a perfect African dad."[172]

A young man replaced Jay and did something no one has ever done. He stood up for his sister, and lectured (in a nice way) his family about their need to honour their daughter. Did they want to drive her away? Did they know how many of their friends' daughters were prostitutes, having being driven out of their families and then having found 'home' with a man who took advantage of them?

A man replaced Kam (the gang leader). This was the first time an intervention recognized Kam's humanity and his struggle to find a way not to have to kill his best friend Sunny. We were all, especially the actor playing Kam, very grateful for the insight of this man. In the intervention, the man really had to work to get Sunny to hear what he was saying – that they had to move slowly and plan Sunny's exit with care, because both their lives were in jeopardy. As is often the case, this led to a conversation about what actual avenues there are for the Sunnys of the world to get out – there are no formal avenues.

After the Saturday Forum we had a very hard time getting the audience members to go home. Many of them stayed and talked and talked. The room was really alive.

---

[172] This young woman (Mumbi Tindyebwa) then applied for a job opening at Headlines and became, in 2006, the executive assistant in the office.

We are preparing to leave the Temple after tonight's show. It's an emotional moment, leaving the Temple space. It was such a foreign environment when we first got there and now it feels like home.

After the show, we packed up the dressing room, the sound and light booth and the lobby in preparation for the tech crew, who will do the tear-down and the move-out tomorrow. It's going to be very different performing the show at the Surrey Arts Centre. A real theatre.

November 30, 2005
The show looks great in the theatre – the design team did a lovely job. We had from 1:00 PM to 6:00 PM to rework entrances and exits, work a few internal moments in scenes, do a cue to cue and then a run. We were done at 6:30 PM. The Surrey tech people were booked until 10:30 PM, but we were all out of there by 7:00 PM. We 'did good'.

December 1, 2005
A full house for the matinee: just under 130 grades 8, 9 and 10 students from the Sikh Khalsa School. Some of them seemed quite young, but we could have done interventions for hours and hours. They were very rowdy sometimes, but never in a bad way – they were highly engaged.

Interestingly, at the top of the Forum, when I asked them to sit if the issues in the play did not touch their lives, about 60 percent of them sat down. An hour into the Forum, I asked them how many of them knew a 'Jay' character, and about 80 percent raised their hands. They were very frightened, I think, at the beginning.

The gangster scenes got a lot of attention, some of it quite informed. Kam played a very hard-hitting scenario with a young boy who replaced Jay in the restaurant and now didn't want the gun. My heart went out to the boy, who thought it would be easy to just 'say no' – as it got more and more serious, the room got more and more quiet. You could feel them thinking.

There was a very well-thought-out intervention at the very end of the play. A boy replaced Jay after Kam gives him the 'kill Sunny' signal. Jay went to Sunny, as in our play, and put the gun to Sunny's head. When he knew Sunny couldn't pull his own gun, he stopped and explained that Kam had ordered him to kill Sunny, but he didn't want to. Could he and Sunny, he wondered, work together to help each other, because he knew if Jay didn't follow through with killing Sunny, Jay himself would be killed. Sunny took the gun and ordered Jay to leave town. Jay wanted to know what would happen. Sunny explained that he was going to go to Sanjay and tell him that Kam tried to have him killed. This was going to get Kam killed, which, in turn, was likely going to start the very war that Sunny feared.

After the play, the students swamped the stage, wanting actors' autographs. One of the teachers came to me and said, "This is a great thing you are doing – you are saving lives here."

The evening show was very different. Maybe, because it is 'opening night' in Surrey, although we have not advertised it that way at all, the audience was very heavy with politicians, counsellors, therapists and social workers. It was the singularly most frustrating Forum we have had.

When I asked the "if this touches your life question" at the beginning of the Forum, 100 percent of the people in the room remained standing. There were interventions in the first family scene and the first restaurant scene that came fairly easily, but also had elements of magic to them. Jay, for example, is just 'not interested' in the gangster world. Daadi is very understanding and 'makes space' for her daughter-in-law to be Sonya's mother. Both these interventions have good outcomes, but there is a level of wishful thinking in them. I had to really dig with the interveners to talk about the characters' struggles.

Then we got into the harder part of the play and there was nothing. They were so silent. It was scary and frustrating. One woman said, "Well, what do you want us to do? We don't know what to do." I said to her that no one ever knows what to do – we are in the theatre to make discoveries; it's not my place to tell you what to do.

Finally, I told them I had no problem with them leaving the theatre frustrated, and brought the Forum to a close. After we closed the Forum, many of them came to me and the actors privately and had suggestions for interventions.

Here's my theory: these professionals give people advice and, in their positions, have a great deal invested in 'being right', in succeeding. The possibility that they might come on stage and fail in public was too much. And this is, in fact, reflected in the problem with many programs and politicians' proposals: there is so little innovation – so little risk-taking. People feel they need to play it safe.

The politicians, though, wanted photographs of themselves with the cast – proof that they had attended the event.

December 5, 2005
We are once again getting the general public. By that I mean it's not only the activist crowd, the counsellors, etc., who are coming. There are still some very silent moments, but they do not feel like the silence of fear of failure. The silences are leading to extraordinary ideas coming onto the stage.

One young man replaced Jay at the end of the play and refused to kill Sunny. Kam shot him. In discussion after the intervention, the intervener said that he knew he would likely get killed, but he didn't see a way out at that point, and at least his family would know that he 'said no' – and would be proud of him. This seems bleak, but it opens up an understanding of the depth of the moment. I believe these insights affect people's lives – especially, in this instance, those who might possibly be 'Jays', or those who know 'Jays' and can talk with them.

A young man replaced Jay and confronted the father about how much he is working and not spending time with his family. The father's response was very appreciated by the audience: "You want me to stop working so much? Are you ready to move into a one-bedroom basement suite?" The room agreed that part of the issue was the disconnection in the family, but they also understood that the father has both a real and imagined pressure to bring in large sums of money – to live, to prepare for the future and also to prove himself in our very consumer-oriented culture.

Another intervention replaced Daadi in the scene when Jay has the gun. The intervener was very strong. She pushed and pushed, and brought the whole family together to talk with Jay. The pressure made him dig his heels in and finally he just left the house, left them all standing there.

This is such an interesting part of the play, because the interveners want to 'give him space' and Jay uses that to guilt them into letting him go. He is afraid to tell them anything, although he actually really wants to be convinced to tell them everything. Of course, if he does, this makes a 'bomb explode' in the family, which they then have to deal with somehow. It comes up over and over again that they cannot go to the police, who have no way to protect them.

Another intervention replaced Sunny in the Kam/Sunny final scene and was like others, except for the beautiful language in it. The audience-member-Sunny wants out and tells Kam that he will always support him. He tells him he "has a couch, and someday, when you are bloody and beaten, you are going to need my couch." It sounds corny as I write it, but our Sunny was offstage with tears in his eyes, and Kam told me later that he had to force himself not to cry.

These heartfelt interventions between the gangsters are important. I have come to understand what we are doing in this part of the play: we are reframing people's ideas of gangsters being alien monsters. They are our brothers, cousins, sons, the kids next door. Once they are in the gangster life, how do we help them get out?

We are gearing up now for the live tele/webcast. Rehearsal is on Saturday. Tele/webcast and final performance is on Sunday.

December 9, 2005
We had an intervention from Herb Dhaliwal tonight. Mr. Dhaliwal is a well-known federal politician (Liberal) and an ex-cabinet minister. He replaced Daadi in the scene when Jay has the gun and almost convinced Jay to tell the truth. He took Jay in his arms and wouldn't let go. He told him how much his family loved him, even if there were fights.

When Mr. Dhaliwal had finished trying his idea, we got into a discussion of what would happen if Jay did tell the truth. Mr. Dhaliwal said that he would call the police. I called Kam out and he talked about how, unfortunately, this would put the family in great danger. The reality is that the police cannot protect Jay. They will want information from him and this puts him and the family in extreme danger. It was, I am certain, very interesting for Mr. Dhaliwal to hear this and he dealt with it very graciously – a difficult position for him to be in as a senior politician in the government. He came to me twice after the evening was done and commented on how powerful the event had been, and said that he had learned things tonight.

the tele/webcast

December 11, 2005
In order to understand the set-up for this live tele/webcast, you might want to read the section on *Television and the World Wide Web* in the *Appendix*.

We had a great night. Another sold-out house. The build-up to 7:30 PM and the house opening included:

> I gave the actors notes from the run last night: try to keep the pacing up and the cues tight; also be very concise during analysis after interventions.

> Then we rehearsed the tele/web-actors. These are the actors who are going to receive and then act out the interventions from people making interventions via the telephones and the Web. Rehearsal includes giving each of them an intervention to do. The tele/web-actors have a very delicate task: they have to be the conduit for an intervention. So we gave them rehearsal interventions and I was able to ask them questions afterwards about how much what they did on the stage was their own impulse and how much was them trying to be true to what had been requested of them. They have to be able to embrace the request and to 'fill in the blanks' themselves, or the intervention can become very shallow.

> After this rehearsal, we ran our first two scenes, a ritual we have been doing to get ready for the run.

The cast did a great run of the play. There were some very powerful interventions, including one in the theatre from a 10 or 12-year-old boy who replaced Jay in the scene with Daadi when he has the gun. He 'confessed'. This is only the second time this has happened in the run. A complex series of events was set into motion from this, which made it possible to talk about how this was exactly what Shawn, the actor playing Jay, did in his real life (we had Shawn's permission).

The live *telecast* was seen by an estimated 15,000 people in the Lower Mainland. Our web-counter indicates that 660 computers logged into the video page of the live *webcast*. We understand that there is usually more than one person at a computer for a viewing like this, so, while it is impossible to know exactly, we can estimate about 1,200 international web-viewers. Web-viewers did not have to log into chat space to see the production.

Web-viewers did have to log into chat to make interventions. The chat log contains entries from Vancouver, Surrey and other communities throughout British Columbia, Calgary and Edmonton, Regina, communities throughout Ontario, and Montreal (all in Canada); Bellingham, New York City, San Francisco and an unnamed community in Tennessee (all in the US); Berlin and communities in Belgium, Holland, Spain and the UK; as well as Japan, the Philippines and numerous communities in Australia.

The tele/web-actors took interventions from these places: Vancouver (10), Surrey, BC (5), Aldergrove, BC (2), Fernie, BC (2), Windsor, ON (1), Toronto, ON (1), San Francisco, CA (1), New York City (2), Perth, Australia (1), Brisbane, Australia (1). Only a portion of these made it to the stage; there were also many interventions live, in the theatre, from that night's audience.

There was a prolonged and enthusiastic standing ovation at the end of the tele/webcast Forum, which was also closing night – and then much celebrating for hours, first in the dressing rooms, and then at the party in the theatre foyer.

legacy

Here and Now (ਏਥੇ ਤੇ ਹੁਣ) was a great critical and audience success, in both art and issue terms. The play succeeded in changing the texture of the conversations about gangs that we see and hear in the media. We noticed, as did others who mentioned it to us at Headlines, that gang violence news items at the time, and for months after, stopped identifying the ethnicity of the gang members.

Sadly, this shift from the media didn't last. But the fact that it happened for a while – because of a four-week run of a play – is a signal that a shift like this in news reporter behaviour is possible. If the behaviour changes for a long enough period of time, will the structures of the media that the behaviour creates and supports also change?

The comprehensive *Community Action Report*, written by Kashmir Besla,[173] was taken up by community-based organizations in the Lower Mainland. One outcome that, in 2006, is in the early planning stages is a 24-hour-a-day confidential phone line for people who have entered gang life and want to get out. Another suggestion, which went to the federal government, but has not been acted upon, is the establishment of 'safe houses' for ex-gang members.

Part of the legacy of a project is what remains in people's hearts and minds. We received a great deal of verbal and written feedback. Here is just a small sample:

> "The *Here and Now* (ਏਥੇ ਤੇ ਹੁਣ) project holds a great deal of value within our local community and within our larger global community. As a member of the local Indo-Canadian community, to introduce this production with a discussion on the politics of race was valuable. By illustrating this point with an example of the non-racial identification of a 'white'/'Caucasian' gang like the Hell's Angels – it does hit home with individuals that have never considered the racial profiling conducted by the media. And the exercise of interrupting the play and replacing one of the performers and performing the 'choice' was extremely useful. Many of us can sit back and judge what needs to be done, but by performing the actions, you become involved in not only critical evaluation, but the common sense factor. I think this project was highly effective and positive on multiple levels.
>
> I came with my mother, brother and partner. Sitting within the family context was important to me, as many of the issues were mirrored in our lives. As much as that exact story doesn't live out in my reality – it is far too close of a possibility in my world. I think it is important to see how something may play out. Personally, I found mirrors for all of us – and perhaps not embedded

[173] See http://www.headlinestheatre.com/Hereandnow/finalreports.html

within one specific character, but with certain mental constructions or characteristics. It is so easy for many of us to stand back and say "call the cops" – but it isn't as easy as that. There are so many strings that are interwoven, and if you tug one, it impacts all of the rest – there isn't one almighty fix-all. Thank you for allowing us, as a family, to view this."

Bindy Kang, audience member, December 22, 2005

"I was a workshop participant for the Headlines Theatre production of *Here and Now (ਏਥੇ ਤੇ ਹੁਣੇ)*. I was amazed at how all of the material that was covered in this play was a vital mirror of my own personal experiences inside my home and of the South Asian community abroad. I think that the content of the performance was very timely. It was exquisitely displayed onstage."

Shyam Wazir, workshop participant, December 27, 2005

"I saw *Here and Now (ਏਥੇ ਤੇ ਹੁਣੇ)* on Thursday night and stepped in for a character. It was an amazing experience. This was my first exposure to Forum Theatre and it is incredibly powerful. It really gave me a greater perspective on the issue of gangs and the individual struggles that encompass it. And what is so cool, is that this form allows, and even forces, the audience to think about it, struggle with it and explore problem-solving. It is very empowering to be reminded that we all have choices."

Shana Orlowsky, audience member/intervener,
December 10, 2005

"*Here and Now (ਏਥੇ ਤੇ ਹੁਣੇ)* is a genuinely gripping piece, which is powerful enough to prompt heartfelt responses that can only help deal with the problem."

Peter Birnie, "Critic's Picks", *Vancouver Sun*, November 24, 2005

EPILOGUE

During late 2006 and early 2007 I directed and Joked *Meth*,[174] a Headlines Theatre production created and performed by people who had struggled with methamphetamine addiction.[175] The Forum Theatre production had a very successful Vancouver run and live tele/webcast, and also had a 28-community tour throughout British Columbia.

During the build-up to the project, and throughout the creation and rehearsal process, I faced my own struggles, as is often the case, both as producer and director/Joker. We had been encouraged to do the project by a broad community consensus. However, as vitally important as the subject matter of this project was, I wondered if we (Headlines Theatre) were focusing our attention on the most important issue possible for today. In particular, my personal attention is more and more on the issue of climate change, which strikes me as singularly important for humanity as a whole.

As we developed the *Meth* project, initially through conversations with people across BC and then in a week-long *Theatre for Living* workshop with people who were living the issues of meth addiction, it became

---

[174] *Meth* was created and performed by: Kayla Cardinal, Cody Gray, Jordan Fields, Betsy Ludwig, Sophie Merasty and Herb Varley. Director/Joker: David Diamond. Stage Manager: Nicole Hawreschuk. Technical Director/Lighting Designer: Tim Cardinal. Set and Props Designer: Yvan Morissette. Costume Designer: Jane Henry. Sound Designer: Chris Hind. Slide Designer: Lincoln Clarkes. Project Support: Gwendolyn Matwick.

[175] Our definition of "struggled with Meth addiction" was that participants had either experienced addiction personally or through the lives of loved ones.

apparent the most useful catalyst for the community would be to use methamphetamines as a window into the broader issue of addiction. As a result of this insight, each character in the play suffered from some kind of addiction. Some of the characters were addicted to meth, others to alcohol, to gambling, to work, to codependency, to secrets... The play presented characters living in an interconnected web of addiction, much like the overarching, addicted culture in which we all live. It strikes me now that working on the issue of addiction is connected to working on the issue of climate change.

The debate about whether or not climate change is real is 'officially' over. On February 2, 2007, against the background of the most conclusive scientific evidence to date that the warming of the climate system is unequivocal and accelerating, the executive secretary of the United Nations Framework Convention on Climate Change, Yvo de Boer, called for "speedy and decisive international action to combat the phenomenon."[176]

We have been seeing the results of climate change all over the world for years in changing weather patterns, receding ice, drought, severe weather, increasing infestations of non-indigenous plant and insect life, and many other phenomena. Here in North America, the report-age in the media has shifted in the past year and has shifted dramatically in the past few months. Momentum is building on this crucial issue, but as the winter of 2007 flows into spring, it remains extremely difficult to see that people are embracing the kind of real behavioural change that will be necessary to have an effect on the degradation of our environment. Why?

Writing the *Epilogue* of this book brings me back to the *Preface*. Could it be that one of the hurdles humanity faces is our culturally embedded addiction to the mechanistic image we have of the universe functioning like a machine? Isn't this central image, in which "mind/spirit" is disconnected from "body/matter", at the very root of the industrialized and industrializing world's insatiable impulse to consume at rates that are clearly unsustainable and pollute at rates that are clearly suicidal? Is it not also the case that the phenomenon of being unable to face an

---

[176] From the UN Framework Convention on Climate Change website: http://unfccc.int/2860.php

addictive situation one is in, and, as a response, 'partying until one drops', is another manifestation of addictive behaviour?

One of the insights from doing *Meth* has been the realization that addiction (to substances, consumption, work, etc.) fills the spaces that open up between us and inside us; spaces that were once filled with a sense of 'home', of belonging and of true interconnectedness.

We will never succeed at either reversing or slowing down climate change, or even coping with the inevitable reality of it, from within the current mechanical model. We need a dramatic paradigm shift – a profound reshaping of our culture of consuming, such as Capra suggests is beginning in his foreword. This shift, however, needs to escalate urgently.

Patterns of behaviour create structure.[177] We must investigate, at a deep and urgent level, our addictive attachment to the mechanistic model and radically change our patterns of behaviour.

One way to encourage this shift is to find ways to tell and honour our collective stories, stories of living communities, stories that help us recognize that on our tiny planet, there is no "us" and "them". As happens so often during Forum Theatre events, we must come to understand that our own stories are intricately woven into the plots of others' stories. We must understand that the decisions we make and the actions we take – both publicly and in the privacy of our lives – affect not only ourselves and our immediate circles, but people, situations and locations far outside our own perceived boundaries. We are all actors in our universal, collective story.

---

[177] See the section *Patterns and structure* in the chapter *The Living Community*.

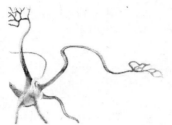

REFERENCE LISTS

Articles, Papers

Khanna, Mukti. "Embracing the Earth Charter: Community Transformation Through Inter-Being." International Conference on Conflict Resolution, St. Petersburg, Russia, 2003.

Varela, Francisco J., Nathalie Depraz, and Pierre Vermersch. "The Gesture of Awareness: An Account of Its Structural Dynamics." *Investigating Phenomenal Consciousness*. Ed. Max Velmans. Amsterdam: John Benjamins Publishing Company, 1999. 121-136.

Books

Bloom, Mia. *Dying to Kill: The Allure of Suicide Terror*. New York: Columbia University Press, 2005.

Boal, Augusto. *Games for Actors and Non-Actors*. Oxford: Routledge, 1992.

Boal, Augusto. *Rainbow of Desire*. Oxford: Routledge, 1995.

Boal, Augusto. *Theatre of the Oppressed*. New York: Theatre Communications Group Inc., 1974; London: Pluto Classics, 1993.

Capra, Fritjof. *The Hidden Connections*. New York: Doubleday, 2002.

Capra, Fritjof. *The Turning Point*. New York: Simon and Schuster, 1982.

Freire, Paulo. *Pedagogy of Hope*. Lanham, MD: Sheed and Ward, 1972; New York: Continuum Publishing Company, 1994.

Freire, Paulo. *Pedagogy of the Oppressed*. Lanham, MD: Sheed and Ward; UK: Penguin, 1972; New York: Continuum, 1997.

Gramsci, Antonio. *Letters from Prison*. New York: Harper and Row, 1973; New York: Columbia University Press, 1994.

Lakoff, George and Mark Johnson. *Philosophy in the Flesh: The Embodied Mind and Its Challenge to Western Thought*. New York: Basic Books, 1999.

Lasn, Kalle. *Culture JAM: The Uncooling of America*. New York: Eagle Brook, 1999.

Luhmann, Niklas. *Social Systems*. Stanford, CA: Stanford University Press, 1990.

Sheldrake, Rupert. *A New Science of Life*. Los Angeles: Tarcher, 1991.

Sheldrake, Rupert. *The Presence of the Past*. New York: Times Books, 1988.

Schutzman, Mady and Jan Cohen-Cruz, eds. *Playing Boal: Theatre, Therapy and Activism*. London/New York: Routledge, 1994.

Interview

Laura Lynch. Interview with Mia Bloom and Dr. Eyel-Sarraj. *The Current*. Canadian Broadcasting Corporation. 7 Jul. 2003.

Internet Resources

Adbusters
http://www.adbusters.org

Cardboard Citizens, Artistic Director, Adrian Jackson
http://www.cardboardcitizens.org.uk

Centre for Complex Quantum Systems (formerly the Ilya Prigogine
Centre for Studies in Statistical Mechanics and Complex Systems)
http://www.order.ph.utexas.edu

Centre for Ecoliteracy
http://www.ecoliteracy.org

Check Your Head
http://www.checkyourhead.org

David Cooper Photography
http://www.davidcooperphotography.com

Delgamuukw/Gisday'wa National Process
http://www.delgamuukw.org

Formaat, Artistic Director, Luc Opdebeeck
http://www.formaat.org/inenglish/index.php

Forum 2000
http://www.forum2000.cz

Fractal images
http://www.softsource.com/fractal.html

Gaza Community Mental Health Program
http://www.gcmhp.net

Gitxsan Chiefs' Office
http://www.gitxsan.com

grunt gallery
http://www.grunt.bc.ca

Headlines Theatre
http://www.headlinestheatre.com

Indian Residential School Survivors Society
http://www.irsss.ca

International Theatre of the Oppressed Organization (ITO)
http://www.theatreoftheoppressed.org

Judith Marcuse Projects
http://www.jmprojects.ca

Nuu-chah-nulth Tribal Council
http://nuuchahnulth.org

Office of the Wet'suwete'en
http://wetsuweten.com

Principia Cybernetica Web
http://pespmc1.vub.ac.be

Street Spirits Theatre Company
http://www.streetspirits.com

United Nations Framework Convention on Climate Change
http://unfccc.int/2860.php

Wild, Nettie (filmmaker), Canada Wild Productions
http://www.canadawildproductions.com

SUGGESTED READING LIST

Boal, Augusto. *Games for Actors and Non-Actors*. Oxford: Routledge, 1992.

Boal, Augusto. *Rainbow of Desire*. Oxford: Routledge, 1995.

Boal, Augusto. *Theatre of the Oppressed*. New York: Theatre Communications Group Inc., 1974; London: Pluto Classics, 1993.

Capra, Fritjof. *The Hidden Connections*. New York: Doubleday, 2002.

Capra, Fritjof. *The Turning Point*. New York: Simon and Schuster, 1982.

Capra, Fritjof. *The Web of Life*. New York: Doubleday, 1996/1997.

Chopra, Deepak. *Quantum Healing: Exploring the Frontiers of Mind/Body Medicine*. New York: Bantam Books, 1990.

Freire, Paulo. *Pedagogy of Hope*. Lanham, MD: Sheed and Ward, 1972; New York: Continuum Publishing Company, 1994.

Freire, Paulo. *Pedagogy of the Oppressed*. Lanham, MD: Sheed and Ward; UK: Penguin, 1972; New York: Continuum Publishing Company, 1997.

Johnstone, Keith. *Impro: Improvisation and the Theatre*. New York: Routledge, 1989.

Levine, Stephen. *Healing into Life and Death*. New York: Anchor Press/Doubleday, 1987.

Lovelock, James E. *Gaia: A New Look at Life on Earth*. 3rd ed. Oxford: Oxford University Press, 2000.

Murchie, Guy. *The Seven Mysteries of Life*: *An Exploration in Science and Philosophy*. Boston: Houghton Mifflin, 1999.

Schutzman, Mady and Jan Cohen-Cruz, eds. *Playing Boal: Theatre, Therapy and Activism*. London/New York: Routledge, 1994.

Varela, Francisco J., Nathalie Depraz, and Pierre Vermersch. "The Gesture of Awareness: An Account of Its Structural Dynamics." *Investigating Phenomenal Consciousness*. Ed. Max Velmans. Amsterdam: John Benjamins Publishing Company, 1999. 121-136.

Wheatley, Margaret J. *Leadership and the New Science*. San Francisco: Berrett-Koehler, 1992.

APPENDIX

Television and the World Wide Web

Headlines Theatre takes, on average, one of our Forum Theatre events to live television and/or the Web each year.[178] This arrangement was originally developed through Rogers Cable Community TV (now SHAW) in Vancouver. The community television station is a creation of the Canadian Radio and Television Commission (CRTC). In exchange for a broadcast licence, the cable company agrees to open up a channel to create and broadcast community-based programming. The community channel is run mostly by volunteers, with a core of paid staff.

I remember very well sitting with Augusto Boal in Sydney, Nova Scotia, in 1987, and explaining that I wanted to take Forums onto live TV. The World Wide Web didn't really exist then. He laughed a very good-natured laugh and said, "You're such a North American!"

Augusto was right – I am a North American. And the most pervasive medium of communication in my culture at that time was television.

---

[178] Telecasts include: ¿Sanctuary? (1989); *Out of the Silence* (1992); *Generations* (1997); *The Dying Game* (1998); *Squeegee* (1999); *Corporate U* (2000); *Don't Say a Word* (2003); *Practicing Democracy* (2004); *Here and Now (ਏਥੇ ਤੇ ਹੁਣੇ)* (2005); *Meth* (2006).

The messages on television were, and still are, most often determined by big corporate interests. This does not need to be the case. There are lessons for artists who are interested in creating community dialogue in the way the anti-globalization movement has used the Web to forge a new way of organizing globally. The technology is moving very fast with the innovation of *podcasts*, and in Web access like *YouTube* and *MySpace*.

A Headlines' *telecast* is just like a normal Forum Theatre event. The added layer is that it is being broadcast live. The live audience can make interventions in the theatre as usual. At the same time, people watching at home in the Vancouver and surrounding area can call in and explain the intervention they want to make to an actor on the telephone: a *tele-actor*.[179] The tele-actor then runs into the theatre and yells, "Stop! – I have an intervention from 'x', who lives in 'y'," and does the intervention on that person's behalf.

If we are also doing a *webcast* along with the live theatre event and the telecast, a home viewer anywhere in the world can watch the play live on their computer and can enter chat space, created specifically for this event, to talk with other viewers from around the world. In the chat space, there are also actors on computers: *web-actors*.[180] The web-viewer can enter private chat space with a web-actor, explain their intervention, and then the web-actor runs into the theatre and yells, "Stop! – I have an intervention from 'x', who lives in 'y'," and does the intervention on that person's behalf.

Having an actor do an intervention on behalf of an 'at-home viewer' creates a filter in between the intervener and the play. Technology just hasn't caught up, in this instance, to desire. Until it does, my choice is to accept this limitation of the tele/webcast.

The televised event needs its own director from the TV world. Mike Keeping has been the TV director for all but one satellite broadcast of *Out of the Silence*, which aired on the Knowledge Network in 1992.

---

[179] The tele-actors are usually a mix of people, some from the community workshop that led to the particular production being performed, and some who already have experience as tele-actors from previous productions.

[180] The web-actors are hired the same way as the tele-actors. They do need to be familiar with basic computer chat software.

The TV viewer's vocabulary is very sophisticated because of a constant diet of highly produced TV shows. We try to achieve a TV product that is as professional looking as possible, without the budget of professional TV. Mike and I have a clear and mutual understanding, though, that while we want to broadcast the best television possible, we are taking *live theatre* to television. Mike works in two different styles during the two-hour event. He shoots the core play as drama, with close-ups and camera angles that take us as close into the rehearsed action as possible. Once the Forum starts, it's more like a sporting event – he and the camera and sound people capture spontaneous action.

The theatre/television collaboration is a marriage of two very different mediums. All the TV crew must be familiar with the short play from viewings and/or rehearsals. They should have seen it in Forum at least once before broadcast.

If we are going to have a tele/webcast, we plan to have at least three performances of the play in order to go to broadcast. It has most often been the case that a broadcast is at the end of a run of at least 10 performances. The first performances will have no cameras or sound in the room. It is the cast's first public performance(s), and I feel they have enough to think about without all of it going on air.

We then have at least one public performance with cameras and lights but no broadcast, in which the TV crew have a dry run to rehearse camera angles, catch any sound issues, etc.

We work in a theatre or a community hall, usually in the community in which the *Theatre for Living* workshop has happened. This means that the TV people need a mobile broadcast studio that they can bring to where we are. They bring in at least five cameras: two of them on platforms behind the audience, one on each side of the audience, and one or two hand-held that can roam. The hand-held cameras need both camera operators and cable-pullers. We have body microphones for the cast and Joker, and boom mikes for audience discussion. Until recently, we have also had a wireless hand-held mike so the Joker can capture what interveners are saying on stage.

Luc Opdebeeck, from the Netherlands, who is artistic director of Formaat,[181] and also one of the co-founders of the International Theatre of the Oppressed Organization (ITO) website,[182] gave us a great suggestion (which we are now using) after he watched the webcast of *Here and Now (ਏਥੇ ਤੇ ਹੁਣ)* in 2005. Instead of having a cordless microphone that the Joker uses like a talk show host for interveners, we have built a sash that the audience member can easily wear over one shoulder. At the bottom of the sash, there is a pocket for a battery and antennae. At the shoulder area, we clip a small microphone. This greatly frees up both the Joker and the audience member during interventions.

All the cameras and sound feed into the remote studio, where the TV director handles the live switching from one camera to the other (like live editing). The signal is then sent to the main studio, where it is fed to the network.

The theatre space needs phones. We get cell phones, sometimes borrowing them from friends. If we are doing a webcast, then the theatre also needs a high-speed internet connection, as we are also streaming video live to a large server. Sometimes we get the server donated, and other times we've had to rent the server space for the two-hour event.

For a webcast, we also have six computers at the performance space, so that the two of the web-actors can each have their own terminal at any given time, and so both the streaming video and the chat can be monitored in both Windows and Mac environments.

It is important to note that we have been doing this with very little money. The TV studio and all the broadcast equipment comes as part of our collaboration with SHAW Community Television. The camera and sound operators have been SHAW Community TV volunteers. The computers are a mix of Headlines' office computers and others borrowed for a few days from people involved in the project. The cell phones are borrowed.

---

[181] http://www.formaat.org/inenglish/index.php
[182] http://www.theatreoftheoppressed.org

We now have a growing group of ex-workshop participants who have experience doing both the tele-actor and web-actor roles. It is an art in and of itself to be the filter for an intervention from someone who is not in the theatre and who may, in fact, be on the other side of the planet!

The tele/web-actor's job is a complex one. On the Web she is visible and waiting in chat space, with a name of web-actor #1, #2 or #3. She is answering questions and waiting for someone who wants to do an intervention. When someone does, she takes the web-intervener into private chat and asks questions about the intervention. The tele-actor asks the same questions to potential interveners on the phone:

- Where are you (location)?
- What is your name and age?
- Where in the play are you yelling "Stop"?
- Which character do you want to replace?
- What do you want?
- Why? What do you hope to accomplish?
- What are you afraid of (as the character you are replacing)?

These questions are designed to help the tele/web-actor understand the intervener's intervention. She is going to run into the theatre and attempt to do the intervention on that person's behalf.

Because of the time pressures of live television, there is also the need for a mid-point (or intermediary) Joker. The tele/web-actor goes to this person and explains the intervention. This is necessary because of the lag between the live action on the stage (audience members are intervening live in the theatre) and the time it takes to ask the questions on the telephone or in chat. The mid-point Joker decides if the intervention will go to the stage. An intervention may not be done if it has already been done, if the Forum has moved on to another scene and the mid-point Joker decides that (again, because of time) it is impossible to go back, or if the intervention is early and therefore relevant to a moment later on in the play – in which case, it is held until the relevant moment comes. The mid-point Joker must be careful about making narrow judgments. As with the live audience in the theatre, sometimes an intervention will have a slightly different angle than one that has already been done, and investigating it will be worthwhile.

The tele/web event is very pressurized for everyone. Not only are there the regular things to deal with in a Forum, but the TV floor manager is counting down air time. Live TV starts exactly on time and, in our case, finishes *exactly two hours* later, regardless of where in the event we are. There are microphones strapped to the Joker and cast's bodies, camera-people trying to get close-ups, and any number of other distractions. In the midst of this, the most important thing for the Joker to do is keep connected to the live audience in the theatre. This is the only way the magic in the room will get transmitted onto the air and the Web.

The viewing audience outside the theatre does not appear by magic. They need to know the event is happening, when it is happening, and how to view it. This work starts anywhere from two to three months before the tele/webcast.

We have developed a web template after years of programming and design work. We are able to adapt the template with new design that reflects the imagery of each project. E-mails go out through Headlines' extensive networks, with requests to forward the notice to anyone, anywhere in the world, who might be interested. We stream video in both high and low bandwidths so people who are on 56k modems can view the project. In the e-mail that we send out, there's a link to the web page,[183] where the viewer will find these items:

- an explanation of how the webcast works
- technical requirements and a link to test the viewer's computer to see if it has the necessary applications installed
- if the test fails, a link to download a free PC or Mac video viewer, which will be necessary to view the show, as well as a link for the latest free Java plugin, necessary for the chat space
- a link to a time zone chart, which will tell the viewer what local time we will be broadcasting
- a link to view the webcast

You might ask why we put ourselves through all the work that it takes to do this once a year. The answer is simple: we reach a tremendously large and varied audience with theatre about issues that are very rarely discussed in an honest way on television. We estimate that, on SHAW

---

[183] See http://www.headlinestheatre.com/Meth/webcast/webcastintro.htm

Community TV, we reach approximately 15,000 people via a broadcast. Many of the productions have been rebroadcast, doubling and tripling that number. In the year 2000, when we webcast *Corporate U,* a project on globalization, we took our first international intervention – from Croatia!

A man named Sasha, viewing from Croatia, intervened on behalf of the character in the play, a young mother who has been working in the high-tech factory in Vancouver. She has lost her job because the company has been taken over by an overseas transnational. The mother has not been able to find work and has resorted to panhandling in the street (asking strangers for spare change). This is a story that plays out too often in Vancouver, a city that has a ever-widening gap between the monetarily wealthy and the poor.

The mother's child sits alone in their apartment watching television for hours. The television is portrayed by an actor wearing a TV set on his head. The TV fills the child with images of violence and consumption, with desires for things that are made by other children in sweatshops, with items her mother cannot afford. In the scene in which Sasha intervenes, the mother comes home disheartened, and she and the child have an argument because the child will not turn off the television. The mother, already under a great deal of stress, snaps and hits her child.

In the theatre we had been taking interventions that investigated the realities of pan-handling; we had worked on the situation inside the office and the ethics of transnational business dealings; we had also spent time in an overseas sweatshop.

Sasha's intervention tried to get inside the struggle of the mother and the way that her terrible situation was affecting her parenting. Sasha wanted, even from within the mother's struggle, to take time to talk with the child. He recognized that, while there are much larger employment and financial issues outside the home – issues we must not lose sight of and must work to resolve – we cannot sacrifice the smaller relationship moments for the larger, global issue. We must find healthy ways to function within the larger struggle.

Corporate U reached out through the Web from Vancouver, Canada, as did Sasha sitting at his computer in Croatia. From different parts of the planet, we used a theatrical moment to focus into the home and the relationship between parent and child, and into the connections between consumption and the absence of healthy relationship that are apparent in the scene.

Sasha's intervention was not a magic solution, but it was a first step towards a healthier relationship between the two characters. The intervention opened up questions and discussion in the theatre about the way the mother was dealing with the terrible situation in which she found herself. This was a global intervention on a play about the global and local stresses of globalization.

In 2003, when we webcast *Don't Say a Word*, a production on violence in the schools, we developed a collaboration with the Regina School District, two time zones east of our location. Lori Whiteman, an educator there, brought groups of students together around computers in Regina to participate in the Vancouver event.

As was mentioned in the *Here and Now (ਏਥੇ ਤੇ ਹੁਣ)* case study, the tele/webcast in 2005 was seen by an estimated 15,000 people in the Vancouver area, and approximately 1,200 international web-viewers. The chat log for this webcast contains entries from around the world.

The 2006 figures for the *Meth* tele/webcast are similar, with web log-ins from: Burnaby, Calgary, Coquitlam, Fort Nelson, Kitimat, Montreal, Ottawa, Prince George, Saskatoon, Terrace, Toronto, Vancouver, Victoria and Winnipeg, all in Canada; Bellingham, Everett, Milwaukee, Norfolk, New York City, Sacramento, Washington DC, and unnamed cities in the states of Arizona and Honolulu, all in the US; Armidale, Brisbane, Canberra, Hobart, Perth and Sydney, all in Australia; as well as Osaka, Japan; Scheemda, Netherlands; and Tel Aviv, Israel.

As well as the interventions in the theatre, we took interventions live from Australia, Honolulu, Israel and Winnipeg, Manitoba (Canada).

Once we recognize that a community is a living entity, it doesn't take long to start seeing that individual communities are part of even larger living organisms that comprise the human community that spans the planet. If the intent of our theatre is to create dialogue within the 'living community', then it seems to me we have a responsibility to keep doing these live tele/webcasts and, each time, to learn better ways to make them work.

Games and Exercises

Numerous games and exercises have been detailed in the body of the book. Following are some more that I use often. Many have come from Boal, some have come from other practitioners and participants, and others I have created myself.

Almost all of the games and exercises that I use that come from Boal have been adapted from the original in some way. This has happened slowly, over many years, as my work has evolved from the model of oppressor and oppressed to the systems theory model explained throughout the book. Many of these games, in different versions, can be found in Boal's *Games for Actors and Non-Actors*, published by Routledge in 1992. I encountered the games and exercises of Boal's that I am using before the publication of *Games for Actors and Non-Actors*. Upon writing this book and cross-referencing the activities, I have discovered many now have names that are different than what I remember and notated when I first encountered them. Having used these names for over 20 years, I am keeping my names and cross-referencing them to Boal's. Some games have no cross-referencing. In these instances, I have searched both my written and memory archives, and can't find a source.

Games and exercises should always be adapted and evolving in order to remain relevant to the situations in which a person is working.

A game or an exercise is an opportunity for movement of some kind. The Joker can't know what exactly will come out of any game or exercise, but can choose the activity to provide the group with an opportunity to make certain kinds of discoveries, at specific points in the project development process. These will build on previous discoveries and lead to future discoveries. In a *Power Play* process, which takes a living community from zero to performance in six days, the journey from walking into the workshop room on the first day, to performing collectively created plays on local issues together on the sixth day, demands that the Joker choose activities that move the group's journey forward.

Each game, each exercise, is an opportunity for movement towards individual and group epoché (suspension, conversion and letting go/receptivity).[184] In the process of stimulating the group consciousness to collectively create plays, each game and exercise must be chosen carefully to follow from the previous one and also to provide an opportunity for group reflection, *without being prescriptive*. The *Knots* game, for instance, may have very different meaning for group 'A' than for group 'B', and may take them a step in different directions. The Joker isn't trying to determine the conclusion that the group comes to – she simply provides the opportunity for the group to move in a direction together.

The games in Boal's *Theatre of the Oppressed* are divided into categories by sense: *See all that we look at* (because all day long we see things, but we don't really look at them), *Listen to all that we hear* (because all day long we listen to things, but we don't really hear them), *Feel all that we touch* (because all day long we touch things, but we don't really feel them), and *Several senses* (games that do not fit into one category). This is a wonderful way to think about these games, because they relate so strongly to the sense demands of an actor.

Sometimes people have the idea that the best actors are people who can 'turn on a performance'. I do not believe this is true. The best actors have the ability to really see, to really listen and to really feel 'in this moment'. "Acting is not acting – acting is being" might sound like a cliché, but it's true. All of the games in this book help us find new ways to see, listen and feel. They can be used both by professional actors and by people who have never thought of themselves as actors; in other words, by all humans.

---

[184] See the section on *Epoché* in the chapter *Awakening the Group Consciousness*.

I have kept Boal's game categories and, when encountering and incorporating games from others that I find useful, or inventing activities myself, have tried to fit them into these sense categories. The usefulness of this is that it helps me to keep the activity of the game focused. I believe that this, in turn, helps create safely defined space in which the workshop participants can explore.

I have made two other game categories: *Trust games* and *Games that are just fun*. The former are important to use each day and deserve their own category. The latter I use primarily as ways to release group tension.

I think the best way to explain how to do the games and exercises is to write, as I have been in the body of the book, as if you (the reader) are a participant in a workshop.

setting up the games

After each game, I ask the participants a question: "What's inside this for you"? When I ask this question, I am really asking two questions:

1. What does doing the game make you think about and feel personally?
2. Does the symbolism of the game create any insights for you, large or small, about the issues we are here to investigate?

I am not asking this question looking for a right answer. This is not a test. I am asking because the individual participants are going to be thinking and feeling things as we work. It is important to share these things with the group as much as possible. Then we can start to understand the different perspectives in the room and also start to listen to the larger consciousness, the consciousness of the living community, of which each participant is a part.[185]

---

[185] This circular activity of praxis (planning, action, reflection) is an integral part of creating the potential for group epoché. For explanations of praxis and epoché see the chapter *Awakening the Group Consciousness*.

See all that we look at

animals

> **Joker Tip:** This needs an even number of participants. Write the names of animals on pieces of paper, with an 'm' (male) or an 'f' (female) for each animal. Each animal should have both genders represented. There should be only as many animals as there are participants. Each participant chooses a piece of paper and does not show it to anyone else.

Everyone lie down on the floor. Know what animal you are, but don't tell anyone. How does this animal sleep? Sleep like the animal. Have a dream as the animal. Wake up as the animal. What does that look like? Feel like? Be thirsty and find water and drink. Be hungry and find food as the animal – no hunting of the other animals (!). And now, it is time to mate. Seek out your counterpart, male or female. You cannot talk. How do you find each other? Do you agree with the person who is trying to mate with you? If so, invent a mating dance and dance it together as the animals. If not, try to find a way to ward off these advances. You can make sounds, but no human talking.

After everyone has found their mate: Will one of the couples show us their mating dance? What animals are these? (Do a few – it's a lot of fun for the group.)

boxing[186]

Take a partner.[187] This is a boxing game. You can kick, scratch, bite, pull hair, hit below the belt – you can be as nasty and dirty and disgusting as you want. There are two rules: you must move in slow motion, and you cannot touch your partner. Begin. Move slowly. Keep focused. Move more and more slowly. (Let this go on for a while.)

---

[186] There is a version of this game called *Boxing match* in Boal's *Games for Actors and Non-Actors*, p. 131.
[187] For activities that need partners, always encourage the participants to work with people with whom they have not yet worked. This helps develop more connections and trust in the room.

Freeze. Everyone take three steps away from your partner. This is as close as you can get. Continue. Stay connected to each other. (Let this go on for a while.)

Freeze. Everyone take another three steps away from your partner. This is as close as you can get. Continue. Stay connected to each other. (Let this go on for a while.)

Now it is a barroom brawl. Anyone can go after anyone and from all the way across the room. Be alert. Go! Slow motion!

> **Joker Tip:** Apart from being a good tension release, and building physical awareness, this game has tremendous value in Forum Theatre. I am often in situations where the plays being made contain some form of violence. In order to be effective, this must look as real as possible in the play. We rehearse violence like dance – making it safe and exactly the same every time. In the Forum event, though, the interveners from the audience have not been in the workshop. They have had no rehearsal and are often in an enhanced state, nervous, emotional in some way. In order for the Forum to be valuable, we cannot shy away from an exploration of violence, but we are not there, of course, to hurt each other. The boxing game provides the rules under which we can explore violence in Forum. The actors have done the game and have also used the technique in rehearsal. Part of their role, along with the Joker, becomes helping the audience theatricalize the violent interventions. In this way we can explore what we need to and stay safe.
>
> The boxing game became very important to me in 1989 during the BC tour of ¿SANCTUARY?. We had performed the play and Forum many times. One night, a woman yelled "Stop!" at the point where the death squad bursts into the house looking for the student. The intervener was a small, elderly woman, and she chose to replace the woman whose house the student was hiding in. The intervener hid behind the door. When the death squad leader burst through the door, she ran out from behind and *jumped onto his back and started pummelling*

his head with her fists. Fortunately, the actor kept his wits about him and did not throw her off of him, potentially breaking some of her bones in the process. Here we were, doing a Forum play with violence in it, but had no mechanism to actually deal with an intervention that incorporated violence. The techniques in *Boxing* serve this purpose.

build an object[188]

Stand in a circle, please. Without speaking and as fast as possible, use your bodies to build a: telephone! car! coat hanger! etc.

> **Joker Tip:** This is a good game for encouraging creativity – thinking outside the box – and for group building.

choose a leader

Everyone stand in a tight circle, shoulder to shoulder. Close your eyes. As I walk around the outside of this circle, I am going to choose one of you to be 'the leader'. You will know you've been chosen to be the leader when I touch you on the back. Your leader, though, is going to lie to you. It will be the job of the leader to hide the fact that she is the leader. It will be the job of the rest of you to try to figure out who the leader is. When you think you know, stand in front of that person. Leader, you can do whatever you need to do (without actual violence or talking) to deflect the attention of the group away from you. OK. Open your eyes and break the circle. You can walk around the room. Who is hiding? Who is the leader?

> **Joker Tip:** This game is done in two parts. The first time, choose no one to be leader. After a while, bring the group back into the circle and repeat the process of choosing, this time choosing everyone.

---

[188] This game is from Joey Ayalla and the Philippine Education Theatre Association (PETA).

(During the second time, after the group has tried to find the leader for a while): OK, now, leader, be a leader. Without talking, get them to follow you. What does a leader do? What does a leader look like?

> **Joker Tip:** After you have done both parts, ask the group about what happened, what was different between the two times? Then tell them what you did.
>
> I often do this game after the group has made its plays and before we start rehearsals. I use it as a way for them to understand how powerful it is for characters to have secrets — just like people. (Because of the nature of this game, you can only really do it with a group once.)

energy clap

Let's gather together in as large a circle as possible. I have a large ball of energy in my hands. We are going to throw it around the circle. It works like this: we receive like this (clapping inward, towards your chest) and we give like this (clapping outward, in the direction of the person you are throwing the energy to). I throw the ball of energy across the circle to someone, that person receives it and throws to someone else, who receives it...

Try not to be too generous. Really focus your hands and your gaze on the person you are throwing the ball to. If you generalize, no one will know where the ball is going. (Let this go on for a while until the group has the hang of it.) Now do it faster.

fear/protector[189]

This is a game. Everyone stand, eyes open. Without talking, and keeping it a secret, choose someone who you are going to pretend to be afraid of. It's not someone you are really afraid of. Now, choose a different person who you are going to pretend is your protector — also

---

[189] There is a version of this game called *One person we fear, one person is our protector* in Boal's *Games for Actors and Non-Actors*, p. 132.

without talking. Keep it a secret. Your task is to keep your protector in between you and the person you are afraid of. Ready? Go!

> **Joker Tip:** I love this game. Sit back at a party or large social gathering sometime and watch the 'people currents' flow in the room. Many are chasing after some, running away from others, without talking about it. This happens in communities, too. If we can see this action and what it creates in the game, can we get a perspective on what it does in our lives?

fill the empty space[190]

Everyone walk around the room, eyes open, relaxed. Be aware of each other. Now, be aware of the spaces in between you and the other people and you and the walls. Fill the empty spaces. Don't let there be any empty space. (Let them do this for a while.) Do it faster. Be careful not to run into each other. And faster... (Let them do this for a while.) Freeze. In partners, arms linked, continue filling the empty space. (Let them do this for a while.) Faster...freeze. In threes. Some of you will have to split up and form new groups. Figure it out. Fill the empty space... Faster... (Let them do this for a while.) Freeze. Now, alone again, as fast as you can, fill the empty space. Don't let there be any empty spaces. Run as fast as you can, without bumping into other people.

> **Joker Tip:** This is a good game to do very early on in a workshop or if the group needs to change spaces sometime during the workshop – say, moving from the workshop space to a larger performance space.

---

[190] This version of this game came from Michael Rohd's Hope Is Vital workshop. There is a different version called *Without leaving empty a single space in the room* in Boal's *Games for Actors and Non-Actors*, p. 116.

hypnosis[191]

Take a partner – someone you haven't worked with yet. You are both going to do both parts of this, but don't change over until I ask you to. For now, decide who will be the hypnotizer 'A' and who will be hypnotized 'B'.

'A' holds her hand in front of 'B's face. As 'A' slowly moves her hand, 'B' keeps his face at the same plane as her palm, in the same relationship to the hand – tips of fingers to forehead, bottom of hand to chin. It is important not to place the hand too close to the other person's face, as he will go cross-eyed and be uncomfortable. The idea is to help your partner move his body into positions that he would not normally get into, to warm the partner up and to challenge him. While you are doing this, play nice – take care of him. Use the whole room – different levels – move through the room and the traffic of the other people working.

> **Joker Tip:** This is also possible, if there is an uneven number in the room, for one group to do with three people, 'A' using both hands for 'B' and 'C'.

After 'A' has led for a good while: Keep working and listen to these directions. I am going to clap my hands. When I do, switch over – leader becomes the follower – but don't break the rhythm. Clap!

After 'B' has led for a while: Freeze! Leaders – look around the room. In the same way your partner's face is attached to your hand, attach your face to the body part of someone else in the room – a knee, an elbow, a shoulder, etc. Don't forget your partner is still attached to your hand. OK. Continue.

> **Joker Tip:** In all the games that have partners, encourage the participants to work with someone they have not worked with before. This actively breaks down the cliques that will always exist in a group of people.

---

[191] There is a version of this game called *Colombian hypnosis* in Boal's *Games for Actors and Non-Actors*, p. 63.

mirror[192]

> **Joker Tip:** Many acting classes use mirror exercises. I first encountered them in high school drama, and then again in professional acting training. They are great for stimulating physical awareness and creating connections between people.

Take a partner and face each other. One leads; the other follows. No speaking. Make your movements slow and fluid. Mirror every aspect of your partner's movement. Change leaders. No leaders. The point is to synchronize thought and movement, not to trick each other. Move into groups of four and move, silently, with no leaders. Groups of eight (and so on until the whole group is facing each other). People in each line join hands, creating two long 'organisms' facing each other with no leaders. Break the group apart – find a new partner out of the chaos. Begin again...

parisian sword[193]

Stand in two groups facing each other. Each group should have a leader who will come forward and stand in front of their group. The leaders mime having broadswords. There are four possible movements: chopping off the head (high horizontal), chopping off the feet (low horizontal), chopping off either arm at the shoulder (left and right vertical). Each leader, and all the team members behind the leader, has to jump out of the way of the opposite leader's sword swings. That is: if the leader chops at the right arm, the whole group jumps to the left, away from the swing. If at the feet, the whole group jumps into the air.

If a member of the group gets 'chopped', he falls down in a very dramatic death. If the leader dies, someone from that group replaces her. The winning group is the last to have people standing.

---

[192] There is a sequence of *Mirror games* in Boal's *Games for Actors and Non-Actors*, starting on p. 120.

[193] There is a version of this game called *The wooden sword of Paris* in Boal's *Games for Actors and Non-Actors*, p. 81.

the plate[194]

Let's all stand in a large circle. (This game needs an even number.) Let's divide the circle in half, one side being 'A's and the other 'B's. In the case of 30 participants, we number off 1 to 15 (A) and 1 to 15 (B). 'A's and 'B's are partners, facing each other across the circle.

Imagine, in the middle of the circle, there is a ball the size of a basketball. Sitting on the ball, is a large plate, the size of the circle. Because the plate is on the ball, it will tip to one side or the other very easily. Opposing partners will come onto the plate and must keep the plate balanced. They cannot speak.

#2s, enter the plate...keeping it balanced...and now find your way off. #10s, enter the plate...keeping it balanced. #4s...etc.... Everyone, onto the plate. Keep it balanced.

Listen to all that we hear

> **Joker Tip:** Listening games are great for people who are preparing to be in a play. Sometimes people think that the best actors are those who can 'perform' the best – great pretenders. This is not true. The best actors are those who have the ability to centre themselves in a moment and really listen. Listening is one of the most difficult things an actor is asked to do. Listening means you are not on stage thinking about what your next line is, how much you like or hate your costume, the bills you have to pay, or how strange it is to be doing these things in front of all these people, or any number of other possible distractions.

---

[194] There is a version of this game called *Balancing circle* in Boal's *Games for Actors and Non-Actors*, p. 137.

lead the blind[195]

Take a partner. You are both going to do both parts of this, but don't switch over until I ask you to. One of you is going to be the leader (eyes open); the other will be blind (eyes closed). Decide on a sound together. No words; not language. Also not a mechanical sound, not clapping or stamping feet, but something you can make with your breath. The leader makes the sound and the blind partner follows. The leader has two signals: sound and no sound. No sound means stop. Everyone is going to be doing this at the same time, so you really have to listen! Take your blind partner around the room and don't have any collisions.

After a couple of minutes: Freeze. Take four or five steps away from each other. This is the closest you can get to each other. Continue.

After a couple of minutes: Freeze. Leaders, go as far away from your partners as you can. Not behind any furniture, please, and you must stay in the room. Leaders, stay where you are now, and start making your sounds, bringing your partner 'home' to you. Partners, once you reach 'home', please just wait silently until everyone is finished.

leader of the orchestra

Everyone sit in a circle. This is a listening game. Someone is going to offer to leave the room for a moment. Then, someone else will silently offer to be the leader. The leader will set up a rhythm (clapping, snapping fingers, whatever). All of us in the circle will do the rhythm with the leader. When the person outside hears us start, he will come back into the room and stand in the middle of the circle. He has three tries to figure out who the leader is. It's our job to protect the leader from being found out – so we should be looking at anyone in the circle other than the leader. The leader has to take risks and change the rhythm.

---

[195] There is a version of this game called *Noises* in Boal's *Games for Actors and Non-Actors*, p. 107.

Feel all that we touch

before doing blind games

Joker Tip: I have some strict rules for groups working with their eyes closed:

1. Hands are either by your sides, in your pockets or across your chest. They are not stretched out in front of you. This is to respect people's eyes (which can get poked) and people's privacy.

2. Heads are up. If two heads meet, it hurts a lot.

3. Speed is determined by the person doing the walking.

4. Don't forget to breathe.

Also, when doing blind games in which *everyone* has their eyes closed, it is a good idea to have 'spotters', people who ensure that the participants do not walk into dangerous areas of the room, if these exist. The spotter will gently turn the person back into the centre of the room. A coffee area, sharp furniture, etc. are dangerous; walls are not.

stand blind

Everyone find a space in the room. Stand with your eyes closed, hands by your sides. Find your centre of gravity by keeping your feet firmly on the floor and shifting your weight slightly forward, sideways and back. Play with it, leaning over almost to that point of falling, then come back to centre. Again...

Joker Tip: This is a preliminary to the first blind game. I will almost always follow this activity with *Find the Spot Blind*.

find the spot blind[196]

Each of you, please stand, on your own, anywhere in the room. Find a spot as far away from you as possible, at about eye level – not behind any furniture; someplace you can get to. Close your eyes. Without speaking, go there. If you encounter someone, don't open your eyes, just make your way around that person.

Joker Tip: I use this game to *start* doing blind work.

blind cars[197]

Take a partner. One of you is going to be the car and the other the driver. Driver, stand behind your car. Car, close your eyes. Driver, here are the signals: Patting on the top of the head means go forward. Patting on the left shoulder means turn left – on the right shoulder means turn right. Patting on the back means reverse. No pats means stop. This is a very important signal – no pats means stop. The speed of the car is determined by the car. Patting your car faster does not mean go faster. Really try to do this without talking. Communicate through the pats. Ready? Go. Move through traffic and try not to have any crashes. (Let this go on for a while.)

Freeze! The car becomes the driver; the driver becomes the car.

blind busses

(This is an adaptation of *Blind Cars* that is a lot of fun for groups.) Stand in lines of four or five people. The driver is the person in the back. He has his eyes open. All the others have their eyes closed. The signals work the same way as above. In blind busses, the driver pats the person in front of him, who pats the person in front of her, who pats the person in front of him, who starts to move forward. Move your

---

[196] There is a version of this game called *The point* in Boal's *Games for Actors and Non-Actors*, p. 106.
[197] There is a version of this game called *The blind car* in Boal's *Games for Actors and Non-Actors*, p. 111.

busses though traffic and try not to have any crashes or have your bus disintegrate.

> **Joker Tip:** After a while: "Person in front goes to the back." Repeat until everyone has had a chance to drive the bus.

blind hugs

This game needs an even number. Find a place in the room to stand on your own, close your eyes, find your centre, hands by your sides or across your front. Now, walk in silence. You will encounter people. As you do, very gently and respectfully, give them a hug. (Let the group do this for a while.) The next time you meet someone, stay in the hug. Each person needs to find a hug, but no three or more people together. Now, keeping your eyes closed, take two steps back from each other. Now find the same hug again. Now, five steps back from each other and find the same hug again. Now 10 steps away from each other and find the same hug again. Now as far away as possible and find the same hug again.

blind sculpture[198]

Make two equal lines, facing each other, about 10 feet apart: side 'A' and side 'B'. The person opposite you is your partner. Make sure you know their name. 'A's, close your eyes. 'B's, each person make a shape, with your own body, that you can hold for a while. Now, 'B's, call your partner's name until your partner touches you, then stop. 'A's, keeping your eyes closed, feel the shape that your partner has made with their body. When you believe you understand it fully, including facial expression, make your way back across the room and, using your own body, make a *mirror image* of the shape your partner is in. When you are finished open your eyes and compare. Once everyone is done, change over.

---

[198] There is a version of this game as a variation of *One blind line, one sighted line* in Boal's *Games for Actors and Non-Actors*, p. 109.

Joker Tip: If a group is working well together, I might also do a variation of this called *Group Blind Sculpture*. This works the same way as above, but each person in side 'B' will need to be touching at least one other person in side 'B', so that they form a group sculpture. When the 'A's come to the 'B's, eyes closed, their task is not only to explore the shape of their partner, but where their partner is within the larger group. 'A's must then go back and make a *mirror image* of the entire group sculpture.

electric current

     Joker Tip: This is a good group-centring game.

Stand in a circle, cross your arms over the front of your body and hold the hands of the people beside you. I am going to start a pulse going around the circle. A pulse is a hand squeeze that travels from one person to the next. Let's see if it can travel around the circle. Good. And now, in the other direction. Good. Now, with eyes closed, I will send many, many pulses around the circle in both directions. Your job is to keep the pulses moving through you; do not let any get trapped inside you.

glass cobra[199]

Find a place in the room to stand, eyes closed. Start to walk. As you walk and encounter people, give them a gentle, respectful hug from behind. Then move along. (Do this for a while.) Now, next time you find a hug, keep it until the whole group has formed a long line (or a circle) of people hugging each other from behind. Now, get to know the hug. Feel the shoulders and back; become aware of the texture of the clothing.

I am going to clap my hands. When I do, without violence, the cobra will shatter into as many pieces as there are people in the exercise. (Ready? Clap!) Now, keeping your eyes closed, and without speaking, find the same hug again. Be gentle and respectful with each other.

---

[199] There is a version of this game (same name) in Boal's *Games for Actors and Non-Actors*, p. 108.

Several senses

american football[200]

> **Joker Tip:** This needs a large group and a large room. I use it as a warm-up game and also as a tension release game.

Everyone, except one, go to one side of the room, against the wall. The one person go to the opposite wall. When I say "go," the group runs across the room to the opposite wall. The lone person has to catch one person of the group. Now there are two catchers. "Go" again... Now there are three or four catchers... Etc.

bears and tree planters[201]

One person needs to volunteer to be the bear. The rest are going to mime being tree planters. In silence, do what tree planters do in the forest. (No, not that, they plant trees!) When you hear the bear make a loud roar, all the tree planters play dead. The bear can do whatever he wants (being respectful, non-violent and without talking or tickling) to see if a tree planter is really 'dead'. If the tree planter moves, laughs, etc., she becomes a bear and works with the first bear on the tree planters. As we progress, there are more and more bears. When you hear the chirping of birds (this sound from the Joker), it is time for the bears to go back to their cave and strategize. It is also time for the tree planters to strategize. Another loud roar from the bears signals another round of investigating the tree planters. Bears can work together. Tree planters can work together. The aim is to be the last tree planter.

---

200 There is a version of this game (same name) in Boal's *Games for Actors and Non-Actors*, p. 82.
201 There is a version of this game called *The bear of Poitiers* in Boal's *Games for Actors and Non-Actors*, p. 79.

knots[202]

Everyone stand in a tight circle, shoulder to shoulder. Raise your hands above your heads, and step in further, breaking the circle, so the group is bunched up now, but still facing the centre. Now reach across the centre and each hand take a hand. Don't take the same person's two hands. (The Joker often has to check and bring the last few 'orphan' hands together.) *Without talking,* and *without letting go of the hands,* undo the knot.

> **Joker Tip:** Some groups are very good at this. For a real challenge, do the game with eyes closed.

person to person[203]

This needs an even number of participants. Everyone walk quickly, eyes open, around the room. When I yell "Person to person!" stand with the person who is closest to you. This is your partner. When I yell (e.g.) "Finger to knee!" – without discussion, one finger goes to one knee. Then (e.g.) "Foot to waist!" – one foot to one waist. I will call out body parts until it appears to be impossible to continue. Then, I will again call out "Person to person!" This is the signal for partners to disengage and to start walking again until the next "Person to person!"

> **Joker Tip:** After a while of doing this, either take someone out or add yourself in to make an odd number. Then, when you yell "Person to person!", the person who is left with no partner calls the body parts.

---

[202] There is a version of this game called *Circle of knots* in Boal's *Games for Actors and Non-Actors*, p. 67.
[203] There is a version of this game (same name) in Boal's *Games for Actors and Non-Actors*, p. 78.

the journey[204]

Everyone take a partner. You are both going to do both parts of this, but don't switch over until you are asked to. Decide who is going to lead (#1) and who is going to follow (#2). #1 is going to take #2 on a journey. #2 has his eyes closed. #1 has her eyes open. #1 is responsible for *everything* – all the movement, the environment, the sounds, the weather, the textures, everything. The journey does not have to be linear, but make each moment as detailed and as physical (but safe!) as possible. There can be no language used – no explaining. When you are finished the journey, do not discuss anything, just sit quietly and wait until everyone is finished working. Once everyone has finished, #2 explains to #1 his interpretation of the journey. Then #1 responds with what she created for #2. Then, when everyone is finished talking and comparing different interpretations, change over.

walk sitting[205]

Tricky, this one. Everyone stand in a tight circle. Now, turn to the right and tighten the circle more. Now, slowly and gently, everyone sit down (!) into each other's laps. In unison (left, right, left, right) start to walk. This needs a large group.

west side story[206]

Make two equal lines facing each other, about six feet apart, on one end of the room. One person from the (Joker's) right side of each line comes into the centre space and stands in front of their group (opposite the other group). These are the leaders of group #1 (closest to the wall) and group #2 (backs facing the rest of the room).

Leader #1 does a rhythmic sound and gesture (no language) that is a challenge to the other leader and her group. This challenge must be

---

[204] There is a version of this game called *Imaginary journey* in Boal's *Games for Actors and Non-Actors*, p. 107.
[205] There is a version of this game called *The chair* in Boal's *Games for Actors and Non-Actors*, p. 79.
[206] There is a version of this game (same name) in Boal's *Games for Actors and Non-Actors*, p. 93.

able to travel forward. Leader #1's group, having seen the challenge, copies it and does it with their leader, as loud and big as possible, backing leader #2 and his group up until they reach the opposite wall of the room. Then leader #2 responds with another sound-and-gesture challenge, which his group copies and does with him, backing leader #1 and her group to the far wall. Then both leaders #1 and #2 join the lines on the (Joker's) far left side and two new leaders come to the centre from the right. Leader #1 makes a challenge, which his group repeats, backing up leader #2 and her group... And back and forth and back and forth. This is best when it is done quickly and loudly. Really make the challenges as big and 'scary' as possible. Don't think too much!!

Trust games

Joker Tip: Following is a series of trust games, in the sequence that I would usually do them, during a *Theatre for Living Power Play* workshop – that is, a six-day process that takes a group to Forum Theatre performance. Generally, I start trust games on the second day. I have some very strict rules in the trust games:

1.   People *volunteer themselves*, not each other. No one will be coerced to do a trust game.
2.   The games must be done in complete silence, directions coming only from the Joker. If there is whispering and talking in a trust game, it breaks what can be a meditative experience for the person in the centre of the moment.
3.   The Joker is always the first to do the trust game. I don't ask people to do something that I will not do myself.
4.   No one in the room is ever too little or too big to do the game.

glass bottle[207]

We need circles of five to eight people. One person stands in the middle of the circle, hands by his sides or across his front, eyes closed, body completely stiff. The people in the circle stand with your strong leg behind you, hands extended but not stiff. Your arms should be like shock absorbers in a car.

The people in the circle gently place your hands on the shoulders of the person in the centre. This is the signal that you are there, ready and focused. Hands off now, and arms ready to catch. The person in the middle then tips, giving his weight to someone in the circle. The people in the circle can move – always two people supporting the person in the middle, really taking his weight and then *placing him gently back into centre – NOT pushing him over*. The person in the centre – go where gravity takes you.

> **Joker Tip:** Let this go on for a long while. It is very important that the person in the middle be allowed to *surrender to gravity* – not be pushed across or around the circle. Each person's turn can end in one of three ways:
>
> 1. the person in the middle says they want to stop
> 2. the group feels the natural rhythm of the person's turn
> 3. if it goes on too long, the Joker signals the end to the turn

To finish: people in the circle place your hands back onto the shoulders of the person in the middle – a grounding moment before that person rejoins the circle and someone else volunteers to go in the middle.

---

[207] I first encountered this game as an acting student in 1981. There is a version called *Joe Egg* in Boal's *Games for Actors and Non-Actors*, p. 67.

the intestine

This needs around 20 people to be effective, the more the better. Form two lines facing each other. Stand close together in the lines so the sides of your arms touch; arms extended out towards the line opposite, arms interspersed, but not linked. The lines form a tube-like conveyer belt – the intestine.

This exercise needs to happen in absolute, pin-drop silence. Now, one of the people at this end of the line (which end is designated by the Joker), please volunteer to go through the intestine. Stand with your back to the opening, hands crossed over your chest, body completely stiff but neck relaxed, eyes closed. The group's arms will support your head as you move through. Now, lie back into the opening, your upper body supported by the first two people in line, as the Joker lifts your feet off the ground.

Remember to push up to the ceiling through your pelvis – this will help distribute your weight away from the centre of your body.

With a horizontal movement of the forearms, always supporting his head, move him through the tube. The movement should be fairly fast as this helps keep his weight moving forward.

The Joker will receive you at the other end, your head coming out first.

Support his head and when his body is about half out of the tube, the people at this end of the line gently bring his feet underneath him and into a standing position. Now, join this end of the line and someone else from the other end offer to go through. If it is your turn and you do not want to go through, that's OK – just move to the other end of the line, into the position you would be in at the end of your turn.

the fall

Joker Tip: Bring a sturdy table into the middle of the room, or this also can be done off of a two or three-foot-high stage. If you are using a table, one person should sit on the other end of the table, so it doesn't tip.

Six people form two lines facing each other, please, at the end of the table, with hands and forearms extended in front of your bodies so a flat surface like a stretcher is created at one end of the table. Stand shoulder to shoulder. Wrist jewelry should come off.

Who wants to fall? Join me on the table, please, with your back to the six catchers. Make your body completely stiff and cross your arms over your chest, clasping your shoulders and tucking in your elbows, eyes closed. Breathe in deeply and on the exhale, fall back, off the table, into the catchers' arms. I will not, under any circumstances, push you – even if you ask me to.

> **Joker Tip:** The person falling must be completely stiff, being careful not to go back with their bum sticking out (creating a wedge) or swinging their arms out (a reflex action when falling), hitting the catchers in the face. The catchers need to take the weight in their legs, not their backs. If any of the catchers get tired, they should be replaced by other people from the group.

catch me

Ten or 12 of the group stand on one side of the room with eyes open, making an inverted 'U' with your bodies. Stretch your arms out, palms facing outward. Your arms should not be tense; make then relaxed – soft like clouds. You are the catchers. Who wants to run? Come here, to the other side of the room, as far away from them as possible.

Take aim at the opening of the inverted 'U', close your eyes, now run as fast as you can (keeping your arms by your sides or across your chest, so they don't churn as you run) until you reach the group's arms. The group will 'absorb' you.

It is not the runner's job to bulldoze to the end of the group, but merely to reach the hands. The runner has their eyes closed, so if they veer off course, the catchers must move, as silently as possible, so they can catch the runner.

group walking[208]

Who wants to walk above the group? Take your shoes off, please. The group – surround the walker, people on all sides. Walker, raise one foot. Group – hands come under to support the foot. Walker – bring one of your hands out in front of you – and there are group hands to support it. Another hand; more hands. The second foot now, hands to support that foot... Now, walker, moving very slowly, climb up on top of the group! Each time you move a foot or a hand, wait for the group to respond with support.

> **Joker Tip:** It is the group's responsibility to support the walker wherever he wants to go. If the walker does a forward roll (or anything else) the group should move underneath him to support. The walker must move very slowly, spreading his weight out between his hands and feet, not standing upright. When he is done, the group can very gently bring him back to the floor.

Games that are just fun

> **Joker Tip:** These games are good to use any time a tension release seems appropriate.

bellies[209]

Someone, lie down on your back. Now, a second person lie down, at a right angle, with your head on the first person's belly. A third person lie down, at a right angle, with your head on the belly of the second. A fourth lie down, at a right angle, with your head on the belly of the third. Etc., until you are all lying down, on your backs, with your head on someone's belly.

Now, everyone, breathe. Don't talk; just breathe together.

---

[208] I experienced this game in a workshop with Boal, but can find no written reference.
[209] Suzie Payne, a co-founder of Headlines Theatre, did this game with us in rehearsal for Headlines' first play, *Buy, Buy Vancouver*, in 1981.

Joker Tip: Now, wait in silence. After a while, almost certainly, someone will start to laugh, and their belly will move up and down, moving the head of the person lying on them – who will start to laugh... This is a wonderful, infectious tension release for a group. It can sometimes lead to wave after wave after wave of deep laughter.

cat and mouse[210]

Everyone stand on your own in the room, with as much space between you as possible. Who wants to be the cat? OK. Who wants to be the mouse? OK. The mouse is safe and cannot be tagged if the mouse stands behind someone. When the mouse does stand behind someone, the person in front becomes the mouse and runs from the cat. If the mouse is tagged by the cat, the mouse turns into the cat and chases the old cat, who is now the mouse, who is trying to stand behind someone...

fox in the hole[211]

Everyone needs a partner. Spread out in the room, but no one against a wall. Stand facing your partner, holding her hands so that the two of you create a horizontal 'O' with your arms. I am going to choose two of you to be a Fox and a Hound. OK. The Hound chases the Fox. This is a tag game. The Fox is safe if he gets into one of the holes (the 'O' of people's arms). The fox gets into a hole, takes the hands of the person he is facing, and pushes the one at his back out, which turns him into a Fox who is now being chased by the Hound. If the Hound tags the Fox, they switch roles and the 'new' Fox must get into a hole before being re-tagged.

Joker Tip: Groups (both youth and adults) *love* this game and sometimes ask to do it many times a day!

---

[210] This game is from Takayama Lisa and the Theatre Workshop Network in Japan.
[211] This game is from workshop participants at F.H. Collins School in Whitehorse, Yukon (1991).

group yell

> **Joker Tip:** At the end of a particularly emotional day, after the final circle, it seemed we needed something more to end the workshop session, but we were out of time. I suggested the following and now use it in almost every workshop.

Stand in a large circle, holding hands. Everyone together: Exhale. Inhale. Now, let's rush together into the centre of the circle, with our arms up in the air, and everyone yell as loud as you can, shooting your voices up through the ceiling. Now that we understand the mechanics of it, let's do it again.

hug tag

This is a tag game. Who wants to be 'it'? OK. You can tag anyone. People are safe from being tagged as long as they are in a hug. People can stay in a hug up to the count of three, and then they must separate. If a person is tagged, they become 'it'.

massage and run[212]

> **Joker Tip:** I use this at the end of a day, after a final circle.

Stand in a circle. Everyone turn to your right. Start walking slowly, and very gently massage the shoulders and back of the person in front of you. Keep it gentle. (After a while) Now, turn around and go the other way, massaging the person who was massaging you. (After a while) Now, go the other way. (A shorter time) The other way. (A shorter time) The other way! The other way!

---

[212] This is a game from Kevin Finnan of Motionhouse Dance Theatre in Leamington Spa, UK.

Joker Tip: Give the group enough space so that the circle starts to extend further than people's arms can reach. This will make it necessary for the participants to run to catch up to each other, faster and faster, until it all collapses into chaos.

the serpent[213]

Get into groups of three, please, standing in straight lines. The person in front is the mouth and uses her arms like jaws. She has her eyes closed. The person in the middle is the heart. She has her eyes open and steers the mouth and tries to protect the tail (the person in the back), who has his eyes closed. Tails can be eaten (tagged) by mouths. If a serpent's tail is tagged, the serpent is 'out'. The task is to be the last serpent. Go!

More exercises

Numerous exercises have been detailed in the body of the book. Here are some more.

autosculpting[214]

Joker Tip: I will sometimes use this exercise in the *early stages* of exploration in a week-long *Power Play* process. It can be very effective in exploring emotionally charged material and the creation of fairly generic (non-specific) improvisations.

Everyone lie down in a circle, with your heads facing inwards, your feet pointing out. Yes, it looks like a human daisy. Close your eyes. I want you to think of a moment in your own life – not a friend's life, not a relative's life, not the movies or TV – when you were engaged in a

---

[213] This game is from Takayama Lisa and the Theatre Workshop Network in Japan.
[214] This begins in a similar way as the second method of model development of Boal's *Illustrating a subject with your body* on p. 165 of *Games for Actors and Non-Actors*, but then it goes in a very different direction.

struggle about (the focus of the workshop). This could be a struggle with another person or a struggle within yourself.

See the situation clearly. Where does it take place? Who are the players? What are the relationships between the people? Where are you in the moment? What are you thinking? What are you feeling? What do you want? What are you afraid of?

I want you to think about the strongest emotion that you feel in the moment, and turn that emotion into a shape that you can see in your mind. Take some time to find this, keeping your eyes closed. Be specific. There is a difference, for instance, between frustration and anger.

Now, still with your eyes closed, everyone roll over onto your right side. And now, everyone onto all fours, and then onto your feet, keeping your eyes closed. I am going to clap my hands. When you hear the handclap, I want each of you, still with your eyes closed, to make the shape you have in your mind, using as much of your body as you can. Ready? Clap!

Now, staying in your shape as much as possible, and without speaking, look around the room. Are there shapes that you think you fit together with? Shapes that resemble your shape somehow, either on a physical or emotional level? If so, go to that shape, and if that shape goes to another shape, go with it. Do this while keeping in your shapes as much as you can.

Good. We have made 'x' number of groups.[215] Each group sit in a circle please, with space between the groups so you don't bother each other. In your circles, I want you to talk about the emotions that went into your shapes. If you have personal stories that you want to tell, that's OK, but you don't have to tell personal stories if you don't want to. I do want you to discuss the emotions, though. What did your struggle with this issue make you feel? As you talk, you are going to find that there is something that you share, that links the individuals in this group together. Seek it out. Name it. Talk about it. Define it as a kind of struggle.

---

[215] There is no way for the Joker to predetermine how many groups will be created in *Autosculpting*.

Then, I want one person from each group to come forward; someone willing to work from his/her own original shape. The person who comes forward is not representing her group, but the work she does will be informed by the conversation she has had with her group. We will do sound and gesture work, to create characters.

Who wants to come forward? (It is now this person and the Joker in front of all the other participants.) Show us your original shape. This is the shape of the Protagonist. As the Protagonist, can you offer a gesture, one movement, that goes from a neutral position into a gesture of the Protagonist? (Sometimes this will mean going from hands by sides into the shape, or going from the shape into another shape – whatever the participant offers.) OK. And can you make a sound that goes with that shape? No language, no talking, just a sound that goes with this gesture of the Protagonist. Good. Do it three times now, from neutral to sound and gesture – neutral, sound and gesture – neutral, sound and gesture – and back to neutral. Great. Let's leave that over there, and move to another spot in the playing area.

In this moment there is also an Antagonist. Can you offer a gesture, starting from neutral, that represents the Antagonist? Good. And a sound? Good. Do that three times.

So now we have a sound and gesture of the Protagonist and of the Antagonist. The person creating the image is the Protagonist. Can someone, not from this person's group (they have inside knowledge) offer to play the Antagonist? That is, learn the sound and gesture and then turn that into a character? OK, come.

Protagonist, teach this new person the sound and gesture of the Antagonist, by example only, please. No explaining. When the Protagonist is satisfied, we'll continue.

OK. I am going to ask you now to play a scene with each other, just using the sounds and gestures. First, the Protagonist will make his sound and gesture and the Antagonist will respond with her sound and gesture. Three times, please.

Now again, but this time the Antagonist will make her sound and gesture and the Protagonist will respond with his sound and gesture. Three times, please.

(To the rest of the group) Which order makes the most sense? The Protagonist initiating or the Antagonist initiating? OK – we'll do it that way.

So now I am going to ask the two of you to have this conversation, with just the sound and gesture, and *keep going* until I clap my hands. Keep eye contact with each other as much as you can. Stay focused; let whatever these characters are thinking and feeling build up inside you and when I clap my hands, one of you (I will let you know who at that moment) will talk first. Tell the truth of the character as you feel it. This is a very important moment. The other one of you must be very flexible in this moment. The first person might say something that takes you completely off guard. Try to accept the reality that has been created in the moment and respond – try not to go "No... That's not what this is about..." Accept the reality and respond. Once each of you has spoken, keep going – let's see if there is a scene here. Ready? Here we go.

> **Joker Tip:** Sometimes, depending on how the group has been working, I may have done *Speed Gestures*[216] before this exercise.
>
> To animate *Autosculpting*, I will place myself on the floor below the Protagonist and Antagonist and speak softly as they have the sound and gesture conversation. "Keep going...again...do it a little faster...keep eye contact as much as possible...allow the movement and sound to create a character...when I clap my hands 'y' speaks...once you start, try to keep it going..."
>
> This process often leads to very deeply emotional improvisations that are about the heart of a generic moment of struggle, but not about the details. We are seeking an emotional truth at this point in the workshop process. This can be a very valuable part of the larger process of finding the core of the living community's story.

---

[216] *Speed gestures* is explained in the section *an example in Iqaluit, Nunavut* in the chapter *In the Workshop Room*.

It is also possible, after the animation has been done with the Antagonist and Protagonist, to ask these two to freeze in their gestures as in a frozen image and then to do Image Theatre work.

Joker Tip 2: Sometimes in exercises like this there will be people who do not feel they belong with anyone. They are alone. No one will be able to relate to them and/or they cannot relate to anyone else. They are the 'loners', or 'outcasts'. Acknowledge this with them, and ask them to be a group. They will, most often, find things they have in common. As it is very hard to work alone in this exercise, if there is only one loner/outcast, ask this person to try to join a group.

build tableaux

Can anyone in the group, using anyone else in the group that they want, sculpt an image? Sculpting only – no speaking, no explaining (naming the image). Remember the concept of 'intelligent clay'.[217]

improvise with your family[218]

Everyone walk around the room, eyes open, just as yourself. As you do that, think of a person – it could be someone you know in your life, someone from the news, even someone iconic, who you believe is part of the problem in regard to the issue we are exploring.[219] You never have to tell anyone who this person is, unless you want to. Walk like that character. How does she walk – in short steps or long steps? Quick or slow steps? Where is her centre of gravity? Which part of the body does she lead from? Develop the walk of this character. Now, think of a

---

[217] For an explanation of 'intelligent clay' see the exercise *sculpting partners/build an image* in the *Making images* section of the chapter *In the Workshop Room*.
[218] This exercise came out of an experiment, working with Judith Marcuse of Judith Marcuse Projects (then called Dance Arts Vancouver) in 1999. I was doing a workshop for her with youth, which was part of a research process for her production *Fire...where there's smoke*, a large dance piece on issues of youth violence. See http://www.jmprojects.ca/
[219] This invitation can be adapted in various ways: think about a politician, or a cartoon character, etc.

gesture that represents this person. One movement, with a hand, arm, face, head, shoulder, etc., that you can do over and over, that represents the character. Now, a sound – not language – it could be a sound this person actually makes or it could be symbolic of the person – a sound that represents the character.

So now you have a broad character – a caricature – that is made up of this walk, gesture and sound.

As you walk around the room as this character, I want you to start to recognize and acknowledge the other characters in the room. If you see someone who you believe is a member of your 'family' – someone who you think you belong with, walk with that character. If someone joins you, you have to let them. Let's form some groups this way.

> **Joker Tip:** Give this a while and then take the time to understand where the boundaries between the groups are. It's OK to have a group of two, but not a group of one. If there are people who are alone, not joined to any group, bring them together into a family of 'loners'. As it is very hard to work alone in this exercise, if there is only one loner/outcast, ask this person to try to join a group.

Now, sit in small circles and talk with each other. You can tell people who you are if you want, but you don't have to. I do want you to share your character's desires, fears, actions, motivations. Then, working together, make an improvisation, a short skit, that shows us these characters in a situation of conflict or dysfunction – dealing with some kind of internal, *relevant* 'family' crisis.[220]

> **Joker Tip:** I do not give groups a lot of time to work in this exercise. I may say to them that I want to see the improvisations in 10 or 15 minutes. They must work very quickly.

---

[220] An example: in one workshop a small group of cartoon super-villains ended up in a crisis, not able to agree on how they were going to destroy the world. The improvisation was very rich and full of analysis of the various forms of violence and disaster that currently appear on the planet. It generated both great characters and material for later in the process.

OK. Let's see each other's improvisations.

> **Joker Tip:** Treat each improvisation like an image. Ask
> the audience what they see, what their interpretations of
> the characters and their actions are. There is often a ter-
> rific richness in the different perspectives and analysis
> that come from the group.

a photo exhibit

> This is not an exercise per se, but I am including it here as an
> example of the kinds of exciting projects that can happen if we
> are willing to collaborate outside our known discipline.

In 1997, Headlines Theatre and the grunt gallery[221] worked together on
a project called *Positive+*. We gathered a group of artists, all of whom
were either HIV+ or who had loved ones who were HIV+, and who
wanted to create a photographic exhibition as a way to tell stories of
HIV and AIDS.

We used *Theatre for Living* techniques for a week to explore issues in
the group. A professional photographer was in the workshop with us,
taking photographs of the images that we made. During the course of
the week, we started to understand the differences in physical language
needed to create images for the theatre and images for photography.
The images for photography, for instance, needed to take up less
physical space than they would in the theatre in order to be effective.
We also realized that we could work with much more subtle facial
expressions, due to the nature of photography close-ups, than we could
in broader, theatrical images.

The result was a very powerful photographic exhibit that was hung at
the Roundhouse Community Centre in Vancouver.

---

221 The grunt is an artist-run centre formed in 1984 in Vancouver, BC.
See http://www.grunt.bc.ca/

Image Theatre animation techniques

Numerous animation techniques[222] have been detailed in the body of the book. Here are some more.

ideal image

We have an image in front of us that is an image of characters engaged in a struggle. Can someone from outside the image imagine these characters in a new, ideal image in which they have achieved 'a healthy community', or 'respect', or 'safety'? (The language of this question changes, depending on the investigation being made.)[223] We are looking for an idea that is possible, not 'magic'.[224]

You have an idea? Come and re-sculpt the people in the image into your ideal image. Be as specific as you can with body shapes, facial expressions, etc., and don't forget the relationship of one character to another.

People in the image: Remember this new image, try to understand what you are thinking and feeling in it. Now, return to the original image. On a series of handclaps, one step at a time, let's see if you can get from the original image to the ideal, but you must remain true to your character in the original image. This means you might get to the ideal and you might not; your character might want to or might not; your character might feel fine about other people getting there, and he might not. Keep in mind that you can also affect each other. Don't be afraid to touch. Each step is a new image; use as much of your bodies as you can.

---

[222] There are numerous other animation techniques in Boal's *Games for Actors and Non-Actors*, pp. 164-200.

[223] I purposefully keep this language vague. One person's 'safety' may very well be another person's 'danger'. Inside the workshop environment and also Forum Theatre events, the conversations about this are very valuable for helping us get beyond the symptoms of issues and into the root causes.

[224] 'Magic' is a term that is used to describe those moments when a participant or an audience member creates a solution in which the problem vanishes as if by 'magic'. For example, a character who is carrying a gun, is suddenly against carrying a weapon.

> **Joker Tip:** Take at least six handclaps to explore this, depending on the complexity of the image, the spaces in between the characters, and the intensity of what happens.

(To the audience) What do we see when we watch this? What insights do we have from the symbolism of the journey? Did we get to the ideal? How? Why? Why not? Other ideal image ideas?

image into dance[225]

Be in the image, please, and do an internal monologue,[226] just inside you, not out loud. What is the essence of your character? An animal, a bird, an insect, a tree or other plant, a flower, water, wind, fire, smoke, etc.? What is the sound of the essence? Let that sound be inside you. As you hear the sound inside you, what rhythm does that sound create inside you? Let the sound and the rhythm build up, like an internal monologue – without words, but with emotion and desire. Do this just inside you; don't make it out loud or with your body.

Now, with your eyes closed, let your bodies move in the rhythm. After a while, let the sound out with the movement.

(To the audience) What do we see when we watch this? What insights do we have from the symbolism of the physical journey?

The results of this exercise are raw movement, which, during discussion, we may discover are attached to narrative. This movement and narrative can be choreographed, like any play can be directed, into dance that is about issues in the community's life.

---

225 This technique was developed in 1998 with Hal Blackwater, in a *Theatre for Living* workshop with Dancers of the Mist in Kispiox, BC. See the *Dancers of the Mist* case study for a detailed explanation.
226 See the *Image activation* section of the chapter *In the Workshop Room.*

orchestra of emotion

Each of you, settle into the strongest emotion that you are feeling as the character inside this image. Now, hear a sound, just inside you – don't make it out loud – that expresses the emotion. No words – not a mechanical sound – something you can make with your breath. Each time I touch you, make the sound out loud. It is OK for the sound to evolve, to change, as the animation progresses and you hear the other characters' sounds. Have a conversation with the sounds, making your sound each time I touch you.

stepping into the future

> This technique is good to use if an image seems unclear. What would it look like one or two steps further down the road to the crisis? Make sure the people in the image have an idea for themselves of what their desires are. What do their characters want?

On a series of handclaps, one step at a time, each step being a frozen image, move in the direction of getting what you want. Keep in mind that, while you cannot talk, you can affect each other physically.

> This can also be done in reverse – stepping into the past to see where the characters have come from in their journey into the crisis.

Rehearsal techniques[227]

> **Joker Tip:** I want to stress that when the time comes for participants to give birth to their plays, very often as the end result of either the *Song of the Mermaid* or the *Magnetic Image* exercises, I will not help them. Very occasionally, groups complain bitterly about this. However,

---

[227] There are various rehearsal techniques in Boal's *Games for Actors and Non-Actors*, pp. 201-222.

after all the group-building work, the trust games and the exploration of issues through Image Theatre, they have the ability to put the skills they have been acquiring into practice; they can do this. The plays do not have to be long or even fully formed. Sometimes the plays groups make are 30 seconds long and incredibly rough. However, the group has had to figure out how to work together and how to use a theatrical language to tell its collective story. They now *own the play* because they have made it together, on their own. This ownership is extremely important.

Once they have made their plays, the Joker, who has done the workshop with the participants, must now be able to get inside the plays with them and make the plays work for Forum Theatre. This can mean editing out, suggesting or extending moments, clarifying characters, layering subtext, directing audience focus, and many other tasks. Each *Theatre for Living* workshop has its own surprises. The important thing is to accomplish this clarifying, layering, etc., while remaining true to the intent of the piece that the participants made.

Leaving the group to its own devices, or suggesting that whatever comes from the group is what goes before an audience, is, in my opinion, abrogating one's responsibilities to the group. Once the group has made their core plays, if the Joker is not going to help them make the best theatre possible with these plays under the circumstances in which they are working, why is he there?

Once the participants have made their core plays, the Joker's role must change from being a workshop facilitator to being a theatre director. I am very clear at this point that a play can only have one director and that person is the Joker. I ask the group to refrain from directing each other, and to allow the Joker to work with the actors. It is the actor who must know what he is doing in every moment. No one will give him advice on how to respond in the Forum.

I generally see the play(s) they have created and then have a break, coming back with ideas that I will work on with the group. My method of working is to move through the play very slowly, sometimes in five or 10-second segments, getting those moments to work, going back to the beginning, running another segment, getting those moments to work and setting them, running from the beginning again... When we are done this process, the cast knows all their lines and can usually pick up the action from anywhere in the play, which will be essential in the Forum. Pen has never gone to paper during any of this process to create the script.

Numerous rehearsal techniques have been detailed in the body of the book. Following are some more techniques that I use once the creation process (above) is finished. Keep in mind that, often, the best thing to do in rehearsal is to make it up as you go along and experiment with ideas that are appropriate to the material. This is how the work evolves.

analysis by emotion[228]

Play a scene focusing on *one emotion only*, such as 'love' or 'hate' or 'joy'. Primal emotions work the best. This layers the characters' relationships with each other. Subtext discoveries become possible.

contrary thought[229]

Joker Tip: How many times in a day, while rising out of a chair, do you think, "Oh good, now I am going to get up out of this chair!"? Chances are you are thinking something else, perhaps something opposite to what you are doing. This is a simple exercise that charges scenes

---

[228] I first encountered this exercise in theatre school in 1971. There is a version called *Analytical rehearsal of emotion* in Boal's *Games for Actors and Non-Actors*, p. 214.

[229] I first encountered this exercise in theatre school in 1971. There is a version called *Opposite thought* in Boal's *Games for Actors and Non-Actors*, p. 215.

with subtext. It is also very basic to the core of all theatre making. All scenes must contain dramatic tension, not just *between* the characters, but *inside* the characters. It becomes apparent, through an investigation of this, that all people contain these basic elements of fear and desire, will and counter will, often at the same time.

Let's play the scene. If you are going to stand up, pause and think about how you don't want to. If you are going to strike someone, pause and think about how much you love him. If you are making an entrance, pause and think about how much/why you don't want to be there. Etc. In the pauses, speak this contrary thought like an internal monologue. What do we discover? What can we use?

magnify[230]

> **Joker Tip:** While we are making theatre about real life, the theatre is not real life, it is the theatre. Our actions, our voices, sometimes our emotions, need to be bigger in the theatre than in real life – and bigger than in film or television. An audience needs to be able to receive the live play across the space between the audience and the actors, even if that physical space is small. If the magnification gets too large, it's possible to pull it back, but the actors will have experienced something of great value for performance.

Play the scene with all the actions, emotions, fears, desires, as big as possible. Bigger! Don't stop doing it... It's an exercise... Make it bigger.

rituals

> **Joker Tip:** This is a good technique for helping the actors set up and understand the rituals, the repetitive actions (perhaps so ingrained they have become unconscious) of their characters; also to understand the

---

230 I first encountered this exercise in theatre school in 1971. There is a version called *Exaggeration* in Boal's *Games for Actors and Non-Actors*, p. 219.

physical space of the play. I find this technique works best with one actor, usually the one who's character 'owns' the location of the play, but I have also used it with entire casts.[231] For example, if a scene takes place in an office, or a kitchen, what are the habitual things that the character does?

Without talking, explore all of the physical movements that your character does in this space. Take your time and be as specific as possible. Do it again but faster. And again, but with more detail. Now, try to play the scene, keeping as much of the movement as possible.

roshomon[232]

"This technique is based on the Akira Kurosawa film of the same name, in which the story of a rape is told from five points of view – that of the rapist, the victim, witnesses, etc. It is particularly useful when analyzing a scene with several people, all of whom may have different versions of what is happening."[233]

Joker Tip: I used this wonderful technique of Boal's extensively in rehearsals for a mainstage play on dying with dignity called *The Dying Game*.[234] Along with the cast, I invited 15 people from the community who were living the issues under investigation into the rehearsal hall.

After showing a scene in a play, ask the workshop participants who are watching if anyone can sculpt the actors into an image, realistic or symbolic, that represents the underlying truth of the scene. The Joker can also make suggestions. The actors then play the scene, frozen in this image. The purpose of the improvisation is to explore the emotions, psychology, hidden relationships, hidden intentions, desires and fears that are in the symbolism of the scene.

---

[231] This exercise led to the discovery of the 'family ritual' scene in *Here and Now* (ਏਥੇ ਤੇ ਹੁਣੇ). See the *Case Studies* chapter.

[232] There is a version of this exercise (same name) in Boal's *Rainbow of Desire* on p. 115.

[233] Boal, *Rainbow of Desire*, p. 115.

[234] For details see the section *Authenticity and a true voice* in the chapter *The Art of Interactive Theatre*.

Joker Tip: For example: in *The Dying Game*, during a scene between the mother and son in the hospital, a participant placed the dying mother in a coffin, and the son sitting on the coffin, keeping her from escaping. Exploring this dynamic unlocked a layer of truth about the son's desire for the ordeal to end, so that they could both be released from the turmoil of dealing with the medical system.

In another scene – a confrontation between the son and the doctor in the doctor's office – a workshop participant placed the mother, who was not originally in the scene, lying on the doctor's desk in between the doctor and the son. This improvisation was so rich, we ended up staging the final production with this very powerful symbolic reality on the stage.

stop and think[235]

It is very important that all the characters on stage always know what they are doing and what they are thinking and feeling. In a Forum, the Joker may ask them why they responded to an intervention the way they did, or what the consequences of an action would be, or what they were thinking or feeling when something happened.

Play the scene. When I yell "Stop!" everyone freezes. At "Think!", everyone starts an internal monologue, speaking the thoughts of your character out loud. Keep this going until "Action!", at which point you all pick up exactly where you left off, as if you had never frozen.

---

[235] There is a version of this exercise called *Stop! Think!* in Boal's *Games for Actors and Non-Actors*, p. 211.

tableau - monologue - dialogue - action[236]

> **Joker Tip:** This can also be used in Image Theatre. I use it often as an animation technique that leads to improvisation from the *Magnetic Image* exercise.

Be in this frozen image that represents the characters' relationships to each other.

All of you do an internal monologue – your thoughts and feelings as the character – frozen in place. Keep going. Try not to repeat the same things over and over again. Use the monologue to explore your character's thoughts and feelings, fears and desires towards the other characters, the situation and yourself. Keep digging.

Now, frozen in shape, I am going to touch one of you. That person say a sentence, speaking as the character. Everyone listen to what this person says. Now, the next person I touch, *respond* to the first character's sentence. And then next person I touch, *respond* to what has been said so far. We will do this until each character has said a sentence.

Now, still frozen in shape, you cannot move, but you can listen and speak to each other. Talk to each other, in character, keeping in mind that you have to leave enough space for everyone to speak. This will be artificially slow, but keep focused. Have a dialogue, trying to get what you want from each other, but frozen in place.

Now the image can walk and talk. "Action!" Play the scene. Try to tell the truth of the character.

---

[236] There is a version of this exercise called *Dynamisation* in Boal's *Games for Actors and Non-Actors*, p. 192.

David Diamond is a 1975 graduate of the University of Alberta, with a BFA in acting. He worked as a professional actor in theatre, television and film throughout Western Canada until 1981 when he co-founded Headlines Theatre. Between 1981 and 2007, David directed almost 400 community-specific theatre projects on issues such as racism, gender roles, violence, addiction, self-esteem, residential schools, globalization, language reclamation and many others. In 1996 he was the first individual recipient of the City of Vancouver's Cultural Harmony Award. In 2001 he received an Honorary Doctorate of Letters from the University College of the Fraser Valley.

Photo: David Cooper

Fritjof Capra, PhD, physicist and systems theorist, is the author of several international bestsellers, including *The Tao of Physics*, *The Web of Life* and *The Hidden Connections*. His new book, *The Science of Leonardo*, will be published in October 2007 by Doubleday in the United States and by Rizzoli in Italy.

Photo: Karl Grossman

ISBN 142512458-5